Africa

Phrasebook & Dictionary

D1408003

Acknowledgments
Product Editor Will Allen
Book Designer Jessica Rose
Language Writers Daniel Aboye Aberra, Harrison Adeniyi, Martin
Benjamin, Thanduxolo Fatyi, Derek Gowlett, Michael Janes, Russell
Kaschula, Shalome Knoll, Robert Landon, Wilna Liebenberg, Fiona
McLaughlin, Vololona Rasolofoson, Chenjerai Shire, Izabela Will
Cover Image Researcher Naomi Parker

Published by Lonely Planet Global Limited
CRN 554153

3rd Edition – December 2019
ISBN 978 1 78657 476 3
Text © Lonely Planet 2019
Cover Image Masai warrior, Lewa Conservancy, Kenya; Joe Sohm/
Getty ©
Printed in China 10 9 8 7 6 5 4 3 2 1

Contact lonelyplanet.com/contact

Although the authors and Lonely Planet try to make the information
as accurate as possible, we accept no responsibility for any loss, injury
or inconvenience sustained by anyone using this book.

Paper in this book is certified against the Forest Stewardship Council™
standards. FSC™ promotes environmentally responsible, socially
beneficial and economically viable management of the world's forests.

MIX
Paper from
responsible sources
FSC™ C021741

acknowledgments

This book is based on existing editions of Lonely Planet's phrasebooks as well as new content. It was developed with the help of the following people:

- Wilna Liebenberg for the Afrikaans chapter
- Daniel Aboye Aberra for the Amharic chapter
- Shalome Knoll for the Arabic chapter
- Michael Janes for the French chapter
- Izabela Will for the Hausa chapter
- Vololona Rasolofoson for the Malagasy chapter
- Robert Landon for the Portuguese chapter
- Chenjerai Shire for the Shona chapter
- Martin Benjamin for the Swahili chapter
- Fiona McLaughlin for the Wolof chapter
- Harrison Adeniyi for the Yoruba chapter
- Russell Kaschula and Thanduxolo Fatyi for the Xhosa chapter
- Derek Gowlett for the Zulu chapter

Thanks also to Jean-Pierre Masclef (French) and Yukiyoshi Kamimura (Portuguese) for additional language expertise.

contents

CONTENTS

5

Africa

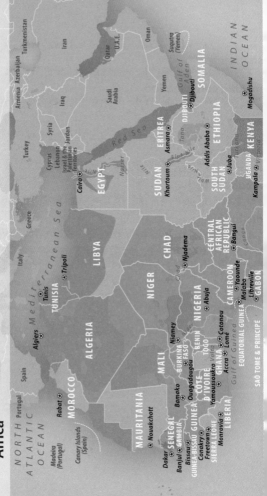

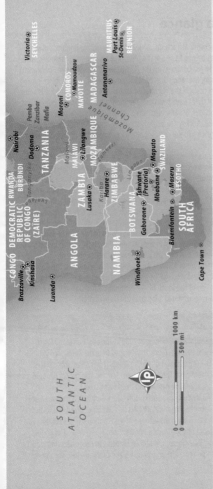

LANGUAGE MAP

- Afrikaans
- Amharic
- Arabic
- French
- Hausa
- Malagasy
- Portuguese
- Shona
- Swahili
- Wolof
- Xhosa
- Yoruba
- Zulu

Note: Language areas are approximate only. For more detail see the relevant introduction.

SOUTH ATLANTIC OCEAN

CONGO
Brazzaville⊕
Kinshasa⊕
DEMOCRATIC REPUBLIC OF CONGO (ZAIRE)
RWANDA
BURUNDI
Nairobi⊕
Dodoma⊕
TANZANIA
Pemba
Zanzibar
Mafia
Moroni⊕
COMOROS
MAYOTTE ⊕Mamoudzou
Victoria⊕
SEYCHELLES
MAURITIUS
Port Louis⊕
St-Denis⊕
RÉUNION
Antananarivo⊕
MADAGASCAR
Mozambique Channel
Luanda⊕
ANGOLA
Malawi
MALAWI
Lilongwe⊕
ZAMBIA
Lusaka⊕
Kariba
Harare⊕
ZIMBABWE
MOZAMBIQUE
Maputo⊕
Mbabane⊕
SWAZILAND
Maseru⊕
LESOTHO
Zambezi
NAMIBIA
Windhoek⊕
BOTSWANA
Gaborone⊕
Tshwane (Pretoria)⊕
Bloemfontein⊕
SOUTH AFRICA
Cape Town⊕

0   500 mi
0   1000 km

africa – at a glance

In addition to its many other attractions, Africa offers incredible linguistic diversity. Most African languages belong to one of the following four language families: Afro-Asiatic, Nilo-Saharan, Niger-Congo (with the Bantu languages as the major branch) and Khoisan. In addition, the languages of Madagascar belong to the Austronesian language family. Even though the number of languages spoken in Africa is huge (around 1000), most of them have less than a million speakers. On the other hand, more prominent languages usually also serve as regional lingua francas – such as Swahili in East Africa. Luckily for English speakers, most African languages use Roman script and there's a general correspondence between the pronunciation and the written form of words.

Arabic has a particularly important status in the north and northeast of the continent, due to its proximity to the Middle East and the Arab conquests of North Africa from the 7th century. Among the African languages, Amharic is linguistically closest to Arabic, as they both belong to the Semitic group of the Afro-Asiatic family. In addition, they're both script languages, but the two scripts are quite different.

Due to the 19th-century European colonisation of Africa, a few European languages (particularly English, French and Portuguese) are still influential in various African countries and even share official status with native African languages. English is predominantly represented in the east and the south, French in the north and the west, and Portuguese in the east and the west of the continent.

A unique linguistic feature of Africa is Afrikaans, which belongs to the Germanic branch of the Indo-European language family. It was created as a result of the 17th-century Dutch colonisation of the south of the continent. Although still very similar to Dutch, Afrikaans is now considered a language in its own right.

did you know?

- The African Union (AU) was established in 2000 by the adoption of the Constitutive Act at the Lome Summit (Togo). It developed from the African Economic Community and the Organisation of African Unity. It has 55 member states, covering the entire continent. The AU is governed by the Assembly of Heads of State and Government and the Pan-African Parliament.
- The home of the AU is Addis Ababa in Ethiopia. The AU anthem is the song 'Let Us All Unite and Celebrate Together'. The AU flag combines green, white and gold colours, with the emblem showing the African continent in the middle.
- The official languages of the AU are all African languages, as well as Arabic, English, French and Portuguese. The African Academy of Languages (founded in 2001) strives to preserve African languages and promote their use among the African people.

Afrikaans

pronunciation

Vowels		Consonants	
Symbol	**English sound**	**Symbol**	**English sound**
a	**run**	b	**bed**
aa	**father**	ch	**cheat**
ai	**aisle**	d	**dog**
aw	**law**	f	**fun**
ay	**say**	g	**go**
e	**bet**	h	**hat**
ee	**see**	k	**kit**
eu	**nurse**	kh	as the 'ch' in the Scottish *loch*
ew	**ee** with rounded lips	l	**lot**
ey	as in **bet**, but longer	m	**man**
i	**hit**	n	**not**
o	**pot**	ng	**ring**
oh	**cold**	p	**pet**
oo	**poor**	r	**run** (trilled)
oy	**toy**	s	**sun**
u	**put**	sh	**shot**
uh	**ago**	t	**top**
		v	**very**
		w	**win**
		y	**yes**
		z	**zero**
		zh	**pleasure**

In this chapter, the Afrikaans pronunciation is given in blue after each phrase.

Each syllable is separated by a dot, and the syllable stressed in each word is italicised. For example:

Dankie. dang·kee

AFRIKAANS
afrikaans

introduction

You don't need to look hard for evidence of Afrikaans in English: *aardvark*, the name of a termite-eating mammal native to Africa, is one of the first words in any English dictionary. English has also borrowed the Afrikaans words *commando* and *trek*, among others. Afrikaans (*Afrikaans* a·free·kans) belongs to the Germanic branch of the Indo-European language family – just like English. It's closely related to the 17th-century Dutch brought to South Africa from 1652 onward, when The Dutch East India Company established the first European settlement at the Cape of Good Hope. Afrikaans derives from the dialect that developed among these settlers, most of whom were from the Netherlands. Until the late 19th century, Afrikaans was considered a Dutch dialect and was known as 'Cape Dutch' – in fact, it wasn't until 1925 that it became one of the official languages of South Africa. Today, it's the first language of some six million people, and is spoken in Botswana, Malawi, Namibia and Zambia as well as South Africa.

 afrikaans (native language) 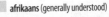 **afrikaans** (generally understood)

introduction – AFRIKAANS

11

language difficulties

Do you speak English?
Praat jy Engels? praat yay *eng*·ils

Do you understand?
Verstaan jy? vir·*staan* yay

I (don't) understand.
Ek verstaan (nie). ek vir·*staan* (nee)

Could you please ...? *Kan jy asseblief ...?* kan yay a·si·*bleef* ...
  repeat that *dit herhaal* dit her·*haal*
  speak more slowly *stadiger praat* *staa*·di·khir praat
  write it down *dit neerskryf* dit *neyr*·skrayf

time, dates & numbers

What time is it?	*Hoe laat is dit?*	hu laat is dit
It's one o'clock.	*Dis een-uur.*	dis *eyn*·ewr
It's (two) o'clock.	*Dis (twee-)uur.*	dis (*twey*)ewr
Quarter past (one).	*Kwart oor (een).*	kwart oor (eyn)
Half past (one).	*Half (twee).*	half (twey)
Quarter to (eight).	*Kwart voor (agt).*	kwart voor (akht)
At what time ...?	*Hoe laat ...?*	hu laat ...
At ...	*Om ...*	om ...
It's (15 December).	*Dis (vyftien Desember).*	dis (*fayf*·teen dey·*sem*·bir)

yesterday	*gister*	*khis*·tir
today	*vandag*	fin·*dakh*
tomorrow	*môre*	*mo*·ri

Monday	*Maandag*	*maan*·dakh
Tuesday	*Dinsdag*	*dins*·dakh
Wednesday	*Woensdag*	*wuns*·dakh
Thursday	*Donderdag*	*don*·ir·dakh
Friday	*Vrydag*	*vray*·dakh
Saturday	*Saterdag*	*sa*·tir·dakh
Sunday	*Sondag*	*son*·dakh

numbers

0	*nul*	neul	16	*sestien*	ses·teen
1	*een*	eyn	17	*sewentien*	sey·vin·teen
2	*twee*	twey	18	*agtien*	akh·teen
3	*drie*	dree	19	*negentien*	ney·khin·teen
4	*vier*	feer	20	*twintig*	twin·tikh
5	*vyf*	fayf	21	*een en twintig*	eyn en twin·tikh
6	*ses*	ses	22	*twee en twintig*	twey en twin·tikh
7	*sewe*	see·vi	30	*dertig*	der·tikh
8	*agt*	akht	40	*veertig*	feyr·tikh
9	*nege*	ney·khi	50	*vyftig*	fayf·tikh
10	*tien*	teen	60	*sestig*	ses·tikh
11	*elf*	elf	70	*sewentig*	sey·vin·tikh
12	*twaalf*	twaalf	80	*tagtig*	takh·tikh
13	*dertien*	der·teen	90	*negentig*	ney·khin·tikh
14	*veertien*	feyr·teen	100	*honderd*	hon·dirt
15	*vyftien*	fayf·teen	1000	*duisend*	day·sint

border crossing

I'm here ...	*Ek is hier ...*	ek is heer ...
in transit	*onderweg*	on·dir·*wekh*
on business	*vir besigheid*	fir *bey*·sikh·hayt
on holiday	*met vakansie*	met fi·*kan*·see

I'm here for ...	*Ek is hier vir ...*	ek is heer fir ...
(10) days	*(tien) dae*	(teen) *daa*·i
(three) weeks	*(drie) weke*	(dree) *vey*·ki
(two) months	*(twee) maande*	(twey) *maan*·di

I'm going to (Johannesburg).
Ek gaan na (Johannesburg). ek khaan naa (yu·*ha*·nis·birkh)

I'm staying at the (Ritz).
Ek bly in die (Ritz). ek blay in dee (rits)

tickets

A ... ticket (to Cape Town), please.	Een ... kaartjie (na Kaapstad), asseblief.	eyn ... kaar·kee (naa kaap·stat) a·si·bleef
one-way	eenrigting	eyn·rikh·ting
return	retoer	ri·tur

I'd like to ... my ticket, please.	Ek wil my kaartjie, asseblief ...	ek vil may kaar·kee a·si·bleef ...
cancel	kanselleer	kan·si·leyr
change	verander	fir·an·dir
collect	afhaal	af·haal

I'd like a (non)smoking seat, please.
Ek wil asseblief 'n (nie-)rook-sitplek hê.
ek vil a·si·bleef i (nee-)rook·sit·plek he

Is there a toilet/air conditioning?
Is daar 'n toilet/lugreëling?
is daar i toy·let/likh·rey·ling

How long does the trip take?
Hoe lank neem die reis?
hu langk neym dee rays

Is it a direct route?
Is dit 'n direkte roete?
is dit i dee·rek·ti ru·ti

transport

Where does flight (MN367) arrive?
Waar kom vlug (MN367) aan?
vaar kom flikh (em en dree ses sey·vi) aan

Where does flight (MN367) depart?
Waar vertrek vlug (MN367)?
vaar fir·trek flikh (em en dree ses see·vi)

How long will it be delayed?
Hoe lank sal dit vertraag word?
hu langk sal dit fir·traakh vort

Is this the ... to (Durban)?	Is dit die ... na (Durban)?	is dit dee ... naa (dir·ban)?
boat	boot	boot
bus	bus	bis
plane	vliegtuig	flikh·tayg
train	trein	trayn

How much is it to …?
Hoeveel kos dit na …?   hu·fil kos dit naa …

Please take me to (this address).
Neem my asseblief na (hierdie adres).   neym may a·si·bleef naa (*heer*·dee a·*dres*)

I'd like to hire a car/4WD (with air conditioning).
Ek wil 'n motor/4-by-4   ek vil i *moo*·tir/feer·bay·feer
(met lugreëling) huur.   (met *likh*·rey·ling) hewr

How much is it for (three) days/weeks?
Hoeveel kos dit vir (drie) dae/weke?   hu·fil kos dit fir (dree) *daa*·i/*vey*·ki

directions

Where's the	*Waar's die*	vaars dee
(nearest) …?	*(naaste) …?*	(*naas*·ti) …
internet café	*Internet-kafee*	*in*·tir·net·ka·*fey*
market	*mark*	mark

Is this the road to (Cape Town)?
Is dit die pad na (Kaapstad)?   is dit dee pat naa (*kaap*·stat)

Can you show me (on the map)?
Kan jy my (op die kaart) wys?   kan yay may (op dee kaart) vays

What's the address?
Wat is die adres?   vat is dee a·*dres*

How far is it?
Hoe ver is dit?   hu fer is dit

How do I get there?
Hoe kom ek daar?   hu kom ek daar

Turn left/right.
Draai links/regs.   drai lings/rekhs

It's …	*Dis …*	dis …
behind …	*agter …*	*akh*·tir …
in front of …	*voor …*	foor …
near (to) …	*naby …*	*naa*·bay …
next to …	*langs …*	langs …
on the corner	*op die hoek*	op dee huk
opposite …	*oorkant …*	*oor*·kant …
straight ahead	*reguit aan*	*rekh*·ayt aan
there	*daar*	daar

accommodation

Where's a ...?	Waar's 'n ...?	vaars i ...
camping ground	kampeerplek	kam·*peyr*·plek
guesthouse	gastehuis	*khas*·ti·hays
hotel	hotel	hu·*tel*
youth hostel	jeugtuiste	*yeykh*·tays·ti

Can you recommend somewhere cheap/good?
Kan jy 'n goedkoop/goeie   kan yay i *khut*·koop/*khoy*·i
plek aanbeveel?   plek *aan*·bi·feyl

I'd like to book a room, please.
Ek wil 'n kamer bespreek, asseblief.   ek vil i *kaa*·mir bi·*spreyk* a·si·*bleef*

I have a reservation.
Ek het 'n bespreking.   ek het i bi·*sprey*·king

Do you have	Het jy	het yay
a ... room?	'n ... kamer?	i ... *kaa*·mir
single	enkel	*eng*·kil
double	dubbel	*di*·bil
twin	dubbelkamer met	*di*·bil·*kaa*·mir met
	twee enkelbeddens	twey *eng*·kil·*be*·dins

How much is it per night/person?
Hoeveel kos dit per nag/   *hu*·fil kos dit pir nakh/
persoon?   pir·*soon*

I'd like to stay for (two) nights.
Ek wil vir (twee) nagte bly.   ek vil fir (twey) *nakh*·ti blay

What time is check-out?
Hoe laat moet ek uit my   hu laat mut ek ayt may
kamer wees?   *kaa*·mir veys

Am I allowed to camp here?
Mag ek hier kampeer?   makh ek heer kam·*peyr*

banking & communications

I'd like to ...	Ek wil asseblief ...	ek vil a·si·*bleef* ...
arrange a transfer	'n oorplasing reël	i *oor*·plaa·sing reyl
cash a cheque	'n tjek wissel	i chek *vi*·sil
change a travellers cheque	'n reisigerstjek wissel	i *ray*·si·khirs·chek *vi*·sil
change money	geld ruil	khelt rayl
withdraw money	geld trek	khelt trek

I want to ...	Ek wil asseblief ...	ek vil a·si·*bleef* ...
buy a phonecard	'n foonkaart koop	i *foon*·kaart koop
call (Singapore)	(Singapoer) skakel	(*seeng*·ga·pur) *skaa*·kil
reverse the charges	'n kollekteeroproep maak	i ko·lek·*teyr*·op·rup maak
use a printer	'n drukker gebruik	i *dri*·kir khi·*brayk*
use the internet	die Internet gebruik	dee *in*·tir·net khi·*brayk*

How much is it per hour?
Hoeveel kos dit per uur?   *hu*·fil kos dit pir ewr

How much does a (three-minute) call cost?
Hoeveel kos 'n oproep (van drie minute)?   *hu*·fil kos i *op*·rup (fan dree mi·*nee*·ti)

(One rand/cent) per minute/hour.
(Een rand/sent) per minuut/uur.   (eyn rant/sent) pir mi·*newt*/ewr

tours

When's the next ...?	Wanneer is die volgende ...?	*va*·nir is dee *fol*·khin·di ...
day trip	dagrit	*dakh*·rit
tour	toer	tur

Is ... included?	Is ... ingesluit?	is ... *in*·khi·slayt
accommodation	verblyf	fir·*blayf*
the admission charge	die toegangsgeld	dee *tu*·khangs·khelt
food	kos	kos
transport	vervoer	fir·*fur*

How long is the tour?
Hoe lank is die toer?   hu langk is dee tur

What time should we be back?
Hoe laat sal ons terug wees?   hu laat sal ons trig veys

shopping

I'm looking for ...
Ek soek na ...   ek suk naa ...

I need film for this camera.
Ek het film vir my kamera nodig.   ek het *fi*·lim vir may *ka*·mi·ra *noo*·dikh

Can I listen to this?
Kan ek hierna luister?   kan ek *heer*·naa *lays*·tir

Can I have my ... repaired?
Kan ek my ... laat regmaak?   kan ek may ... laat *rekh*·maak

When will it be ready?
Wanneer sal dit rekh wees?   *va*·nir sal dit rekh veys

How much is it?
Hoeveel kos dit?   *hu*·fil kos dit

What's your lowest price?
Wat is jou laagste prys?   vat is yoh *laakh*·sti prays

I'll give you (five) rand.
Ek sal jou (vyf) rand gee.   ek sal yoh (fayf) rant khey

There's a mistake in the bill.
Daar's 'n fout op die rekening.   daars i foht op dee *rey*·ki·ning

It's faulty.
Dis stukkend.   dis *sti*·kint

I'd like a ..., please.   *Ek wil asseblief 'n ...*   ek vil a·si·*bleef* i ...
  receipt   *kwitansie hê*   kwi·*tan*·see he
  refund   *my geld terug hê*   may khelt trikh he

Do you accept ...?   *Aanvaar jy ...?*   aan·*faar* yay ...
  credit cards   *kredietkaarte*   kri·*deet*·kaar·ti
  debit cards   *debietkaarte*   di·*beet*·kaar·ti
  travellers cheques   *reisigerstjeks*   *ray*·si·khirs·cheks

Could you ...?	Kan jy ...?	kan yay ...
burn a CD from	'n CD van my	i *sey*·dey fan may
my memory card	geheuekaart brand	khi·*hee*·i·kaart brant
develop this film	hierdie film ontwikkel	*heer*·dee *fi*·lim ont·*vi*·kil

making conversation

Hello.	Hallo.	ha·*loh*
Good night.	Goeienag.	*khoy*·i·nakh
Goodbye.	Totsiens.	tot·*seens*

Mr	Meneer	mi·*neyr*
Mrs	Mevrou	mi·*froh*
Miss	Juffrou	*yi*·froh

How are you?
Hoe gaan dit? — hu khaan dit

Fine, and you?
Goed dankie, en jy? — khut *dang*·kee en yay

What's your name?
Wat's jou naam? — vats yoh naam

My name's ...
My naam is ... — may naam is ...

I'm pleased to meet you.
Bly te kenne. — blay ti *ke*·ni

This is my ...	Dit is my ...	dit is may ...
boyfriend	kêrel	*ke*·ril
brother	broer	brur
daughter	dogter	*dokh*·tir
father	pa	paa
friend	vriend m	freend
	vriendin f	freen·*din*
girlfriend	meisie	*may*·see
husband	man	man
mother	ma	maa
partner	maat	maat
sister	suster	*sis*·tir
son	seun	seyn
wife	vrou	froh

Here's my ...	Hier's my ...	heers may ...
What's your ...?	Wat's jou ...?	vats yoh ...
address	adres	a-dres
email address	e-posadres	ey-paws-a-dres
phone number	foonnommer	foon-no-mir

| Where are you from? | | |
| Waarvandaan kom jy? | | vaar-fan-daan kom yay |

I'm from ...	Ek kom van ...	ek kom fan ...
Australia	Australië	oh-stra-lee-i
Canada	Kanada	ka-na-da
New Zealand	Nieu-Seeland	new-sey-lant
the UK	Brittanje	bri-tan-yi
the USA	die VSA	dee fey-es-aa

| I'm (not) married. | | |
| Ek's (nie) getroud (nie). | | eks (nee) khi-troht (nee) |

| Can I take a photo (of you)? | | |
| Kan ek 'n foto (van jou) neem? | | kan ek i foo-tu (fan yoh) neym |

eating out

Can you	Kan jy 'n ...	kan yay i ...
recommend a ...?	aanbeveel?	aan-bi-feyl
bar	kroeg	krukh
dish	gereg	khi-rekh
place to eat	eetplek	eyt-plek

I'd like ..., please.	Ek wil asseblief ... hê.	ek vil a-si-bleef ... he
the bill	die rekening	dee rey-ki-ning
the menu	die spyskaart	dee spays-kaart
a table for (two)	'n tafel vir (twee)	i taa-fil fir (twey)
that dish	daardie gereg	daar-dee khi-rekh

| Do you have | Het julle | het yi-li |
| vegetarian food? | vegetariese kos? | fe-gee-taa-ree-si kos |

Could you prepare a meal without ...?	Kan julle 'n maaltyd sonder ... bedien?	kan *yi*-li i *maal*-tayt *son*-dir ... bi-*deen*
eggs	eiers	*ay*-irs
meat stock	vleisaftreksel	*flays*-af-trek-sil
(cup of) coffee ...	(koppie) koffie ...	(*ko*-pee) *ko*-fee ...
(cup of) tea ...	(koppie) tee ...	(*ko*-pee) tey ...
with milk	met melk	met melk
without sugar	sonder suiker	*son*-dir *say*-kir
boiled water	kookwater	*kook*-vaa-tir

emergencies

Help!	Help!	help
Call ...!	Kry ...!	kray ...
an ambulance	'n ambulans	i am-bew-*lans*
a doctor	'n dokter	i *dok*-tir
the police	die polisie	dee pu-*lee*-see

Could you help me, please?
Kan jy my help, asseblief?   kan yay may help a-si-*bleef*

I'm lost.
Ek is verdwaal.   ek is fir-*dwaal*

Where are the toilets?
Waar is die toilette?   vaar is dee toy-*le*-ti

I want to report an offence.
Ek wil 'n misdaad aanmeld.   ek vil i *mis*-daat *aan*-melt

I have insurance.
Ek het versekering.   ek het fir-*sey*-ki-ring

I want to contact my consulate/embassy.
Ek wil my konsulaat/   ek vil may kon-sew-*laat*/
ambassade kontak.   am-ba-*saa*-di *kon*-tak

I've been ...	Ek is ...	ek is ...
assaulted	aangerand	aan-khi-rant
raped	verkrag	fir-krakh
robbed	beroof	bi-roof

I've lost my ...	Ek het my ... verloor.	ek het may ... vir-loor
My ... was/were stolen.	My ... is gesteel.	may ... is khi-steyl
bags	bagasie	bi-khaa-see
credit card	kredietkaart	kri-deet-kaart
handbag	handsak	hant-sak
jewellery	juwele	yu-vee-li
money	geld	khelt
passport	paspoort	pas-poort
travellers cheques	reisigerstjeks	ray-si-khirs-cheks
wallet	beursie	beyr-see

medical needs

Where's the nearest ...?	Waar's die naaste ...?	vaars dee naas-ti ...
dentist	tandarts	tant-arts
doctor	dokter	dok-tir
hospital	hospitaal	hos-pee-taal
pharmacy	apteek	ap-teyk

I need a doctor (who speaks English).
Ek het 'n dokter nodig (wat Engels praat).
ek het i dok-tir noo-dikh (vat eng-ils praat)

Could I see a female doctor?
Kan ek 'n vroulike dokter sien?
kan ek i froh-li-ki dok-tir seen

It hurts here.
Dis hier seer.
dis heer seyr

I'm allergic to (penicillin).
Ek's allergies vir (penisillien).
eks a-ler-khees fir (pi-ni-si-leen)

english–afrikaans dictionary

In this dictionary, words are marked as n (noun), a (adjective), v (verb), sg (singular), pl (plural), inf (informal) and pol (polite) where necessary.

A

accommodation *akkommodasie* a-kaw-maw-daa-see
adaptor *adaptor* i-*dep*-tir
after *na* naa
airport *lughawe* leukh-haa-vi
alcohol *alkohol* al-ku-hawl
all *alle* a-li
allergy *allergie* a-ler-*khee*
and *en* en
ankle *enkel* eng-kil
antibiotics *antibiotika* an-tee-bee-oo-tee-ka
anti-inflammatories *anti-inflammatoriese middels* an-tee-in-fla-ma-*too*-ree-si *mi*-dils
arm *arm* a-rim
aspirin *aspirien* as-pi-*reen*
asthma *asma* as-ma
ATM *OTM* oo-tey-em

B

baby *baba* baa-ba
back (body) *rug* reukh
backpack *rugsak* reukh-sak
bad *sleg* slekh
baggage claim *bagasiebewys* bi-khaa-see-bi-vays
bank *bank* bank
bathroom *badkamer* bat-kaa-mir
battery *battery* ba-ti-*ray*
beautiful *mooi* moy
bed *bed* bet
beer *bier* beer
bees *bye* bay-i
before *voor* foor
bicycle *fiets* feets
big *groot* khroot
blanket *kombers* kawm-*bers*
blood group *bloedgroep* blut-khrup
bottle *bottel* baw-til
bottle opener *botteloopmaker* baw-til-oop-maa-kir
boy *seun* seyn
brakes (car) *remme* re-mi

breakfast *ontbyt* awnt-*bayt*
bronchitis *bronchitis* brawn-*khee*-tis

C

café *kafee* ka-*fey*
cancel *kanselleer* kan-si-*leyr*
can opener *blikoopmaker* blik-oop-maa-kir
cash n *kontant* kawn-*tant*
cell phone *selfoon* sel-foon
centre n *sentrum* sen-treum
cheap *goedkoop* khut-koop
check (bill) *rekening* rey-ki-ning
check-in n *aanmeld* aan-melt
chest *bors* bawrs
child *kind* kint
cigarette *sigaret* see-kha-*ret*
city *stad* stat
clean a *skoon* skoon
closed *toe* tu
codeine *kodeïen* koo-dey-*heen*
cold a *koud* koht
collect call *kollekteeroproep* kaw-lek-*teyr*-awp-rup
condom *kondoom* kawn-*doom*
constipation *hardlywigheid* hart-*lay*-vikh-hayt
contact lenses *kontaklense* kawn-tak-len-si
cough n *hoes* hus
currency exchange *valutawinkel* va-*lew*-ta-ving-kil
customs (immigration) *doeane* du-*haa*-ni

D

dairy products *suiwelprodukte* soy-vil-pru-dik-ti
dangerous *gevaarlik* khi-*faar*-lik
date (time) *datum* daa-tim
day *dag* dakh
diaper *doek* duk
diarrhoea *diarree* dee-ha-*rey*
dinner *aandete* aant-ey-ti
dirty *vuil* vayl
disabled *gestremd* khi-*stremt*
double bed *dubbelbed* di-bil-bet*

drink n *drankie* drang-kee
drivers licence *bestuurderslisensie* bi-stewr-dirs-li-sen-see
drug (illicit) *dwelm* dwe-lim

E

ear *oor* oor
east *oos* oos
economy class *ekonomiese klas* e-ku-noo-mee-si klas
elevator *hysbak* hays-bak
email n *e-pos* ey-paws
English (language) *Engels* eng-ils
exchange rate *wisselkoers* vi-sil-kurs
exit n *uitgang* ayt-khang
expensive *duur* dewr
eye *oog* ookh

F

fast *vinnig* fi-nikh
fever *koors* koors
finger *vinger* fing-ir
first-aid kit *noodhulpkissie* noot-hilp-ki-see
first class *eerste klas* eyr-sti klas
fish n *vis* fis
food *kos* kaws
foot *voet* fut
fork *vurk* firk
free (of charge) *gratis* khra-tis
fruit *vrugte* frikh-ti
funny *snaaks* snaaks

G

game park *wildtuin* vil-tayn
gift *geskenk* khi-skengk
girl *meisie* may-see
glass (drinking) *glas* khlas
glasses *bril* bril
gluten *gluten* glu-tin
good *goed* khut
gram *gram* khram
guide n *gids* khits

H

hand *hand* hant
happy *gelukkig* khi-leu-kikh

have *het* het
he *hy* hay
head *kop* kawp
headache *hoofpyn* hoof-payn
heart *hart* hart
heart condition *harttoestand* hart-tu-stant
heat n *hitte* hi-ti
here *hier* heer
high *hoog* hookh
highway *hoofpad* hoof-pat
homosexual n *homoseksueel* hoo-mu-sek-see-heyl
homosexual a *homoseksuele* hoo-mu-sek-see-hey-li
hot *warm* va-rim
hungry *honger* hawn-gir

I

I *ek* ek
identification (card) *identifikasie* ee-den-ti-fee-*kaa*-see
ill *siek* seek
important *belangrik* bi-*lang*-rik
internet *Internet* in-tir-net
interpreter *tolk* tawlk

J

job *werk* verk

K

key *sleutel* sley-til
kilogram *kilogram* kee-lu-khram
kitchen *kombuis* kom-*bays*
knife *mes* mes

L

laundry (place) *wassery* va-si-*ray*
lawyer *prokureur* praw-keu-*rewr*
left-luggage office *bagasiekantoor* ba-*kha*-see-kan-toor
leg *been* beyn
lesbian n *lesbiër* les-bee-ir
lesbian a *lesbies* les-bees
less *minder* min-dir
letter (mail) *brief* breef
like v *hou van* hoh fan
lost-property office *verlore goedere kantoor*
    vir-*loo*-ri *khu*-di-ri kan-*toor*

love (romantic) v *lief hê* leef he
lunch *middagete* mi-dakh-ey-ti

M

man *man* man
matches *vuurhoutjies* vewr-hoh-kees
meat *vleis* vlays
medicine *medisyne* mi-di-say-ni
message *boodskap* boot-skap
mobile phone *selfoon* sel-foon
month *maand* maant
morning *oggend* aw-khint
motorcycle *motorfiets* moo-tir-feets
mouth *mond* mawnt
movie *fliek* fleek
MSG *MSG* em es khey
museum *museum* mee-zeym
music *musiek* meu-seek

N

name *naam* naam
napkin *servet* sir-vet
nappy *doek* duk
national park *nasionale park* na-shu-naa-li park
nausea *naarheid* naar-hayt
neck *nek* nek
new *nuut* newt
news *nuus* news
newspaper *koerant* ku-rant
night *nag* nakh
nightclub *nagklub* nakh-kleup
noisy *raserig* raa-si-rikh
nonsmoking *nie-rook* nee-rook
north *noord* noort
nose *neus* neys
now *nou* noh
number *nommer* naw-mir
nuts *neute* ney-ti

O

oil (engine) *olie* oo-lee
OK *goed* khut
old *oud* oht
open a *oop* oop
outside *buite* bay-te

P

package *pakkie* pa-kee
pain *pyn* payn
paper *papier* pa-peer
park (car) v *parkeer* par-keyr
passport *paspoort* pas-poort
pay *betaal* bi-taal
pen *pen* pen
petrol *petrol* pe-trawl
pharmacy *apteek* ap-teyk
plate *plaat* plaat
postcard *poskaart* paws-kaart
post office *poskantoor* paws-kan-toor
pregnant *swanger* swang-ger

Q

quiet *stil* stil

R

rain n *reën* reyn
razor *skeermes* skeyr-mes
registered mail *geregistreerde pos*
    khi-re-khi-streyr-di paws
rent v *huur* hewr
repair v *herstel* her-stel
reservation *bespreking* bi-sprey-king
restaurant *restaurant* res-toh-rant
return v *terugkeer* ti-reukh-keyr
road *pad* pat
room *kamer* kaa-mir

S

sad *hartseer* hart-seyr
safe a *veilig* fay-likh
sanitary napkin *sanitêre doekie* sa-nee-te-ri du-kee
seafood *seekos* sey-kaws
seat *sitplek* sit-plek
send *stuur* stewr
sex *seks* seks
shampoo *sjampoe* sham-pu
share (a dorm, etc) *deel* deyl
shaving cream *skeerroom* skeyr-room
she *sy* say
sheet (bed) *laken* laa-kin

shirt *hemp* hemp
shoes *skoene* sku-ni
shop n *winkel* ving-kil
shower n *stort* stawrt
skin *vel* fel
skirt *romp* rawmp
sleep v *slaap* slaap
small *klein* klayn
smoke (cigarettes) v *rook* rook
soap *seep* seyp
some *'n paar* i paar
soon *gou* khoh
sore throat *seer keel* seyr keyl
south *suid* sayt
souvenir shop *soewenierwinkel* su-vi-*neer*-ving-kil
speak *praat* praat
spoon *lepel* ley-pil
stamp *seël* seyl
stand-by ticket *bystandkaartjie* bay-stant-*kaar*-kee
station (train) *stasie* staa-see
stomach *maag* maakh
stop v *stop* stawp
stop (bus) n *halte* hal-ti
street *straat* straat
student *student* stu-*dent*
sunscreen *sonskerm* sawn-ske-rim
swim v *swem* swem

T

tampons *tampons* tam-pawns
teeth *tande* tan-di
telephone n *telefoon* te-li-*foon*
television *televisie* te-li-vee-see
temperature (weather) *temperatuur* tem-pi-ra-*tewr*
tent *tent* tent
that (one) *daardie* daar-dee
they *hulle* heu-li
thirsty *dors* dawrs
this (one) *hierdie* heer-dee
throat *keel* keyl
ticket *kaartjie* kaar-kee
time n *tyd* tayt
tired *moeg* mukh
tissues *tissues* tee-shus
today *vandag* van-dakh
toilet *toilet* toy-let
tonight *vanaand* vi-naant
toothache *tandpyn* tant-payn
toothbrush *tandeborsel* tan-di-bawr-sil
toothpaste *tandepasta* tan-di-pas-ta
torch (flashlight) *flits* flits

tourist office *toeristekantoor* tu-*ris*-ti-kan-*toor*
towel *handdoek* han-duk
translate *vertaal* fir-taal
travel agency *reisagentskap* rays-a-khent-skap
travellers cheque *reisigerstjek* ray-si-khirs-chek
trousers *broek* bruk
twin beds *twee beddens* twey be-dins
tyre *band* bant

U

underwear *onderklere* on-dir-kley-ri
urgent *dringend* dring-int

V

vacant *leeg* leykh
vegetable n *groente* khrun-ti
vegetarian n *vegetariër* fe-khee-*ta*-ree-ir
visa *visa* vee-sa

W

waiter *kelner* kel-nir
walk v *loop* loop
wallet *beursie* beyr-see
warm a *warm* va-rim
wash (something) *was* vas
watch n *horlosie* oor-*loo*-see
water *water* va-tir
we *ons* awns
weekend *naweek* naa-veyk
west *wes* ves
wheelchair *rolstoel* rawl-stul
when *wanneer* va-nir
where *waar* vaar
who *wie* vee
why *waarom* vaar-awm
window *venster* fens-tir
wine *wyn* vayn
with *met* met
without *sonder* sawn-dir
woman *vrou* froh
write *skryf* skrayf

Y

you sg inf/pol *jy/u* jay/ew
you pl inf/pol *julle/u* yeu-li/ew

Amharic

pronunciation

Vowels		Consonants	
Symbol	**English sound**	**Symbol**	**English sound**
a	**r**u**n**	b	**b**ed
ai	**ai**sle	ch	**ch**eat
e	b**e**t	ch'	strong ch
ee	s**ee**	d	**d**og
i	h**i**t	f	**f**un
o	p**o**t	g	**g**o
ow	n**ow**	h	**h**at
u	p**u**t	j	**j**ar
uh	**a**go	k	**k**it
'	like the pause in 'uh-oh' (comes before a vowel)	k'	strong k
		l	**l**ot
		m	**m**an
		n	**n**ot
		ny	ca**ny**on
		p	**p**et
		p'	**p**opping p
		r	**r**un (trilled)
		s	**s**un
		s'	hissing s
		sh	**sh**ot
		t	**t**op
		t'	spitting t
		v	**v**ery
		w	**w**in
		y	**y**es
		z	**z**ero
		zh	plea**s**ure

In this chapter,
the Amharic pronunciation
is given in light blue after each phrase.

Each syllable is separated
by a dot. For example:

ይቅርታ   yi·k'ir·ta

Amharic's glottalised consonants,
simplified as ch', k', p', s' and t'
in our pronunciation guide,
are made by tightening and releasing
the space between the vocal cords
when you pronounce the sound,
a bit like combining it with
the ' sound listed above.

አማርኛ – pronunciation

introduction

If you're a reggae fan, you already know at least one phrase from Amharic (አማርኛ a·mar·nya), courtesy of Bob Marley and the Wailers' anthem 'One Love/People Get Ready' – *Fiqir bandinet* fi·k'ir band·nuht (one love) expresses the idea of unity or one-ness central to Rastafarianism. Bob Marley wasn't the first to use Amharic for artistic purposes, of course: it's been used to create works of art for centuries. In fact, the earliest known Amharic writings are poems in praise of an emperor dating back to the 14th century AD. A Semitic language belonging to the Afro-Asiatic family, Amharic began to spread in the 10th to 12th centuries, when power shifted to the present Amhara region after the decline of the Aksumite Empire. Most of the world's 27 million Amharic speakers live in Ethiopia, where it's the official language and the most widely used of the more than 80 indigenous Ethiopian languages. Learning just a few basic phrases will smooth your way through this fascinating country.

■ **amharic** (native language)   ■ **amharic** (generally understood)

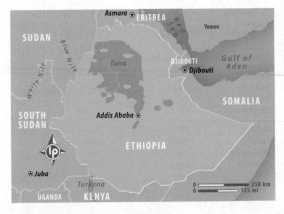

Do you speak English?

እንግሊዘኛ ትችላለህ?	'in·glee·zuh·nya ti·chi·la·luh·hi m
እንግሊዘኛ ትችያለሽ?	'in·glee·zuh·nya ti·chia·luhsh f

Do you understand?

ገባህ/ገባሽ?	guh·bah/guh·bash m/f

I (don't) understand.

(አል)ገባኝ(ም)	('al·)guh·bany(·mi)

Could you please ...?

	እባክህ/እባክሽ ...?	'i·ba·kih/'i·ba·kish ... m/f
repeat that	ድገመው/	di·guh·muhw/
	ድገሚው	di·guh·meew m/f
speak more slowly	በዝግታ አውራ	buh·zi·gi·ta 'ow·ra m
	በዝግታ አውሪ	buh·zi·gi·ta 'ow·ree f
write it down	ጻፈው/ጻፊው	s'a·fuhw/s'a·feew m/f

time, dates & numbers

What time is it?	ስንት ሰአት ነው?	sint suh·'at nuhw
It's (two) o'clock.	(ስምንት) ሰአት ነው	(si·mint) suh·'at nuhw
Quarter past (one).	(ሰባት) ከፉብ ነው	(suh·bat) kuh·rub nuhw
Half past (one).	(ሰባት) ተኩል ነው	(suh·bat) tuh·kul nuhw
Quarter to (eight).	ለ(ሁለት) ሩብ ጉዳይ ነው	luh·(hu·luht) rub gu·dai nuhw
At what time ...?	በስንት ሰአት...?	buh·sint suh·'at ...
At ...	በ ...	buh ...
It's (15 December).	(ታህሳስ አስራ	(ta·hi·sa·'a·si·ra
	አምስት) ነው	'am·mist) nuhw

yesterday	ትላንትና	ti·lan·ti·na
today	ዛሬ	za·re
tomorrow	ነገ	nuh·guh

Monday	ሰኞ	suh·nyo
Tuesday	ማክሰኞ	mak·suh·nyo
Wednesday	ሮብ	rob
Thursday	ሃሙስ	ha·mus
Friday	አርብ	'a·rib
Saturday	ቅዳሜ	k'i·da·me
Sunday	እሁድ	'i·hud

numbers

0	ዜሮ	ze·ro		16	አስራ ስድስት	a·si·ra si·dist
1	አንድ	and		17	አስራ ሰባት	a·si·ra suh·bat
2	ሁለት	hu·luht		18	አስራ ስምንት	a·si·ra si·mint
3	ሶስት	sost		19	አስራ ዘጠኝ	a·si·ra zuh·t'uhny
4	አራት	'ar·at		20	ሃያ	ha·ya
5	አምስት	'am·mist		21	ሃያ አንድ	ha·ya and
6	ስድስት	si·dist		22	ሃያ ሁለት	ha·ya hu·luht
7	ሰባት	suh·bat		30	ሰላሳ	suh·la·sa
8	ስምንት	si·mint		40	አርባ	'ar·ba
9	ዘጠኝ	zuh·t'uhny		50	ሃምሳ	ham·sa
10	አስር	a·sir		60	ስልሳ	sil·sa
11	አስራ አንድ	a·si·ra and		70	ሰባ	suh·ba
12	አስራ ሁለት	a·si·ra hu·luht		80	ሰማንያ	suh·ma·nia
13	አስራ ሶስት	a·si·ra sost		90	ዘጠና	zuh·t'uh·na
14	አስራ አራት	a·si·ra 'ar·at		100	መቶ	muh·to
15	አስራ አምስት	a·si·ra am·mist		1000	ሺ	shee

border crossing

I'm here ...	እዚህ ... ነኝ	'i·zeeh ... nuhny
in transit	በትራንዚት ላይ	buh·tran·zeet lai
on business	በስራ ጉዳይ ላይ	buh·si·ra gu·dai lai
on holiday	በእረፍት ላይ	buh·'i·ruhft lai

I'm here	እዚህ ያለሁት	'i·zeeh ya·luh·hut
for ...	ለ ... ነው	luh ... nuhw
(10) days	(አስር) ቀን	(a·sir) k'uhn
(three) weeks	(ሶስት) ሳምንት	(sost) sa·mint
(two) months	(ሁለት) ወር	(hu·luht) wuhr

I'm going to (Meta Abo).
(ሜታ አቦ) እሄዳለሁ (me·ta 'a·bo) 'i·he·da·luh·hu

I'm staying at the (Hilton Hotel).
(ሂልተን ሆቴል) እቆያለሁ (heel·tuhn ho·tel) 'i·k'o·ya·luh·hu

tickets

A ... ticket (to Bahir Dar), please.	አንድ ... ትኬት (ወደባህር ዳር) እባክህ/እባክሽ?	and ... ti·ket (wuh·duh ba·hir dar) 'i·ba·kih/'i·ba·kish m/f
one-way (going)	የአንድ ጉዞ (መሄጃ) ብቻ	yuh·and gu·zo (muh·he·ja) bi·cha
one-way (returning)	የአንድ ጉዞ (መመለሻ) ብቻ	yuh·and gu·zo (muh·muh·luh·sha) bi·cha
return	ደርሶ መልስ	duh·so muh·lis
I'd like to ... my ticket, please.	... እፈልግ ነበር እባክህ ትኬቴን ስጠኝ	... 'i·fuh·lig nuh·buhr 'i·ba·kih ti·ke·ten si·t'uhny m
	... እፈልግ ነበር እባክሽ ትኬቴን ስጪኝ	... 'i·fuh·lig nuh·buhr 'i·ba·kish ti·ke·ten si·ch'eeny f
cancel	መሰረዝ	muh·suh·ruhz
change	መቀየር	muh·k'uh·yuhr
collect	መውሰድ	muh·suhd

I'd like a smoking/nonsmoking seat, please.

መቀመጫ የሚጫስበት/የማይጫስበት ቦታ ጋ እፈል.ጋለሁ
muh·k'uh·muh·ch'a yuh·mee·ch'uhs·buht/ yuh·mai·ch'uhs·buht bo·ta ga 'i·fuh·li·ga·luh·hu

Is there a toilet?

ሽንት ቤት አለው?
shint bet 'a·luhw

Is there air conditioning?

ቬንትሌተር አለው?
vent·le·tuhr 'a·luhw

How long does the trip take?

ጉዞው ምን ያህል ይፈጃል?
gu·zo·wi min ya·hil yi·fuh·jal

Is it a direct route?

ይሄ ዋናው መንገድ ነው?
yi·he wa·now muhn·guhd nuhw

transport

Where does the flight (to Addis Ababa) arrive/depart?

(የአዲስ አበባ) በረራ መቼ ይደርሳል/ይነሳል?
(yuh·'a·dees 'a·buh·ba) buh·ruh·ra muh·che yi·duhr·sal/yi·nuh·sal

How long will it be delayed?

ምን ያህል ይዘገያል?
min ya·hil yi·zuh·guh·yal

Is this the ... to (Dire Dawa)?	ይህ ... ወደ (ድሬዳዋ) የሚሄደው ነው?	yih ... wuh·duh (di·re da·wa) yuh·mee·he·duhw nuhw
boat	ጀልባ	juhl·ba
bus	አውቶቢስ	'ow·to·bees
plane	አውሮፕላን	ow·rop·lan
train	ባቡር	ba·bur

I'd like to hire a ... (with air conditioning).	እባክህ/እባክሽ (ኤየር ኮንዲሽነር ያለው) ... መከራየት እፈልጋለሁ?	'i·ba·kih/'i·ba·kish ('e·yuhr kon·dee·shi·nuhr ya·luhw) ... muh·kuh·ra·yuht 'i·fuh·li·ga·luh·hu m/f
car	መኪና	muh·kee·na
4WD	ፎር ዊል ድራይቭ	for weel di·ra·yiv

How much is it to ...?

ወደ ... ለመሄድ ዋጋው
ስንት ነው?

wuh·duh ... luh·muh·hed wa·gow
sint nuhw

Please take me to (the museum).

እባክህ/እባክሽ ወደ (ሙዚየም)
ውሰደኝ/ውሰጂኝ

'i·ba·kih/'i·ba·kish wuh·duh (mu·zee·yuhm)
wi·suh·duhny/wi·suh·jeeny m/f

How much is it for (three) days/weeks?

ለ(ሶስት) ቀን/ሳምንት
ዋጋው ስንት ነው?

luh·(sost) k'uhn/sa·mint
wa·gow sint nuhw

directions

Where's the (nearest) ...?	(ቅርብ) ያለ ... የት ነው?	(k'irb) ya·luh ... yuht nuhw
internet café	ኢንተርኔት ካፌ	'een·tuhr·net ka·fe
market	ገበያ	guh·buh·ya

Is this the road to the museum?

ይህ መንገድ ወደ ሙዚየም
ይወስዳል?

yih muhn·guhd wuh·duh mu·zee·yuhm
yi·wuhs·dal

Can you show me (on the map)?

(ካርታ ላይ) ልታሳየኝ
ትችላለህ/ትችያለሽ?

(kar·ta lai) li·ta·sa·yuhny
ti·chi·la·luh/ti·chi·ya·luhsh m/f

What's the address?

አድራሻው የት ነው?

'ad·ra·show yuht nuhw

How far is it?

ምን ያህል ይርቃል? | min yahl yir·k'al

How do I get there?

እዚያ እንዴት መሄድ ይቻላል? | 'i·zee·ya 'in·det muh·hed yi·cha·lal

Turn left/right.

ወደ ግራ/ቀኝ ታጠፍ | wuh·duh gi·ra/k'uhny ta·t'uhf

It's ... | ... ነው | ... nuhw
behind ... | ... ከጀርባ | ... kuh·juhr·ba
in front of ... | ... ፊት ለፊት | ... feet luh·feet
near ... | ... እጠገብ | ... 'a·t'uh·guhb
next to ... | ... ቀጥሎ | ... k'uh·t'i·lo
on the corner | መታጠፊያው ላይ | muh·ta·t'uh·fee·yow lai
opposite ... | ... ትይዩ | ... ti·yi·yu
straight ahead | ቀጥታ | k'uh·t'i·ta
there | እዚያ | 'i·zee·ya

accommodation

Where's a ...? | ... የት ነው? | ... yuht nuhw
camping ground | የድንኳን ቦታ | yuh·din·ku·wa·nu bo·ta
guesthouse | የእንግዳ ማረፊያ | yuh·'in·gi·da ma·ruh·fee·ya
hotel | ሆቴል | ho·te·lu
youth hostel | ሆስቴሉ | hos·te·lu

Can you recommend somewhere (cheap/good)?

(ርካሽ/ጥሩ) ቦታ ልትጠቁመኝ | (ri·kash/t'i·ru) bo·ta li·ti·t'uh·k'u·muhny
ትችላለህ/ትችያለሽ? | ti·chi·la·luh·hi/ti·chi·ya·luhsh m/f

I'd like to book a room, please.

እባክህ/እባክሽ ክፍል ቡክ | 'i·ba·kih/'i·ba·kish ki·fil buk
ማድረግ ፈልጌ ነበር? | mad·ruhg fuh·li·ge nuh·buhr m/f

I have a reservation.

ክፍል ቡክ አድርጌ ነበር | ki·fil buk 'ad·ri·ge nuh·buhr

Do you have a ... room? | ... ክፍል አላችሁ? | ... ki·fil 'a·la·chi·hu
single | አንድ | and
double | ሁለት | hu·luht
twin | ሁለት አልጋ ያለው | hu·luht 'al·ga ya·luhw

How much is it per night/person?

በቀን/በሰው ዋጋው ስንት ነው? | buh·k'uhn/buh·suhw wa·gow sint nuhw

I'd like to stay for (two) nights.

(ሁለት) ቀን መቆየት	(hu·luht) k'uhn muh·k'o·yuht
እፈልጋለሁ	'i·fuh·li·ga·luh·hu

What time is check-out?

ክፍል መልቀቂያው	ki·fil muhl·k'uh·k'ee·yow
ስንት ሰአት ነው?	sint suh·'at nuhw

Am I allowed to camp here?

እዚህ ግቢ ድንኩዋን	'i·zeeh gi·bee din·ku·wan
መትከል እችላለሁ?	muht·kuhl 'i·chi·la·luh·hu

banking & communications

I'd like to ...	እባክህ/እባክሽ ...	i·ba·kih/'i·ba·kish ...
	እፈልጋለሁ	'i·fuh·li·ga·luh·hu m/f
arrange a transfer	ገንዘብ ማዛወር	guhn·zuhb ma·za·wuhr
cash a cheque	ቼክ መመንዘር	chek muh·muhn·zuhr
change a travellers	ትራቭለርስ ቼክ	ti·rav·luhrs chek
cheque	መመንዘር	muh·muhn·zuhr
change money	ገንዘብ	guhn·zuhb
	መመንዘር	muh·muhn·zuhr
withdraw money	ገንዘብ ማውጣት	guhn·zuhb mow·t'at

I want to ...	... እፈልጋለሁ	... 'i·fuh·li·ga·luh·hu
buy a phonecard	የስልክ ካርድ መግዛት	yuh·silk kard muhg·zat
call (Australia)	(አውስትራሊያ)	('owst·ra·lee·ya)
	መደወል	muh·duh·wuhl
reverse the charges	በተዘዋዋሪ	buh·tuh·zuh·wa·wa·ree
	መደወል	muh·duh·wuhl
use a printer	ፕሪንተር	pi·reen·tuhr
	መጠቀም	muh·t'uh·k'uhm
use the internet	ኢንተርኔት	'een·tuhr·net
	መጠቀም	muh·t'uh·k'uhm

How much is it per hour?

በሰአት ስንት ነው?	buh·suh·'at sint nuhw

How much does a (three-minute) call cost?

የ(ሶስት ደቂቃ)	yuh·(sost duh·k'ee·k'a)
ጥሪ ዋጋው ስንት ነው?	t'i·ree wa·gow sint nuhw

(One birr) per minute/hour.

(አንድ ብር) በደቂቃ/በሰአት	(and bir) buh·duh·k'ee·k'a/buh·suh·'at

tours

When's the next ...?	የሚቀጥለው ... መቼ ነው?	yuh·mee·k'uh·t'i·luhw ... muh·che nuhw
day trip	ውሎ ገባ ጉዞ	wi·lo guh·ba gu·zo
tour	ሽርሽር	shi·ri·shir

Is ... included?	... ይጨምራል?	... yi·ch'uh·mi·ral
accommodation	መኝታን	muh·nyi·tan
the admission charge	የአገልግሎት ዋጋን	yuh·'a·guhl·gi·lot wa·gan
food	ምግብን	mi·gib·n
transport	ትራንስፖርትን	ti·rans·por·tin

How long is the tour?
ሽርሽሩ ምን ያህል ጊዜ ይፈጃል?   shi·ri·shi·ru min ya·hil gee·ze yi·fuh·jal

What time should we be back?
በስንት ሰአት እንመለሳለን?   buh·sint suh·'at 'in·muh·luh·sa·luhn

shopping

I'm looking for ...
... እፈልጋለሁ   ... 'i·fuh·li·ga·luh·hu

I need film for this camera.
ለዚህ ካሜራ የሚሆን ፊልም እፈልጋለሁ   luh·zeeh ka·me·ra yuh·mee·hon feelm 'i·fuh·li·ga·luh·hu

Can I listen to this?
ይህንን ማዳመጥ እችላለሁ?   yi·hi·nin ma·da·muht' 'i·chi·la·luh·hu

Can I have my ... repaired?
... ማስጠገን እችላለሁ?   ... mas·t'uh·guhn 'i·chi·la·luh·hu

When will it be ready?
መቼ ይደርሳል?   muh·che yi·duhr·sal

How much is it?
ዋጋው ስንት ነው?   wa·gow sint nuhw

Can you write down the price?
ዋጋውን ልትጽፍልኝ ትችላለህ?   wa·gown li·ti·s'if·liny ti·chi·la·luh

What's your lowest price?
መጨረሻውን ስንት ትለዋለህ?   muh·ch'uh·ruh·sha·win sint ti·luh·wa·luh·hi

I'll give you (five) birr.
(አምስት) ብር እከፍላለሁ ('am·mist) bir 'i·kuhf·la·luh·hu

There's a mistake in the bill.
ቢሉ ላይ ስህተት አለ bee·lu lai sih·tuht 'a·luh

It's faulty.
የተበላሸ ነው yuh·tuh·buh·la·shuh nuhw

I'd like a receipt/refund, please.
እባክህ/እባክሽ ደረሰኝ/ i·ba·kih/'i·ba·kish duh·ruh·suhny/
ገንዘቤ እንዲመለስልኝ guhn·zuh·be 'in·dee·muh·luhs·liny
እፈል.ጋለሁ 'i·fuh·li·ga·luh·hu m/f

Do you accept ...? ... ትቀበላላችሁ? ... ti·k'uh·buh·la·la·chi·hu
  credit cards ክሬዲት ካርድ ki·re·deet kard
  debit cards ዴቢት ካርድ de·beet kard
  travellers cheques ትራ.ቨለርስ ቼክ ti·rav·luhrs chek

Could you ...? ... ትችላለህ? ... ti·chi·la·luh
  burn a CD from ሲዲ ከዮኤስ ቢ see·dee kuh yu 'es bee
    my memory card ኮፒ ko·pee
  develop this film ይህንን ፊልም yi·hi·nin feelm
    ልታጥብልኝ li·ta·t'ib·liny

making conversation

Hello.	ሰላም	suh·lam
Good night.	ደህና እደር/እደሪ	duh·na 'i·duhr/'i·duh·ree m/f
Goodbye.	ደህና ሁን/ ሁኚ	duh·na hun/hun·yee m/f
Mr	አቶ	'a·to
Mrs	ወይዘሮ	wuhy·zuh·ro
Ms/Miss	ወይዘሪት	wuhy·zuh·reet

How are you?
እንዴት ነህ/ነሽ? 'in·det nuh·hi/nuhsh m/f

Fine, and you?
ይመስገነው አንተስ/አንቺስ? yi·muhs·guh·nuhw 'an·tuhs/'an·chees m/f

What's your name?
ማን ትባላለህ?/ትባያለሽ? man ti·ba·la·luh/ti·ba·ya·luhsh m/f

My name's ...
... ነኝ ... nuhny

I'm pleased to meet you.

በመተዋወቃችን ደስ ብሎኛል   buh·muh·tuh·wa·wuh·k'a·chin duhs bi·lon·yal

This is my ...	እሱ ...-ዬ ነው	'i·su ...·ye nuhw
boyfriend	የወንድ ጉዋደኛ	yuh·wuhnd gu·wa·duhn·ya
brother	ወንድም	wuhn·dim
daughter	ሴት ልጅ	set lij
father	አባት	'a·bat
friend	ጉዋደኛ	gu·wa·duh·nya
girlfriend	የሴት ጉዋደኛ	yuh·set gu·wa·duh·nya
husband	ባል	bal
mother	እናት	'i·nat
partner	ባልንጀራ/ሽርካ	bal·ni·juh·ra/shi·ri·ka m/f
sister	እህት	'i·hit
son	ልጅ	lij
wife	ሚስት	mist

Here's my ...	... ይኸው	... yi·huh·wi
What's your ...?	... ልትሰጠኝ ትችላለህ?	... li·ti·suh·t'uhny ti·chi·la·luh
address	አድራሻህን	'ad·ra·sha·hin
email address	ኢ.ሜልህን	'ee·me·li·hin
phone number	ስልክ ቁጥርህን	silk k'u·t'ir·hin

Where are you from?	ከየት ነህ?	kuh·yuht nuh·hi

I'm from ...	እኔ ከ- ... ነኝ	'i·ne kuh·... nuhny
Australia	አውስትራሊያ	'owst·ra·lee·ya
New Zealand	ኒው ዚላንድ	neew zi·land
the UK	እንግሊዝ	'in·gleez
the USA	አሜሪካ	'a·me·ree·ka

I'm married.	አግብቻሉሁ	'ag·bi·cha·luh·hu
I'm not married.	አላባሁም	'a·la·guh·ba·hum
Can I take a photo (of you)?	ፎቶ ላነሳ(ሁ)/ላነሳ(ሽ) እችላለሁ?	fo·to la·nuh·sa(h)/la·nuh·sa(sh) 'i·chi·la·luh·hu m/f

eating out

Can you recommend a ...?	ጥሩ ... ልትጠቁመኝ ትችላለህ?	t'i·ru ... li·ti·t'uh·k'u·muhny ti·chi·la·luh
bar	ቡና ቤት	bu·na bet
dish	ምግብ	mi·gib
place to eat	ምግብ ቤት	mi·gib bet

I'd like ...,	እባክህ/እባክሽ ...	'i·ba·kih/'i·ba·kish ...
please.	እፈልጋለሁ	'i·fuh·li·ga·luh·hu m/f
the bill	ቢል	beel
the menu	ሜኑ	me·nu
a table for	ጠረጴዛ	t'uh·ruh·p'e·za
(two)	(ለሁለት) ሰው	(luh·hu·luht) suhw
that dish	ያንን ምግብ	ya·nin mi·gib

Do you have	የጻም ምግብ	yuh·s'om mi·gib
vegetarian food?	አላችሁ?	'a·la·chi·hu

Could you	ምግብ ያለ ...	mi·gib ya·luh ...
prepare a meal	ልታዘጋጂልን ትችያለሽ?	li·ta·zuh·ga·jee·lin ti·chi·ya·luhsh f
without ...?	ምግብ ያለ ...	mi·gib ya·luh ...
	ልታዘጋጅልን ትችላለህ?	li·ta·zuh·gaj·lin ti·chi·la·luh·hi m
eggs	እንቁላል	'in·k'u·lal
meat stock	ስጋ	si·ga

(cup of) coffee ...	(አንድ ስኒ) ቡና ...	(and si·nee) bu·na ...
(cup of) tea ...	(አንድ ስኒ) ሻይ ...	(and si·nee) shai ...
with milk	በወተት	buh·wuh·tuht
without sugar	ያለ ስኩዋር	ya·luh si·ku·war

(boiled) water	(የፈላ) ውሃ	(yuh·fuh·la) wi·ha

emergencies

Help!	እርዳታ እርዳታ!	'ir·da·ta 'ir·da·ta
I'm lost.	ጠፋብኝ	t'uh·fa·biny

Call ...!	... ጥራልኝ/ጥሪልኝ	... t'i·ra·liny/t'i·ree·liny m/f
an ambulance	አምቡላንስ	'am·bu·lans
a doctor	ዶክተር	dok·tuhr
the police	ፖሊስ	po·lees

Could you help me, please?
ልትረዳኝ ትችላለህ? — lit·ruh·dany ti·chi·la·luh m
ልትረጂኝ ትችያለሽ? — lit·ruh·jeeny ti·chi·ya·luhsh f

Where are the toilets?
ሽንት ቤት የት ነው? — shint bet yuht nuhw

I want to report an offence.
ጥቃቱን ሪፖርት ማድረግ — t'i·k'a·tun ree·port mad·ruhg
እፈልጋለሁ — 'i·fuh·li·ga·luh·hu

I have insurance.
ኢንሹራንስ አለኝ
'in·shu·rans 'a·luhny

I want to contact my consulate/embassy.
ከቆንስላዬ/ከኤምባሲዬ ጋር
kuh·k'ons·la·ye/kuh·'em·ba·see·ye gar
መገናኘት እፈልጋለሁ
muh·guh·na·nyuht 'i·fuh·li·ga·luh·hu

I've been ...	እኔ ...	'i·ne ...
assaulted	ተጠቃሁ	tuh·t'uh·k'a·hu
raped	ተደፈርኩ	tuh·duh·fuhr·ku
robbed	ተዘረፍኩ	tuh·zuh·ruhf·ku

I've lost my ...	... ጠፋብኝ	... t'uh·fa·biny
My ... was/were stolen.	የኔ ... ተሰረቀ	yuh·ne ... tuh·suh·ruh·k'uh
bags	ሻንጣ	shan·t'a
credit card	ክሬዲት ካርድ	ki·re·deet kard
handbag	የጅ ቦርሳ	yuhj bor·sa
jewellery	ጌጣጌጥ	ge·t'a·get'
money	ገንዘብ	guhn·zuhb
passport	ፓስፖርት	pas·port
travellers cheques	ትራቭለርስ ቼክ	ti·rav·luhrs chek
wallet	የኪስ ቦርሳ	yuh·kees bor·sa

medical needs

Where's the nearest ...?	በቅርብ ያለ ... የት ነው?	buh·k'irb ya·luh ... yuht nuhw
dentist	የጥርስ ሃኪም	yuh·t'irs ha·keem
doctor	ዶክተር	dok·tuhr
hospital	ሆስፒታል	hos·pee·tal
pharmacist	ፋርማሲስት	far·ma·seest

I need a doctor (who speaks English).
(እንግሊዘኛ የሚናገር)
('in·glee·zuhn·ya yuh·mee·na·guhr)
ሃኪም እፈልጋለሁ
ha·keem 'i·fuh·li·ga·luh·hu

Could I see a female doctor?
ሴት ዶክተር ልታየኝ ትችላለች?
set dok·tuhr li·ta·yuhny ti·chi·la·luhch

It hurts here.
እዚህ ጋ ያመኛል
'i·zeeh ga ya·muhn·yal

I'm allergic to (penicillin).
ለ(ፔኒሲሊን) አለርጂ ነኝ
luh·(pe·nee·see·leen) 'a·luhr·jee nuhny

english–amharic dictionary

In this dictionary, words are marked as n (noun), a (adjective), v (verb), ⓜ (masculine), ⓕ (feminine), sg (singular), pl (plural), inf (informal) and pol (polite) where necessary.

A

accommodation ማደሪያ ma-duh-ree-ya
adaptor አዳፕተር a-dap-tuhr
after በኋዋላ buh-hu-wa-la
airport አይሮፕላን ማረፊያ ai-rop-lan ma-ruh-fee-ya
alcohol አልኮል al-kol
all ሁሉ hu-lu
allergy አለርጂ 'a-luhr-jee
and እና i-na
ankle ቁርጭምጭሚት k'ur-ch'im-ch'im-it
antibiotics አንቲባዮቲክ an-tee-ba-yo-teek
arm ክንድ kind
aspirin አስፕሪን asp-ree-in
asthma አስም as-m
ATM ኤቲኤም ey-tee-em

B

baby ህጻን hi-s'an
back (body) ጀርባ juh-ri-ba
backpack ባክ ፓክ bak pak
bad መጥፎ muht'-fo
baggage claim ሻንጣ መጠየቂያ
 shan-t'a muh-t'uh-yuh-k'ee-ya
bathroom መታጠቢያ ቤት muh-ta-t'uh-bi-ya bet
battery ባትሪ ድንጋይ ba-tree din-gai
beautiful ቆንጆ k'on-jo
bed አልጋ al-ga
beer ቢራ bee-ra
bees ንብ nib
before በፊት buh-feet
bicycle ብስክሌት bisk-let
big ትልቅ ti-lik'
blanket ብርድ ልብስ yuh-duhm 'ai-nuht
blood group የደም አይነት yuh-duhm 'ai-nuht
bottle ጠርሙስ t'uhr-mus
bottle opener ጠርሙስ መክፈቻ
 t'uhr-mus muhk-fuh-cha
boy ልጅ lij
brakes (car) ፍሬን fi-ren

breakfast ቁርስ k'urs
bronchitis ብሮንካይትስ bi-ron-kaits

C

cancel መሰረዝ muh-suh-ruhz
can opener ጣሳ መክፈቻ t'a-sa muhk-fuh-cha
cash n ገንዘብ guhn-zuhb
cell phone ሞባይል mo-bail
centre n ማእከል ma-'i-kuhl
cheap ርካሽ ri-kash
check (bill) ቼክ chek
check-in n ቼክ ኢን chek een
chest ደረት duh-ruht
child ልጅ lij
cigarette ሲጋራ see-ga-ra
city ከተማ kuh-tuh-ma
clean a ንጹህ ni-s'uh
closed ዝግ zig
codeine ኮዲን ko-din
cold a ጉንፋን gun-fan
collect call በተዘዋዋሪ buh-tuh-zuh-wa-wa-ree
condom ኮንደም kon-duhm
constipation ድርቀት dir-k'uht
contact lenses የአይን መነጽር
 yuh-ain muh-nuh-s'ir
currency exchange የውጭ ምንዛሪ
 yuh-wich' mi-ni-za-ree
customs (immigration) ጉምሩክ gum-ruk

D

dairy products የወተት ተዋጽኦ
 yuh-wuh-tuht tuh-wa-s'i-'o
dangerous አደገኛ 'a-duh-guhn-ya
date (time) ቀን k'uhn
day ቀን k'uhn
diaper ዳይፐር dai-puhr
diarrhoea ተቅማጥ tuh-k'i-mat'
dinner እራት i-rat
dirty ቆሻሻ k'o-sha-sha
disabled አካለ ስንኩል 'a-ka-luh sin-kul

double bed ሁለት አልጋ በአንድ ክፍል
hu-luht al-ga buh-an-id ki-fil

drink n መጠጥ muh-t'uht

drivers licence መንጃ ፈቃድ muh-ja fuh-k'ad

drug (illicit) አደንዛዥ ዕጽ 'a-duhn-zazh 'is'

E

ear ጆሮ jo-ro

east ምስራቅ mis-rak'

email ኢ.ሜይል 'ee-ma-yil

English (language) እንግሊዘኛ 'ing-lee-zuhn-ya

exchange rate የውጭ ምንዛሪ ዋጋ
yuh-wich' min-za-ree wa-ga

exit n መውጫ muh-wi-ch'a

expensive ውድ wid

eye አይን 'ain

F

fast ፈጣን fuh-t'an

fever ትኩሳት ti-ku-sat

finger ጣት t'at

first class አንደኛ ማዕረግ
'an-duh-nya ma-'i-ruhg

fish n አሳ 'a-sa

food ምግብ mi-gib

foot እግር 'i-gir

fork ሹካ shu-ka

free (of charge) ነጻ nuh-s'a

fruit ፍራፍሬ fi-ra-fi-re

funny አስቂኝ 'as-k'eeny

G

game park ፓርክ park

gift ስጦታ si-t'o-ta

girl ልጃገረድ li-ja-guh-ruhd

glass (drinking) ብርጭቆ bir-ch'i-k'o

glasses መነጽር muh-nuh-s'ir

gluten አንጸባራቂ 'an-s'uh-ba-ra-k'ee

good ጥሩ t'i-ru

guide n መሪ muh-ree

H

hand እጅ 'ij

happy ደስታ duh-si-ta

have አለው/አላት ⒨/ⒻⒺ 'a-luhw/'a-lat

he እሱ 'i-su

head ራስ ras

headache ራስ ምታት ras mi-tat

heart ልብ lib

heart condition የልብ ሁናቴ yuh-lib hu-na-te

heat n ሙቀት mu-k'uht

here እዚህ 'i-zeeh

high ከፍ ያለ kuhf ya-luh

highway የቀለበት መንገድ
yuh-k'uh-luh-buht muhn-guhd

homosexual n&a ሆሞ ho-mo

hot ሙቅ muk'

hungry ረሀብ ruh-hab

I

I እኔ 'i-ne

identification (card) መታወቂያ muh-ta-wuh-k'ee-ya

ill ታመመ ta-muh-muh

important አስፈላጊ 'as-fuh-la-gee

internet ኢንተርኔት 'een-tuhr-net

interpreter አስተርጉዋሚ 'as-tuhr-gu-wa-mee

J

job ስራ si-ra

K

key ቁልፍ k'u-lif

kilogram ኪሎ ግራም kee-lo gi-ram

kitchen ማድ ቤት mad bet

knife ቢላዋ bee-la-wa

L

laundry (place) ላውንደሪ la-win-duh-ree

lawyer ጠበቃ t'uh-buh-k'a

left-luggage office እቃ መርከቢያ መጋዘን
'i-k'a muh-ruh-kuh-bee-ya muh-ga-zuhn

leg እግር 'i-gir

lesbian n&a ሊዝቢያን lez-bee-yan

less ያነሰ ya-nuh-suh

letter (mail) ደብዳቤ duhb-da-be

like v ወደደ wuh-duh-duh

lost-property office ፖሊስ ጣቢያ
po-lees t'a-bee-ya

love v አፈቀረ 'a-fuh-k'uh-ruh

lunch ምሳ mi-sa

M

man ሰው suhw
matches ክብሪት kib-reet
meat ስጋ si-ga
medicine መድሀኒት muhd-ha-neet
message መልእክት muhl-'ikt
month ወር wuhr
morning ጠዋት t'uh-wat
mouth አፍ 'af
movie ሲኒማ see-nee-ma
MSG ሜሳንጀር me-sen-juhr
museum ሙዚየም mu-zee-yuhm
music ሙዚቃ mu-zee-k'a

N

name n ስም sim
napkin ናፕኪን nap-keen
nappy ዳይፐር dai-puhr
national park ብሄራዊ ፓርክ bi-he-ra-wee park
nausea ማጥወልወል mat'-wuhl-wuhl
neck አንገት 'an-guht
new አዲስ 'a-dees
news ዜና ze-na
newspaper ጋዜጣ ga-ze-t'a
night ምሽት mi-shit
nightclub ምሽት ክበብ yuh-mi-shit ki-buhb
noisy የሚረብሽ yuh-mee-ruh-bish
nonsmoking የማይጨስበት yuh-mai-ch'uhs-buht
north ሰሜን suh-men
nose አፍንጫ 'a-fin-ch'a
now አሁን 'a-hun
number ቁጥር k'u-t'ir
nuts እጽሎኒ 'o-cho-lo-nee

O

oil (engine) የሞተር ዘይት yuh-mo-tuhr zuh-yit
OK እሺ 'i-shee
old አሮጌ 'a-ro-ge
open a ክፍት kift
outside ውጪ wi-ch'ee

P

package ፓኬጅ pa-kej
pain ህመም hi-muhm

paper ወረቀት wuh-ruh-k'uht
park (car) v ማቆም ma-k'om
passport ፓስፖርት pas-port
pay v ክፈል ki-fuhl
pen ብእር bi-'ir
petrol ቤንዚን ben-zeen
pharmacy ፋርማሲ far-ma-see
plate ሳህን sa-hin
postcard ፖስት ካርድ post kard
post office ፖስታ ቤት pos-ta bet
pregnant እርጉዝ 'ir-guz

Q

quiet ጸጥ ያለ s'uht' ya-luh

R

rain n ዝናብ zi-nab
razor ምላጭ mi-lach'
registered mail ሪኮማንዴ ree-ko-man-de
rent v ተከራየ tuh-kuh-ra-yuh
repair v ጠገነ t'uh-guh-nuh
reservation መያዣ muh-yaz
restaurant ሬስቶራንት res-to-rant
return v መሰስ/መለስ muh-luh-suh/muh-luh-suhch ⑩/①
road መንገድ muhn-guhd
room ክፍል ki-fil

S

sad ሀዘን ha-zuhn
safe a ሰላም suh-lam
sanitary napkin ሞዴስ mo-des
seafood የባህር ምግቦች yuh-ba-hir mi-gib-och
seat መቀመጫ muh-k'uh-muh-ch'a
send መላክ muh-lak
sex ጾታ s'o-ta
shampoo ሻምፑ sham-pu
share (a dorm, etc) ለህሉት መከራየት luh-hu-luht muh-kuh-ra-yuht
shaving cream የጺም መላጫ ሳሙና yuh-s'eem muh-la-ch'a sa-mu-na
she እሱዋ 'i-su-wa
sheet (bed) አንሶላ 'an-so-la
shirt ሽሚዝ shuh-meez
shoes ጫማ ch'a-ma
shop n ሱቅ suk'

shower n ሻወር sha-wuhr
skin ቆዳ k'o-da
skirt ቀሚስ k'uh-mis
sleep ተኛ Ⓝ tuh-nya
small ትንሽ ti-nish
smoke (cigarettes) v ማጨስ ma-ch'uhs
soap ሳሙና sa-mu-na
some ጥቂት t'i-k'eet
soon በቅርብ buh-k'irb
sore throat የቅስል ጉሮሮ yuh-k'o-suh-luh gu-ro-ro
south ደቡብ dub-bub
speak ተናገር tuh-na-guhr
spoon ማንኪያ man-kee-ya
stamp ቴምብር tem-bir
stand-by ticket የተጠባባቂ ትኬት yuh-tuh-t'uh-ba-ba-k'ee ti-ket
station (train) ጣቢያ t'a-bee-ya
stomach ሆድ hod
stop v ቆመ k'o-muh
stop (bus) n ፌርማታ fer-ma-ta
street መንገድ muhn-guhd
student ተማሪ tuh-ma-ree
sunscreen የጸሀይ መከላከያ yuh-s'uh-hai muh-kuh-la-kuh-ya
swim v ዋኘ wa-nyuh

T

tampons ጎዝ goz
teeth ጥርስ t'irs
telephone ስልክ silk
television ቴሊ tee-vee
temperature (weather) ሙቀት mu-k'uht
tent ድንኩዋን din-ku-wan
that (one) ያ ya
they እነሱ 'i-nuh-su
thirsty መጠማት muh-t'uh-mat
this (one) ይህ yih
throat ጉሮሮ gu-ro-ro
ticket ትኬት ti-ket
time ጊዜ gee-ze
tired ደከመ duh-kuh-muh
tissues ሶፍት soft
today ዛሬ za-re
toilet ሽንት ቤት shint bet
tonight ዛሬ ማታ za-re ma-ta
toothache የጥርስ ህመም yuh-t'irs hi-muhm
toothbrush የጥርስ ብሩሽ yuh-t'irs bi-rush
toothpaste የጥርስ ሳሙና yuh-t'irs sa-mu-na
torch (flashlight) ባትሪ bat-ree

towel ፎጣ fo-t'a
translate መተርጎም muh-tuhr-gom
travel agency የጉዞ ወኪል yuh-gu-zo wuh-keel
trousers ሱሪ su-ree
twin beds ሁለት አልጋ hu-luht al-ga
tyre ጎማ go-ma

U

underwear ቁታንታ bu-tan-ta
urgent አስቸኩዋይ as-chuh-ku-wai

V

vacant ክፍት ቦታ kift bo-ta
vegetable n አትክልት 'at-kilt
vegetarian a አትክልት ተመጋቢ 'at-kilt tuh-muh-ga-bee
visa ቪዛ vee-za

W

waiter አስተናጋጅ as-tuh-na-gaj
walk v በእግር መጓዝ buh-'i-gir muh-gu-waz
wallet የኪስ ቦርሳ yuh-kees bor-sa
warm a ሙቅ muk'
wash (something) ማጠብ ma-t'uhb
watch n ማያት ma-yuht
water ውሀ wi-ha
we እኛ 'i-nya
weekend የሳምንት መጨረሻ yuh-sa-min-tu muh-ch'uh-ruh-sha
west ምእራብ mi-'i-rab
wheelchair ዊል ቸር weel chuhr
when መቼ muh-che
where የት yuht
who ማን man
why ለምን luh-min
window መስኮት muhs-kot
wine ወይን wuh-yin
with ጋር gar
without ያለ ya-luh
woman ሴት set
write መጻፍ muh-s'af

Y

you sg inf አንተ/አንቺ Ⓜ/Ⓕ an-tuh/an-chee
you sg pol እርስዎ 'ir-si-wo
you pl inf&pol እናንተ 'in-an-tuh

Arabic

pronunciation

Vowels		Consonants	
Symbol	**English sound**	**Symbol**	**English sound**
a	**a**ct	b	**b**ed
aa	f**a**ther	d	**d**og
aw	p**aw**	dh	**th**at
ay	s**ay**	f	**f**un
e	b**e**t	gh	a guttural sound, like the French 'r'
ee	s**ee**	h	**h**at
i	h**i**t	j	**j**ar
oo	z**oo**	k	**k**it
u	p**u**t	kh	as the 'ch' in the Scottish 'loch'
'	a pronounced with the throat constricted – like the pause in the middle of 'uh-oh'	l	**l**ot
		m	**m**an
		n	**n**ot
		r	**r**un
		s	**s**un
		sh	**sh**ot
		t	**t**op
		th	**th**in
		w	**w**in
		y	**y**es
		z	**z**ero

In this chapter, the Arabic pronunciation is given in green after each phrase.

Each syllable is separated by a dot, and the syllable stressed in each word is italicised.

For example:

نعم. na·'am

العربية – pronunciation

46

introduction

It may have given us the terms 'algebra' and 'massacre', but we can also thank Arabic for the names of more pleasant things like 'alcohol', 'coffee' and 'jasmine'. Arabic (العربية al·'a·ra·bee·ya) belongs to the Semitic branch of the Afro-Asiatic language family, and is closely related to Hebrew and Aramaic. The language of the Quran (Koran), Arabic owes its wide spread to the advent of Islam and the subsequent rise of the Muslim Empire during the 7th and 8th centuries. It's the fifth-most spoken language in the world, with almost 300 million native speakers worldwide, it's the official language of the Arab nations that spread across the Middle East and North Africa (comprising 423 million people), and it's a national language of Mali, Niger, Senegal and Somalia. Though there are many groups of Arab dialects – which can be broadly divided into North African and Middle Eastern dialects – Modern Standard Arabic (MSA) is the form of Arabic used by the media and taught in schools in the Arab world. So if you're planning to visit an Arabic-speaking country, start getting your mind – and tongue – around some MSA phrases!

■ **arabic** (native language)   ■ **arabic** (generally understood)

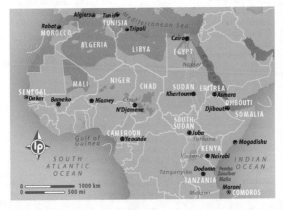

language difficulties

Do you speak English?

هل تتكلّمُ/تتكلّمِينَ
الإنجليزية؟

hal ta·ta·*kal*·la·mu/ta·ta·kal·la·*mee*·na al·'inj·lee·*zee*·ya m/f

Do you understand?

هل تفهمُ/تفهمِينَ؟

hal *taf*·ha·mu/taf·ha·*mee*·na m/f

I (don't) understand.

أنا (لا) أفهم

'a·naa (laa) 'af·ham

Could you	لو سمحتَ	law sa·*mah*·ta
please ...?	يمكنك أن ...؟	yum·*ki*·nu·ka 'an ... m
repeat that	تكرّر ذلك	tu·*ka*·ri·ra *dhaa*·lik
speak more slowly	تتكلّم ببطء	ta·ta·*kal*·la·ma bi·*but*'
write it down	تكتبه على الورقة	tak·*tu*·ba·hu 'a·laa al·*wa*·ra·ka

time, dates & numbers

What time is it?	كم الساعة الآن؟	kam as·*saa*·'a·tul 'aan
It's one o'clock.	الساعة الواحدة.	as·*saa*·'a·tul *waa*·hi·da
It's (two) o'clock.	الساعة (الثانية).	as·*saa*·'a·tu (ath·*thaa*·nee·ya)
Quarter past (two).	(الثانية) والربع.	(ath·thaa·*nee*·ya·tu) war·*rub*·'u
Half past (two).	(الثانية) والنصف.	(ath·thaa·*nee*·ya·tu) wan·*nus*·fu
Quarter to (two).	(الثانية) إلا الربع.	(ath·thaa·*nee*·ya·tu) *'il*·la ar·*rub*·'u
At what time ...?	في أيّ ساعةٍ ...؟	fee *'ay*·yee *saa*·'a·tin ...
At ...	في ...	fee ...
It's (15 December).	انّه (الخامس عشر من ديسمبر).	*'in*·na·hu (al·*khaa*·mis 'a·*shar* min dee·*sem*·bir)

yesterday	أمس	*'am*·si
today	اليوم	al·*yawm*
tomorrow	غداً	*gha*·dan

Monday	يوم الاثنين	yawm al·'ith·*nayn*
Tuesday	يوم الثلاثاء	yawm ath·thu·laa·*thaa*'
Wednesday	يوم الأربعاء	yawm al·'ar·bi·*'aa*
Thursday	يوم الخميس	yawm al·kha·*mees*
Friday	يوم الجمعة	yawm al·*jum*·'a
Saturday	يوم السبت	yawm as·*sabt*
Sunday	يوم الأحد	yawm al·*'a*·had

0	٠	صفر *sifr*	16	١٦	ستة عشر *sit*·ta·ta *'a*·shar
1	١	واحد *waa*·hid	17	١٧	سبعة عشر *sa*·ba·'ta *'a*·shar
2	٢	اثنان *ith*·*naan*	18	١٨	ثمانية عشر *tha*·*maa*·ni·ya·ta *'a*·shar
3	٣	ثلاثة tha·*laa*·tha	19	١٩	تسعة عشر *tis*·'a·ta *'a*·shar
4	٤	أربعة *'ar*·ba·'a	20	٢٠	عشرون *'ish*·roon
5	٥	خمسة *kham*·sa	21	٢١	واحد وعشرون *waa*·hid wa·*'ish*·roon
6	٦	ستة *sit*·ta	22	٢٢	اثنان وعشرون *ith*·*naan* wa·*'ish*·roon
7	٧	سبعة *sa*·b'a	30	٣٠	ثلاثون tha·*laa*·thoon
8	٨	ثمانية tha·*maa*·ni·ya	40	٤٠	أربعون *'ar*·ba·*'oon*
9	٩	تسعة *tis*·'a	50	٥٠	خمسون kham·*soon*
10	١٠	عشرة *'a*·sha·ra	60	٦٠	ستون sit·*toon*
11	١١	احد عشر *'a*·ha·da *'a*·shar	70	٧٠	سبعون sab·*'oon*
12	١٢	اثنا عشر *'ith*·naa·*'a*·shar	80	٨٠	ثمانون tha·maa·*noon*
13	١٣	ثلاثة عشر tha·*laa*·tha·ta *'a*·shar	90	٩٠	تسعون tis·*'oon*
14	١٤	أربعة عشر *'ar*·ba·'a·ta *'a*·shar	100	١٠٠	مائة *mi*·'a
15	١٥	خمسة عشر *kham*·sa·ta *'a*·shar	1000	١٠٠٠	ألف *'alf*

border crossing

I'm here ...	... غرض زيارتي هو	*gha*·ra·du zee·*yaa*·ra·tee *hu*·wa ...
in transit (to) ...	... (العبور (إلى	al·'u·*boo*·ru (*'i*·laa) ...
on business	التجارة	at·ti·*jaa*·ra
on holiday	السياحة	as·see·*yaa*·ha

I'm here for ...	... مدّة إقامتي هنا	*mud*·da·tu *'i·kaa*·ma·tee *hu*·na ...
(10) days	(عشرة) أيّام	(*'a*·sha·ra·tu) *'ay·yaam*
(three) weeks	(ثلاثة) أسابيع	(tha·*laa*·tha·tu) *'a·saa·bee'*
(four) months	(أربعة) أشهر	(*'ar*·ba·'a·tu) *'ash*·hur

I'm going to (Khartoum).

سأسافر إلى (الخرطوم). sa·'u·*saa*·fi·ru *'i*·laa (al·khar·*toom*)

I'm staying at the (Hilton).

سأقيم بـ(فندق الهلتون). sa·'u·*kee*·mu bi·(*fun*·du·kil hil·*toon*)

tickets

A ... ticket (to Cairo), please.	... تذكرة (إلى القاهرة), لو سمحتَ.	*tadh*·ka·ra·tu ... (*'i*·laa al·*kaa*·hi·ra) law sa·*mah*·ta
one-way	ذهاب فقط	dha·*haa*·bu fa·kat
return	ذهاب وإياب	dha·*haa*·bu wa·'ee·*yaab*
I'd like to ... my my ticket, please.	أريد أن ... تذكرتي, لو سمحتَ.	'u·*ree*·du 'an ... tadh·*ki*·ra·tee law sa·*mah*·ta
cancel	ألغيَ	'*ul*·ghi·ya
change	أغيرَ	'u·*ghay*·yi·ra
collect	أجمعَ	'*aj*·ma·'a
I'd like a ... seat, please.	أريد مقعداً ...., لو سمحتَ.	'u·*ree*·du *mak*·'a·dan ... law sa·*mah*·ta
nonsmoking	في قسم غير المدخّنين	fee *kis*·mi *ghay*·ril mu·dakh·khi·*neen*
smoking	في قسم المدخّنين	fee *kis*·mil mu·dakh·khi·*neen*

Is there air conditioning?

هل يوجد مكيف الهواء؟   hal *yoo*·ja·du mu·*kay*·ya·ful ha·*waa'*

Is there a toilet?

هل يوجد دورات المياه؟   hal *yoo*·ja·du daw·*raa*·tul mee·*yaah*

How long does the trip take?

كم مدّة الرحلة   kam *mud*·da·ti ar·*rih*·la

Is it a direct route?

هل الطريق مباشر؟   hal at·ta·*reek* mu·*baa*·shir

transport

Where does flight (CL58) arrive/depart?

من أين تُغادر/ تصل رحلة (سي ال ٥٨)؟   min *'ay*·na tu·*ghaa*·di·ru/*ta*·si·lu *rih*·la (see el tha·*maa*·ni·ya wa kham·*soon*)

How long will it be delayed?

كم ساعةٍ سيتأخر؟   kam *saa*·'a·tin sa·ya·ta·*'akh*·khir

Is this the ...	... هل هذا ال	hal *haa*·dhaa al ...
to (Alexandria)?	إلى (الاسكندرية)؟	*'i*·laa (al·*'is*·kan·da·*ree*·ya)
boat	سفينة	sa·*fee*·na
bus	باص	baas
plane	طائرة	*taa*·'i·ra
train	قطار	ki·*taar*

How much is it to ...?

كم الأجرة إلى ...؟   kam al·*'uj*·ra·ti *'i*·laa ...

Please take me to (this address).

أوصلني عند (هذا العنوان)   '*aw*·sal·nee 'ind (*haa*·dhaa al·'un·*waan*)
لو سمحت.   law sa·*mah*·ta

I'd like to hire a ...	... أريدُ أن أستأجرَ	'*u*·ree·du 'an 'as·*ta*'·ji·ra ...
car	سيارة	say·*yaa*·ra
4WD	سيارة ذات الدفع	say·*yaa*·ra that ad·*daf*·'il
	الرباعي	ru·*baa*·'ee

| with air conditioning | ذات مكيف الهواء | thaat mu·*kay*·ya·ful ha·*waa*' |

How much is it for (three) days/weeks?

كم الأجرة لـ(ثلاثة)   kam al·*'uj*·ra li·(tha·*laa*·tha·ti)
أيام/أسابيع؟   '*ay*·yaam/'a·saa·*bee*

directions

Where's (the nearest) ...?	...؟ أين (أقرب)	'*ay*·na ('*ak*·ra·bu) ...
internet café	مقهى الانترنت	*mak*·ha al·'in·*tir*·net
market	سوق	sook

Is this the road to (Asmara)?

هل هذا الشارع إلى   hal *haa*·dhaa ash·*shaa*·ri·'u *'i*·laa
(اسمره)؟   (*as*·ma·ra)

Can you show me (on the map)?

هل يمكنك أن توضح لي   hal yum·*ki*·nu·ka 'an tu·*wad*·da·ha lee
(على الخريطة)؟ m   ('*a*·laa al·kha·*ree*·ta)

هل يمكنكِ أن توضحي لي   hal yum·*ki*·nu·ki 'an tu·*wad*·da·hee lee
(على الخريطة)؟f   ('*a*·laa al·kha·*ree*·ta)

What's the address?

ما هو العنوان؟   maa *hu*·wa al·'un·*waan*

How far is it?

كم يبعد المكان من هنا؟

kam *yab*·'u·du al·ma·*kaa*·nu min *hu*·naa

How do I get there?

كيف أصِل إلى هناك؟

kay·fa *'a*·si·lu *'i*·laa hu·*naak*

Turn left/right.

اتجه إلى اليمين/اليسار.

'it·ta·jih *'i*·laa al·ya·*meen*/al·ya·*saar* m

اتجهي إلى اليمين/اليسار.

'it·*ta*·ji·hee *'i*·laa al·ya·*meen*/al·ya·*saar* f

It's ...

هو/هي ...

hu·wa/*hi*·ya ... m/f

   behind ...

وراء ...

wa·*raa*' ...

   in front of ...

أمامَ ...

'a·*maam* ...

   near (to ...)

قريب (من ...)

ka·*reeb* (min ...)

   next to ...

بجانب ...

bi·*jaa*·ni·bi ...

   on the corner

عندَ الزاوية

'an·da az·*zaa*·wi·ya

   opposite ...

بمقابل ...

bi·mu·*kaa*·bil ...

   straight ahead

إلى الأمام

'i·laa al·*'a*·*maam*

   there

هناك

hu·*naak*

accommodation

Where's a ...?

أين أجدُ ...؟

'ay·na *'a*·ji·du ...

   camping ground

مخيم

mu·*khay*·yam

   guesthouse

بيت للضيوف

bayt li·du·*yoof*

   hotel

فندق

fun·duk

   youth hostel

فندق شباب

fun·duk sha·*baab*

Can you recommend somewhere cheap/good?

هل يمكنك أن توصيَ بمكان رخيص/جيّد؟

hal yum·*ki*·nu·ka 'an too·*see*·ya bi·ma·*kaan* ra·*khees*/jay·yid m

هل يمكنكِ أن توصي بمكان رخيص/جيّد؟

hal yum·*ki*·nu·ki 'an *too*·see bi·ma·*kaan* ra·*khees*/jay·yid f

I'd like to book a room, please.

أريد أن أحجزَ غرفة لو سمحتَ.

'u·*ree*·du 'an *'ah*·ji·za *ghur*·fa law sa·*mah*·ta

I have a reservation.

عندي حجز.

'in·dee hajz

Do you have	هل عندكم	hal 'in·da·kum
a ... room?	غرفة ...؟	ghur·fa ...
single	بسرير منفرد	bi·sa·ree·rin mun·fa·rid
double	بسرير مزدوّج	bi·sa·ree·rin muz·daw·waj
twin	بسريرين منفردينِ	bi·sa·ree·ray·ni mun·fa·ri·day·ni

How much is	كم ثمنه	kam tha·ma·nu·hu
it per ...?	لِ ...؟	li ...
night	ليلة واحدة	lay·la·tin waa·hid
person	شخصٍ واحد	shakh·sin waa·hid

I'd like to stay for (three) nights.

أريد الإقامة لمدّةِ
(ثلاث) ليالي.

'u·ree·du al·'i·kaa·ma li·mud·da·ti
(tha·laa·thi) lay·yaa·lee

What time is check-out?

في أيّ ساعةِ المغادرة؟

fee 'ay·yee saa·'a·tin al·mu·ghaa·da·ra

Am I allowed to camp here?

هل من الممكن أن أخيمَ هنا؟

hal min al·mum·kin 'an 'u·khay·ya·ma hu·naa

banking & communications

I'd like to ...	أريدُ أن ...	'u·ree·du 'an ...
arrange a transfer	أقومَ بتحويل مالي	'a·koo·ma bi·tah·wee·li maa·lee
cash a cheque	أصرفَ شيك	'as·ru·fa sheek
change a travellers cheque	أحوّلَ شيكاً سياحي	'u·haw·wi·la shee·kan see·yaa·hee
change money	أحوّلَ النقود	'u·haw·wi·la an·nu·kood
withdraw money	أسحبَ نقود	'as·hu·ba nu·kood

I'd like to ...	أريد أن ...	'u·ree·du 'an ...
buy a phonecard	أشتريَ بطاقة تلفونية	'ash·ta·ree·ya bi·taa·ka ti·li·foo·nee·ya
call (Canada)	أتّصلَ بـ(كندا)	'at·ta·si·la bi·(ka·na·daa)
get internet access	أستخدمَ الانترنت	'as·takh·di·ma al·'in·tir·net
reverse the charges	أقومَ باتّصالٍ والأجرة على الشخصِ المتلقي الاتصال	'a·koo·ma bi·'it·ti·saa·li wal·'uj·ra 'a·laa ash·shakh·sil mut·la·kee al·'it·ti·saal
use a printer	أستخدمَ آلة الطباعة	'as·takh·di·ma 'aa·lat at·ta·baa·'a

How much is it per hour?

ما تكلفة الساعة الواحدة؟

maa tak·*li*·fa·tu as·*saa*·'a·til *waa*·hi·da

How much does a (three)-minute call cost?

كم تكلفة الاتصال لمدة (ثلاثِ) دقائق؟

kam tak·*li*·fa·til 'it·ti·*saa*·li li·*mud*·da·ti (tha·*laa*·thi) da·*kaa*·'ik

(One pound) per minute/hour.

(جنيه واحدة) بدقيقةٍ/بساعةٍ.

(ju·*nay*·ha *waa*·hi·da) bi·da·*kee*·ka/ bi·*saa*·'a

tours

When's the next ...?	متى الـ ... القادم؟	*ma*·taa al· ... al·*kaa*·dim
day trip	رحلة يومية	*rih*·la yaw·*mee*·ya
tour	دورة	*daw*·ra

Is ... included?	هل يتضمّنُ على ...؟	hal ya·ta·*dam*·ma·nu 'a·laa ...
accommodation	سكن	sa·kan
the admission charge	ثمن الدخول	tha·man ad·du·*khool*
food	الطعام	at·ta·*'aam*
transport	المواصلات	al·mu·waa·sa·*laat*

How long is the tour?

كم مدّة الدورة؟

kam *mud*·da·ti ad·*daw*·ra

What time should we be back?

في أيِّ ساعةٍ يجب أن نرجعَ إلى هنا؟

fee *'ay*·yee *saa*·'a·tin ya·ji·bu 'an *nar*·ja·'a 'i·laa hu·*naa*

shopping

I'm looking for ...

أبحثُ عن ...

'*ab*·ha·thu 'an ...

I need film for this camera.

حتاج إلى فيلماً لهذِه الكاميرا.

'ah·*taa*·ju 'i·laa *feel*·man li·*haa*·dhi·hil kaa·*mee*·raa

Can I listen to this?

هل يمكنني أن أسمعَ إلى هذا؟

hal yum·*ki*·nu·nee 'an '*as*·ma·'a 'i·laa haa·dhaa

Can I have my ... repaired?

هل يمكنك أن تصلّحَ لي ...؟

hal yum·*ki*·nu·ka 'an tus·*li*·ha lee ...

When will it be ready?

متى يكون جاهز؟   *ma*·taa ya·*koo*·nu *jaa*·hiz

How much is it?

كم سعره؟   kam *si*'·ru·hu

Can you write down the price?

هل يمكنُكَ أن تكتبَ لي السعر؟   hal yum·*ki*·nu·ka 'an *tak*·tu·ba lee as·*si*'r m

هل يمكنكِ أن تكتبي لي السعر؟   hal yum·*ki*·nu·ki 'an tak·tu·*bee* lee as·*si*'r f

What's your lowest price?

ما أحسنُ سعر لديكم؟   maa '*ah*·sa·nu *si*'·ri la·*day*·kum

I'll give you (five pounds).

سأدفع (خمس جنيهات).   sa·'*ad*·fa·'u bi (*kham*·su ju·nay·*haat*)

There's a mistake in the bill.

يوجد خطأ في الحساب.   *yoo*·jad *kha*·ta' feel hi·*saab*

It's faulty.

هذا لا يعمل.   *haa*·dhaa laa *ya*'·mal

I'd like a (receipt/refund).

أريد (وصل/استرداد مال)   'u·*ree*·du (*wa*·sil/'is·tir·*daad* maal)

Do you accept ...?	هل تقبلونَ ...؟	hal tak·ba·*loo*·na ...
credit cards	بطاقات الرصيد	bi·taa·*kaat* ar·ra·*seed*
debit cards	بطاقات الاقتراض	bi·taa·*kaat* al·'ik·ti·*raad*
travellers cheques	شيكات سياحية	shee·*kaat* see·yaa·*hee*·ya
Could you ...?	هل يمكنكَ ...؟	hal yum·*ki*·nu·ka ... m
	هل يمكنكِ ...؟	hal yum·*ki*·nu·ki ... f
burn a CD from	تجهّزَ قرصاً مدمج	tu·*jah*·hi·za *kur*·san mu·*dam*·maj
my memory card	من بطاقتي الذاكرة	min bi·*taa*·ka·tee adh·*dhaa*·ki·ra
develop this film	تحمّضَ هذا الفيلم	tu·*ham*·mi·da *haa*·dhaa al·*feelm*

making conversation

Hello.	السلام عليكم.	as·sa·*laa*·mu '*a*·lay·kum
Good night.	تصبِح على الخير.	*tus*·bi·hu '*a*·laa al·*khayr*
Goodbye.	إلى اللقاء.	'*i*·laa al·li·*kaa*'
Mr	سيد	say·*yeed*
Mrs/Miss	سيدة	say·*yee*·da

How are you?

كيف حالكَ؟   *kay*·fa *haa*·lu·ka m

كيف حالكِ؟   *kay*·fa *haa*·lu·ki f

Fine, thanks. And you?

بخيرٍ شكراً. وأنتَ/وأنتِ؟   bi·*khay*·rin *shuk*·ran wa·*an*·ta/wa·*an*·ti m/f

What's your name?

ما اسمكَ/اسمكِ؟   maa *'is*·mu·ka/*'is*·mu·ki m/f

My name is ...

اسمي ...   *'is*·mee ...

I'm pleased to meet you.

أنا سعيدٌ/سعيدةٌ   *'a*·naa sa·*'ee*·dun/sa·*'ee*·da·tun

بالتعرُّف عليك.   bit·ta·*'ar*·ruf *'a*·layk m/f

This is my ...   هذا/هذه ...   haa·*dhaa*/haa·*dhi*·hi ... m/f

brother	أخي	*'a*·khee
daughter	ابنتي	*'ib*·na·tee
father	أبي	*'a*·bee
friend	صديقي/صديقتي	sa·*dee*·kee/sa·*dee*·ka·tee m/f
husband	زوجي	*zaw*·jee
mother	أمّي	*'um*·mee
sister	أختي	*'ukh*·tee
son	ابني	*'ib*·nee
wife	زوجتي	*zaw*·ja·tee

Here's my ...   هذا ...   haa·*dhaa* ...

What's your ...?   ما ...؟   maa ...

(email) address	عنوانكَ/عنوانكِ	*'un*·waa·nu·ka/*'un*·waa·nu·ki
	(البريد الالكتروني)	(al·ba·*ree*·deel *'i*·lik·*troo*·nee) m/f
phone number	رقم هاتفكَ/	*rak*·mu haa·*ti*·fu·ka/
	هاتفكِ	haa·*ti*·fu·ki m/f

Where are you from?   من أين أنتَ/أنتِ؟   min *'ay*·na *an*·ta/*an*·ti m/f

I'm from ...   أنا من ...   *'a*·naa min ...

Australia	أستراليا	*'us*·traa·li·yaa
Canada	كندا	*ka*·na·daa
New Zealand	نيو زيلندا	nee·*yoo* zee·*lan*·daa
the UK	بريطانيا	ba·*ree*·*taa*·ni·ya
the USA	أمريكا	*'am*·*ree*·kaa

I'm (not) married.   أنا (لستُ)   *'a*·naa (*las*·tu)

متزوّج/متزوّجة.   mu·ta·*zaw*·waj/mu·ta·*zaw*·wa·ja m/f

Can I take   يمكنني أن آخذَ   yum·*ki*·nu·nee *'an* *'aa*·khu·dha

a photo of you?   صورتكَ/صورتكِ؟   soo·*ra*·tu·ka/soo·*ra*·tu·ki m/f

eating out

Can you recommend a ...?	هل يمكنك أن توصي بـ ...؟	hal yum-*ki*-nu-ka 'an *too*-*see*-ya ... m
	هل يمكنك أن توصي بـ ...؟	hal yum-*ki*-ki 'an *too*-see ... f
bar	بارّ	baar
dish	وجبة	*waj*-ba
place to eat	مكان نأكل فيه	ma-*kaa*-nun na'-ku-lu *fee*-hi
I'd like ..., please.	أريدُ ...، لو سمحت.	'u-*ree*-du ... law sa-*mah*-ta
the bill	الحساب	al-hi-*saab*
the menu	قائمة الطعام	kaa-'i-ma-tu at-ta-'*aam*
a table for (four)	طاولة لـ (أربعة) أشخاص	taa-wi-la-tan li-('ar-*ba*-'a-ti) 'ash-*khaas*
that dish	تلك الوجبة	*til*-kal *waj*-ba
Do you have vegetarian food?	هل لديكم طعامٌ نباتيٌّ؟	hal la-*day*-ku-mu ta-'*aa*-mun na-*baa*-tee
Could you prepare a meal without ...?	هل من الممكن أن تعدَّ وجبةً بدونِ ...؟	hal min al-*mum*-kin 'an tu-'*id*-da *waj*-ba-tan bi-*doo*-ni ...
eggs	بيض	bayd
meat stock	مرق اللحم	ma-rak al-*lah*-mi
(cup of) coffee ...	(فنجانُ) قهوة ...	(fin-*jaa*-nu) *kah*-wa ...
(cup of) tea ...	(كأسُ) شاي ...	(ka'-su) *shaa*-ee ...
with milk	بحليب	bi-ha-*leeb*
without sugar	بدونِ سكّر	bi-*doo*-ni *suk*-kar
(boiled) water	ماء (مغلي)	maa' (*magh*-lee)

emergencies

Call ...!	اتصل/اتصلي بـ ...!	'*it*-ta-sil/'*it*-*ta*-si-lee bi- ... m/f
an ambulance	سيارة الإسعاف	say-*yaa*-ra-til 'is-'*aaf*
a doctor	طبيب	ta-*beeb*
the police	الشرطة	ash-*shur*-ta

Could you help me, please?

هل من الممكن أن تساعدني/تساعديني؟

hal min al-*mum*-kin 'an tu-saa-'*i*-du-nee/tu-saa-'*i*-*dee*-na-nee m/f

I'm lost.

أنا ضائع/ضائعة.

'*a*-naa daa-'*i*'/daa-'*i*-'a m/f

Where are the toilets?

أينّ دورات المياه؟   'ay·na daw·raa·tul mee·yaah

I want to report an offence.

أريد أن أبلّغ عن جريمة.   'u·ree·du 'an 'u·bal·li·gha 'an ja·ree·ma

I have insurance.

عندي تأمين.   'in·dee al·ta'·meen

I want to contact my consulate/embassy.

أريد أن اتصل   'u·ree·du 'an 'at·ta·si·la
بقنصليتي/بسفارتي،   bi·kun·su·li·ya·tee/bi·sa·faa·ra·tee

I've been assaulted.	اعتدى عليّ شخص.	i'·ta·daa 'a·la·yee shakhs
I've been raped.	اغتصبني شخص.	'igh·ta·sa·ba·nee shakhs
I've been robbed.	سرّقني شخص.	sa·ra·ka·nee shakhs
My ... was/were	... كان مسروق.	... kaa·na mas·rook m
stolen.	... كانت مسروقة.	... kaa·nat mas·roo·ka f
bag	حقيبتي	ha·kee·ba·tee
money	نقودي	nu·koo·dee
passport	جواز سفري	ja·waa·zu sa·fa·ree
wallet	محفظتي	mah·fa·dha·tee

medical needs

Where's the nearest ...?	أين أقربُ ...؟	'ay·na 'ak·ra·bu ...
dentist	طبيب الأسنان	ta·bee·bul 'as·naan
doctor	طبيب/طبيبة	ta·beeb/ta·bee·ba m/f
hospital	مستشفى	mus·tash·faa
pharmacist	صيدلية	say·da·lee·ya

I need a doctor (who speaks English).

أحتاج إلى طبيب   'ah·taa·ju 'i·laa ta·bee·bin
(يتكلم الانجليزية).   (ya·ta·kal·la·mu al·'inj·lee·zee·ya)

Could I see a female doctor?

هل من الممكن أن أقابلَ طبيبة؟   hal min al·mum·kin 'an 'u·kaa·bi·la ta·bee·ba

It hurts here.

يؤلمني هنا.   yu'·li·mu·nee hu·naa

I've run out of my medication.

لقد نفذتُ جميع أدويتي.   la·kad na·fadh·tu ja·mee·'u 'ad·wi·ya·tee

I'm allergic to (penicillin).

عندي حساسيّة من   'an·dee has·saa·see·ya min
(البنسلين).   (al·bi·ni·si·leen)

english–arabic dictionary

Words in this dictionary are marked as n (noun), a (adjective), v (verb), sg (singular) and pl (plural), ⓜ masculine and ⓕ feminine where necessary. Where both the masculine and the feminine forms of a word are given, they're marked with ⓜ/ⓕ. Verbs are given in the third-person singular, in the present tense.

A

accommodation سكن *sa*-kan ⓜ
adaptor الموصل al-mu-*was*-sil ⓜ
after بعد *ba*'-da
airport مطار ma-*taar* ⓜ
alcohol الكحول al-ku-*hool* ⓜ
all كل *kul*-luⓛ
allergy حساسية has-*saa*-si-ya ⓕ
and و *wa*
ankle كاحل *kaa*-hil ⓕ
antibiotics مضاد حيوي mu-*daa*-dun ha-ya-wee ⓜ
arm ذراع *dhi-raa*' ⓕ
asthma الربو ar-*rabw* ⓜ
ATM جهاز الصرافة ji-*haaz* as-sar-*raa*-fa ⓜ

B

baby طفلٌ صغير/طفلةٌ صغيرة
tif-lu sa-*gheer*/*tif*-la-tun sa-*ghee*-ra ⓜ/ⓕ
back شنطة *shan*-ta
backpack ظهر *shan*-ta-tu dhahr ⓕ
bad سيّئ/سيّئة *say*-yi'/*say*-yi'-a ⓜ/ⓕ
baggage claim مكان لجمع الأمتعة
ma-*kaa*-nun li-*jam*-'il '*am*-ti-'a ⓜ
bank بنك bank ⓜ
bathroom غرفة الحمام *ghur*-fa-tul ham-*maam* ⓕ
battery بطارية ba-*taa*-ri-ya ⓕ
beautiful جميل/جميلة ja-*meel*/ja-*mee*-la ⓜ/ⓕ
bed سرير *sa*-reer ⓜ
beer بيرة *bee*-ra ⓕ
before قبل *kab*-la
bicycle درّاجة dar-*raa*-ja ⓕ
big كبير/كبيرة ka-*beer*/ka-*bee*-ra ⓜ/ⓕ
blanket بطانية ba-*taa*-ni-ya ⓕ
bottle زجاجة zu-*jaa*-ja ⓕ
bottle opener فاتح الزجاجات
faa-ti-hu az-zu-jaa-*jaat* ⓜ
boy ولد *wa*-lad ⓜ
breakfast فطور fu-*toor* ⓜ
bronchitis التهاب الشُعَب il-ti-*haab* ash-*shu*-'ab ⓜ

C

café مقهى *mak*-han ⓜ
cancel يلغي/تلغي *yul*-ghee/*tul*-ghee ⓜ/ⓕ
can opener فاتح التكة *faa*-ti-hu at-*tan*-ka ⓜ
cash n نقد nukd ⓜ
cell phone هاتف محمول *haa*-ti-fu mah-*mool* ⓜ
centre n مركز *mar*-kaz ⓜ
cheap رخيص/رخيصة ra-*khees*/ra-*khee*-sa ⓜ/ⓕ
check (bill) الحساب al-hi-*saab* ⓜ
check-in n مكتب التسجيل *mak*-ta-bu at-tas-*jeel* ⓜ
chest صدر sadr ⓜ
child طفل/طفلة *tif*-lu/*tif*-la ⓜ/ⓕ
cigarette سجارة si-*jaa*-ra ⓕ
city مدينة ma-*dee*-na ⓕ
clean a نظيف/نظيفة na-*dheef*/na-*dhee*-fa ⓜ/ⓕ
closed مغلق/مغلقة *mugh*-lak/*mugh*-la-ka ⓜ/ⓕ
cold a بارد/باردة *baa*-rid/*baa*-ri-da ⓜ/ⓕ
collect call
اتصال والأجرة على الشخص المتلقي الاتصال *it*-ti-saal
wal-'uj-ra 'a-laa al-*shakh*-sil *mut*-la-kee al-'it-ti-*saal*
ⓜ
condom الواقي al-*waa*-kee ⓜ
contact lenses عدسة لاصقة *a*-da-sa-tun laa-*si*-ka ⓕ
cough su-*'aal* سعال ⓜ
currency exchange صرافة *sa*-raa-fa ⓕ
customs (immigration) جمارك ja-*maa*-rik ⓜ

D

dairy products الألبان al-'al-*baan* ⓜ
dangerous خطر/خطرة khatr/*khat*-ra ⓜ/ⓕ
date (time) تاريخ taa-*reekh* ⓜ
day يوم yawm ⓜ
diaper حفاظة طفل ha-*faa*-dha-tu tifl ⓜ
diarrhoea الإسهال al-'is-*haal* ⓜ
dinner عشاء a-*shaa*' ⓜ
dirty وسخ/وسخة waskh/*was*-kha ⓜ/ⓕ
disabled معاق/معاقة mu-'*aak*/mu-'*aa*-ka ⓜ/ⓕ
double bed سرير مزدوج *sa*-ree-run muz-*daw*-waj ⓜ
drink n مشروب mash-*roob* ⓜ
drivers licence
رخصة القيادة
rukh-sa-tul kee-*yaa*-da ⓕ
(drug (illicit) مخدّر mu-*khad*-dir ⓜ

E

ear أذن *u*-dhun ①
east شرق shark
economy class الدرجة العادية
ad-*da*-ra-ja-tul *'aa*-diy-ya ①
elevator مصعد *mas*-'ad ⓜ
email البريد الالكتروني al-ba-*ree*-dul 'i-lik-*troo*-nee ⓜ
English (language) الإنجليزية al-'inj-lee-*zee*-ya ①
exchange rate سعر التحويل *si*-'ru at-tah-*weel* ⓜ
exit ⓜ مخرج *makh*-raj
expensive غال/غالية *ghaa*-lin/ghaa-*lee*-ya ⓜ/①
eye عين *'ayn* ①

F

fast سريع/سريعة sa-*ree*'/sa-*ree*-'a ⓜ/①
fever حمى *hum*-maa ①
finger إصبع *'is*-ba' ①
first-aid kit صندوق للإسعاف الأولي
sun-*doo*-kun lil-'is-*'aa*-fil *'aw*-wa-lee
first class الدرجة الأولى ad-*da*-ra-ja-tul *'oo*-la ①
fish ⓜ سمك *sa*-mak
food طعام ta-*'aam*
foot قدم *ka*-dam
fork شوكة *shaw*-ka ①
free (of charge) مجاناً ma-*jaa*-nan
fruit فاكهة *faa*-ki-ha ①
funny مضحك/مضحكة *mud*-hik/*mud*-hi-ka ⓜ/①

G

game park مدينة ملاه متنقلة
ma-*dee*-na-tu ma-*laa*-hin mu-ta-*nak*-ka-la ①
gift هدية ha-*dee*-ya ①
girl بنت bint ①
glass (drinking) كأس ka's ⓜ
glasses نظارات na-dhaa-*raat* ①
gluten الغلوتين al-ghloo-*teen* ⓜ
good جيّد/جيّدة jay-*yid*/jay-*yi*-da ⓜ/①
gram غرام ghraam

H

hand يد yad ①
happy سعيد/سعيدة sa-*'eed*/sa-*'ee*-da ⓜ/①
have عند *'ind*
he هو *hu*-wa ⓜ
head رأس ra's ⓜ
headache صداع su-*daa*' ⓜ
heart قلب kalb ⓜ
heart condition مشكلة القلب
mush-*ki*-la-tul kalb ①

heat ⓜ حرارة ha-*raa*-ra ①
here هنا *hu*-naa
high عال/عالية *'aa*-lin/*'aa*-li-ya ⓜ/①
highway طريق عام ta-*ree*-ku 'aam ⓜ
homosexual لوطي/سحاقية
loo-tee/su-haa-*kee*-ya ⓜ/①
hot حار/حارة haar/haa-ra ⓜ/①
hungry جائع/جائعة *jaa*-'i'/*jaa*-'i-'a ⓜ/①

I

identification (card) شخصية shakh-*see*-ya ①
ill مريض/مريضة ma-*reed*/ma-*ree*-da ⓜ/①
important مهم/مهمة mu-*him*/mu-*him*-ma ⓜ/①
internet الإنترنت *'in*-tir-net
interpreter مترجم/مترجمة فورية
mu-*tar*-jim faw-*ree*/mu-*tar*-ji-ma faw-*ree*-ya ⓜ/①

J

job عمل *'a*-mal ⓜ

K

key مفتاح mif-*taah*
kilogram كيلوغرام kee-loo-*ghraam*
kitchen مطبخ *mat*-bakh
knife سكين sik-*keen* ⓜ

L

laundry (place) مغسل *magh*-sal ⓜ
lawyer محام/محامية
mu-*haa*-min/mu-haa-*mee*-ya ①/①
left-luggage office مكتب للاحتفاظ بالأمتعة
mak-ta-bun li-li-'ih-ti-*faa*-dhi bil-'am-ti-'a ⓜ
leg رجل rijl ①
lesbian سحاقية su-haa-*kee*-ya ①
less أقل ri-*saa*-la
letter (mail) رسالة ri-*saa*-la ①
like v يحب/تحب yu-*hib*-bu/tu-*hib*-bu ⓜ/①
lost-property office مكتب للأغراض الضائعة
mak-ta-bu lil-'agh-raa-di ad-*daa*-'i-'a ⓜ
love v يحبّ / تحبّ yu-*hib*-bu/tu-*hib*-bu ⓜ/①
lunch غداء gha-*daa*' ⓜ

M

man رجُل *ra*-jul ⓜ
matches كبريت kib-*reet* ⓜ
meat لحم lahm ⓜ
medicine دواء da-*waa*' ⓜ

message رسالة ri-*saa*-la ①
mobile phone هاتف محمول
haa-ti-fun mah-*mool*
month شهر shahr ⓜ
morning صباح sa-*baah*
motorcycle دراجة نارية dar-*raa*-ja-tun naa-*ree*-ya ①
mouth فم famm ⓜ
movie فيلم feelm ⓜ
MSG أحادي الصوديوم الغلوتيناتي
a-ha-dee as-*soo*-dee-oom al-ghloo-tee-*naat* ⓜ
museum المتحف al-*mat*-haf ⓜ
music الموسيقى al-*moo*-see-kaa ①

N

name اسم ism ⓜ
napkin محرمة mah-*ra*-ma
nappy حفاظة طفل ha-*faa*-dha-tu tifl ①
national park حديقة وطنية
ha-*dee*-ka-tun wa-ta-*nee*-ya ①
nausea غثيان gha-tha-*yaan* ⓜ
neck رقبة *ra*-ka-ba ①
new جديد/جديدة ja-*deed*/ja-*dee*-da ⓜ/①
news الأخبار al-*akh*-baar ⓜ
newspaper جريدة ja-*ree*-da ①
night ليل layl ⓜ
nightclub ملهى ليلي *mil*-han lay-*lee*
noisy ضجيج/ضجيجة da-*jeej*/da-*jee*-ja ⓜ/①
nonsmoking غير المدخنين
ghay-ri al-mu-*dakh*-khi-neen
north شمال sha-*maal* ⓜ
nose أنف *anf* ⓜ
now الآن al-*aan* ⓜ
number رقم rakm ⓜ
nuts مكسرات mu-kas-si-*raat* ①

O

oil (engine) نفط naft ⓜ
OK تمام ta-*maam*
old قديم/قديمة ka-*deem*/ka-*dee*-ma ⓜ/①
open مفتوح/مفتوحة maf-*tooh*/maf-*too*-ha ⓜ/①
outside خارج / خارجة *khaa*-rij/*khaa*-ri-ja ⓜ/①

P

package طرد tard ⓜ
pain ألم *a*-lam ⓜ
palace قصر kasr ⓜ
paper ورقة *wa*-ra-ka ①
park (car) v يوقف / توقف *too*-ki-fu/*yoo*-ki-fu ⓜ/①
passport جواز سفر ja-*waa*-zu sa-far ⓜ
pay v يدفع/ يدفع *yad*-fa-'u/*tad*-fa-'u ⓜ/①
pen قلم *ka*-lam ⓜ

petrol نفط naft ⓜ
pharmacy صيدلية say-da-*lee*-ya ①
plate صحن sahn ⓜ
postcard بطاقة المعايدة bi-*taa*-ka-tul mu-*'aa*-ya-da ①
post office مكتب البريد *mak*-ta-bul ba-*reed*
pregnant حامل *haa*-mil ①

Q

quiet هادئ/هادية *haa*-din/haa-*dee*-ya ⓜ/①

R

rain n مطر *ma*-tar ⓜ
razor موسى *moo*-saa ⓜ
registered mail بريد مسجل
ba-*reed* mu-*saj*-jal
rent v يستأجر/تستأجر
yas-*ta*-ji-ru/tas-*ta*-ji-ru ⓜ/①
repair v يُصلح / تصلح *yus*-li-hu/*tus*-li-hu ⓜ/①
reservation حجز hajz ⓜ
restaurant مطعم *mat*-'am ⓜ
return v يرجع/ ترجع *yar*-ja-'u/*tar*-ja-'u ⓜ/①
road شارع *shaa*-ri' ⓜ
room غرفة *ghur*-fa ①

S

sad حزين/حزينة ha-*zeen*/ha-*zee*-na ⓜ/①
safe a آمن/آمنة *'aa*-min/*'aa*-mi-na ⓜ/①
sanitary napkin منديل لصاق
min-*dee*-lun ni-*saa*-'ee ⓜ
seafood الطعام البحري at-ta-*'aa*-mul ba-ha-ree
seat مقعد *mak*-'ad ⓜ
send v يبعث/تبعث *yab*-'a-thu/*tab*-'a-thu ⓜ/①
sex جنس jins ⓜ/①
shampoo الشامبو ash-*shaam*-boo ⓜ
share (a dorm, etc) يشارك/ تشارك
yu-*shaa*-ri-ku/tu-*shaa*-ri-ku ⓜ/①
shaving cream معجون الحلاقة
ma-*'joo*-nul hal-*laa*-ka ⓜ
she هي *hi*-ya ①
sheet (bed) شرف *shar*-shaf ⓜ
shirt قميص ka-*mees* ⓜ
shoes حذاء hi-*dhaa*' ⓜ
shop n دكان duk-*kaan* ⓜ
shower n دوش doosh ⓜ
skin جلد jild ⓜ
skirt تنّورة tan-*noo*-ra ①
sleep v ينام / تنام *ya*-naa-mu/ta-*naa*-mu ⓜ/①
small صغير/صغيرة sa-*gheer*/sa-*ghee*-ra ⓜ/①
smoke (cigarettes) يدخّن/ تدخّن
yu-*dakh*-khi-nu/tu-*dakh*-khi-nu ⓜ/①
soap صابون saa-*boon* ⓜ

N

english–arabic

61

some بعض ba'-du

soon قريباً ka-ree-ban

sore throat ألم في حلقي 'a-la-mu fee hal-kee ⑩

south جنوب ja-noob

souvenir shop دكان التذكارات duk-kaa-nu at-tidh-kaa-raat ⑩

speak يتكلّم / تتكلّم ya-ta-kal-la-mu/ta-ta-kal-la-mu ⑩/ⓕ

spoon ملعقة mal'a-ka ⓕ

stamp طابع taa-bi' ⑩

stand-by ticket تذكرة بديلة tadh-ki-ra-tun ba-dee-la ⓕ

station (train) محطة mu-hat-ta-tu ⓕ

stomach معدة ma'-i-da ⓕ

stop v يقِف / تقِف ya-ki-fu/ta-ki-fu ⑩/ⓕ

stop (bus) موقف maw-ki-fu ⑩

street شارع shaa-ri' ⑩

student طالب/طالبة taa-lib/taa-li-ba ⑩/ⓕ

sunscreen معجون واقي من الشمس ma'-joo-nun waa-kee min ash-shams ⑩

swim v يسبح / تسبح yas-ba-hu/tas-bu-hu ⑩/ⓕ

T

tampons الصمام النسائيّ as-si-maa-mu an-ni-saa-'ee ⑩

teeth أسنان as-naan

telephone n هاتف haa-tif ⑩

television تلفزيون ti-li-fi-si-yoon ⑩

temperature (weather) درجة الحرارة da-ra-ja-tul ha-raa-ra ⓕ

tent خيمة khay-ma ⓕ

that (one) ذلك/تلك dhaa-li-ka/til-ka ⑩/ⓕ

they هم/هنّ hum/hun-na ⑩/ⓕ

thirsty عطشان/عطشانة 'at-shaan/'at-shaa-na ⑩/ⓕ

this (one) هذا/هذه haa-dhaa/haa-dhi-hi ⑩/ⓕ

throat حلق khalk ⑩

ticket تذكرة tadh-ki-ra ⓕ

time وقت wakt ⑩

tired تعبان/تعبانة ta'-baan/ta'-baa-na ⑩/ⓕ

tissues محارم ma-haa-ram ⓕ

today اليوم al-yawm ⑩

toilet دورات المياه daw-raa-tul mi-yaah ⓕ

tonight الليلة اليوم lay-la-tul yawm ⓕ

toothache ألم في الأسنان 'a-la-mu fee-l'as-naan ⑩

toothbrush فرشاة الأسنان far-shaa-tul 'as-naan ⓕ

toothpaste معجون الأسنان ma'-joo-nul as-naan ⑩

torch(flashlight) مِشعَل كهربائي mish-'a-lun kah-ra-baa-'ee ⑩

tourist office مكتب السياحة mak-ta-bu as-si-yaa-ha ⑩

towel منشفة man-sha-fa ⓕ

translate يترجم / تترجم yu-tar-ji-mu/tu-tar-ji-mu ⑩/ⓕ

travel agency وكالة سفر wa-kaa-la-tu sa-far ⓕ

travellers cheque شيك سياحي shee-kun si-yaa-hee ⑩

trousers بنطلون ban-ta-loon ⑩

twin beds سريرين منفردين sa-ree-ray-ni mun-fa-ri-dayn ⑩

tyre إطار السيّارة 'i-taa-ru as-say-yaa-ra ⑩

U

underwear ملابس داخلية ma-laa-bi-sun daa-khi-lee-ya ⓕ

urgent مستعجل/مستعجلة mus-ta'-jal/mus-ta'-ja-la ⑩/ⓕ

V

vacant شاغر/شاغرة shaa-ghir/shaa-ghi-ra ⑩/ⓕ

vegetable n خضراوات khud-raa-waat ⓕ

vegetarian a نباتي/نباتية na-baa-tee/na-baa-tee-ya ⑩/ⓕ

visa تأشيرة ta'-shee-ra ⓕ

W

waiter نادل/نادلة naa-dil/naa-di-la ⑩/ⓕ

walk v يمشي / تمشي yam-shee/tam-shee ⑩/ⓕ

wallet محفظة mah-fa-dha ⓕ

warm a دافئ/دافئة daa-fi'/daa-fi-'a ⑩/ⓕ

wash (something) يغسِل / تغسِل yagh-si-lu/tagh-si-lu ⑩/ⓕ

watch n ساعة اليد saa-'a-tul yad ⓕ

water ماء maa' ⓕ

we نحنُ nah-nu

weekend نهاية الأسبوع ni-haa-ya-tul 'us-boo' ⓕ

west غرب gharb ⑩

wheelchair كرسي المُقعَدين kur-see al-muk-'a-deen ⑩

when متى ma-taa

where أين 'ay-na

who من man

why لماذا li-maa-dhaa

window شبّاك shub-baak ⑩

wine نبيذ na-beedh ⑩

with مع ma'a

without بدُون bi-doo-ni

woman امرأة 'im-ra-'a ⓕ

write يكتُب / تكتُب yak-tu-bu/tak-tu-bu ⑩/ⓕ

Y

you sg أنت/أنتِ 'an-ta/'an-ti ⑩/ⓕ

you pl أنتُم/أنتُنّ 'an-tum/'an-tun-na ⑩/ⓕ

French

pronunciation

Vowels		Consonants	
Symbol	**English sound**	**Symbol**	**English sound**
a	**run**	b	**b**ed
ai	**aisle**	d	**d**og
air	**fair**	f	**f**un
e	**bet**	g	**g**o
ee	**see**	k	**k**it
eu	**nurse**	l	**l**ot
ew	ee with rounded lips	m	**m**an
ey	as in '**bet**', but longer	n	**n**ot
o	**pot**	ny	ca**ny**on
oo	**zoo**	ng	ri**ng**
om/on/ong	as in '**pot**', but nasal	p	**p**et
um/un/ung	as in '**act**', but nasal	r	**r**un (throaty)
		s	**s**un
		sh	**sh**ot
		t	**t**op
		v	**v**ery
		w	**w**in
		y	**y**es
		z	**z**ero
		zh	plea**s**ure

In this chapter, the French pronunciation is given in green after each phrase.

Each syllable is separated by a dot. For example:
Bonjour.   bon·zhoor

French's nasal vowels, simplified as om/on/ong and um/un/ung above, are pronounced as if you're trying to force the sound out of your nose.

FRANÇAIS – pronunciation

64

language difficulties

Do you speak English?	*Parlez-vous anglais?*	par·ley·voo ong·gley
Do you understand?	*Comprenez-vous?*	kom·pre·ney·voo
I understand.	*Je comprends.*	zhe kom·pron
I don't understand.	*Je ne comprends pas.*	zhe ne kom·pron pa
Could you please please ...?	*Pourriez-vous ..., s'il vous plaît?*	poo·ree·yey voo ... seel voo pley
repeat that	*répéter*	rey·pey·tey
speak more slowly	*parler plus lentement*	par·ley plew lon·te·mon
write it down	*l'écrire*	ley·kreer

time, dates & numbers

What time is it?	*Quelle heure est-il?*	kel eur ey·teel
It's one o'clock.	*Il est une heure.*	ee·ley ewn eu
It's (ten) o'clock.	*Il est (dix) heures.*	ee·ley (deez) eu
Quarter past (one).	*Il est (une) heure et quart.*	ee·ley (ewn) eu ey kar
Half past (one).	*Il est (une) heure et demie.*	ee·ley (ewn) eu ey de·mee
Quarter to (one).	*Il est (une) heure moins le quart.*	ee·ley (ewn) eu mwun le kar
At what time ...?	*À quelle heure ...?*	a kel eu ...
At ...	*À ...*	a ...
It's (18 October).	*C'est le (dix-huit octobre).*	sey le (dee·zwee tok·to·bre)

Monday	*lundi*	lun·dee
Tuesday	*mardi*	mar·dee
Wednesday	*mercredi*	mair·kre·dee
Thursday	*jeudi*	zheu·dee
Friday	*vendredi*	von·dre·dee
Saturday	*samedi*	sam·dee
Sunday	*dimanche*	dee·monsh

yesterday	hier	ee-yair
today	aujourd'hui	o-zhoor-dwee
tomorrow	demain	de-mun

numbers

0	zéro	zey-ro	16	seize	sez
1	un	un	17	dix-sept	dee-set
2	deux	deu	18	dix-huit	dee-zweet
3	trois	trwa	19	dix-neuf	deez-neuf
4	quatre	ka-tre	20	vingt	vung
5	cinq	sungk	21	vingt et un	vung tey un
6	six	sees	22	vingt-deux	vung-deu
7	sept	set	30	trente	tront
8	huit	weet	40	quarante	ka-ront
9	neuf	neuf	50	cinquante	sung-kont
10	dix	dees	60	soixante	swa-sont
11	onze	onz	70	soixante-dix	swa-son-dees
12	douze	dooz	80	quatre-vingts	ka-tre-vung
13	treize	trez	90	quatre-vingt-dix	ka-tre-vung-dees
14	quatorze	ka-torz	100	cent	son
15	quinze	kunz	1000	mille	meel

border crossing

I'm here ...	Je suis ici ...	zhe swee zee-see ...
in transit	de passage	de pa-sazh
on business	pour le travail	poor le tra-vai
on holiday	pour les vacances	poor ley va-kons

I'm here for ...	Je suis ici pour ...	zhe swee zee-see poor ...
(10) days	(dix) jours	(dees) zhoor
(three) weeks	(trois) semaines	(trwa) se-men
(two) months	(deux) mois	(deu) mwa

I'm going to (Yaoundé).
Je vais à (Yaoundé).   zhe vey a (ya-oon-dey)

I'm staying at the (Mercure Hotel).
Je loge au (Mercure).   zhe lozh o (mer-kewr)

tickets

One ... ticket (to Douala), please.	Un billet ... (pour Douala), s'il vous plaît.	um bee·yey ... (poor dwa·la) seel voo pley
one-way	simple	sum·ple
return	aller et retour	a·ley ey re·toor
Is there ...?	Est-qu'il y a ...?	es·keel ya ...
air conditioning	la climatisation	la klee·ma·tee·za·syon
a toilet	des toilettes	dey twa·let
I'd like a ... seat, please.	Je voudrais une place ..., s'il vous plaît.	zhe voo·drey ewn plas ... seel voo pley
nonsmoking	non-fumeur	non·few·mer
smoking	fumeur	few·mer

transport

Is this the ... to (Libreville)?	Est-ce le ... pour (Libreville)?	es le ... poor (lee·brer·veel)
boat	bateau	ba·to
bus	bus	bews
train	train	trun

How much is it to ...?
C'est combien pour aller à ...? sey kom·byun poor a·ley a ...

Please take me to (this address).
Conduisez-moi à (cette adresse), s'il vous plaît. kon·dwee·zey mwa a (set a·dres) seel voo pley

I'd like to hire a ...	Je voudrais louer ...	zhe voo·drey loo·wey ...
car (with air conditioning)	une voiture (avec climatisation)	ewn vwa·tewr (a·vek klee·ma·tee·za·syon)
4WD	un quatre-quatre	un ka·tre ka·tre

directions

Where's the nearest ...?	*Où est-ce qu'il y a ... le plus proche?*	oo es·keel ya ... le plew prosh
internet café	*le cybercafé*	le see·bair·ka·fey
market	*le marché*	le mar·shey
It's ...	*C'est ...*	sey ...
behind ...	*derrière ...*	dair·yair ...
in front of ...	*devant ...*	de·von ...
near (to ...)	*près (de ...)*	prey (de ...)
next to ...	*à côté de ...*	a ko·tey de ...
on the corner	*au coin*	o kwun
opposite ...	*en face de ...*	on fas de ...
straight ahead	*tout droit*	too drwa
there	*là*	la

accommodation

I'd like to book a room, please.
Je voudrais réserver une chambre, s'il vous plaît.
zhe voo·drey rey·zair·vey ewn shom·bre seel voo pley

I'd like to stay for (two) nights.
Je voudrais rester pour (deux) nuits.
zhe voo·drey res·tey poor (deu) nwee

Do you have a ... room?	*Avez-vous une chambre ...?*	a·vey·voo ewn shom·bre ...
single	*à un lit*	a un lee
double	*avec un grand lit*	a·vek ung gron lee
twin	*avec des lits jumeaux*	a·vek dey lee zhew·mo
How much is it per ...?	*Quel est le prix par ...?*	kel ey le pree par ...
night	*nuit*	nwee
person	*personne*	pair·son

banking & communications

I'd like to ...	Je voudrais ...	zhe voo·drey ...
change a travellers cheque	changer des chèques de voyage	shon·zhey dey shek de vwa·yazh
change money	changer de l'argent	shon·zhey de lar·zhon
get internet access	me connecter à l'internet	me ko·nek·tey a lun·tair·net
withdraw money	retirer de l'argent	re·tee·rey de lar·zhon

shopping

I'm looking for ...
Je cherche ...   zhe shairsh ...

How much is it?
C'est combien?   sey kom·byun

Can you write down the price?
Pouvez-vous écrire le prix?   poo·vey·voo ey·kreer le pree

Do you accept ...?	Est-ce que je peux payer avec ...?	es·ke zhe pe pey·yey a·vek ...
credit cards	une carte de crédit	ewn kart de krey·dee
travellers cheques	des chèques de voyages	dey shek de vwa·yazh

making conversation

Hello.	Bonjour.	bon·zhoor
Good night.	Bonsoir.	bon·swar
Goodbye.	Au revoir.	o re·vwar

Mr	Monsieur	me·syeu
Mrs	Madame	ma·dam
Miss	Mademoiselle	mad·mwa·zel

| How are you? | Comment allez-vous? | ko·mon ta·ley·voo |
| Fine, thanks. And you? | Bien, merci. Et vous? | byun mair·see ey voo |

What's your name?	Comment vous appelez-vous?	ko·mon voo za·pley·voo
My name's ...	Je m'appelle ...	zhe ma·pel ...
I'm pleased to meet you.	Enchanté(e). m/f	on·shon·tey
This is my ...	Voici mon/ma ... m/f	vwa·see mon/ma ...
boyfriend	petit ami	pe·tee ta·mee
daughter	fille	fee·ye
friend	ami/amie m/f	a·mee
girlfriend	petite amie	pe·tee ta·mee
husband	mari	ma·ree
son	fils	fees
wife	femme	fam
I'm ...	Je suis ...	zhe swee ...
married	marié/mariée m/f	mar·yey
single	célibataire m&f	sey·lee·ba·tair
Here's my ...	Voici mon ...	vwa·see mon ...
What's your ...?	Quel est votre ...? pol	kel ey vo·tre ...
	Quel est ton ...? inf	kel ey ton ...
address	adresse	a·dres
email address	e-mail	ey·mel
phone number	numéro de téléphone	new·mey·ro de tey·ley·fon
Where are you from?	Vous venez d'où? pol	voo ve·ney doo
	Tu viens d'où? inf	tew vyun doo
I'm from ...	Je viens ...	zhe vyun ...
Australia	d'Australie	dos·tra·lee
Canada	du Canada	dew ka·na·da
New Zealand	de la Nouvelle-Zélande	de la noo·vel·zey·lond
the UK	du Royaume-Uni	dew rwa·om ew·nee
the USA	des Etats Unis	dey ey·tas ew·nee
Can I take a photo?	Est-ce que je peux prendre une photo?	es·ke zhe peu pron·dre ewn fo·to

eating out

I'd like . . ., please.	Je voudrais . . ., s'il vous plaît.	zhe voo·drey . . . seel voo pley
the bill	l'addition	la·dee·syon
the menu	la carte	la kart
a table for (two)	une table pour (deux) personnes	ewn ta·ble poor (deu) pair·son
that dish	ce plat	se pla
Do you have vegetarian food?	Vous faites les repas végétariens?	voo fet ley re·pa vey·zhey·ta·ryun
Could you prepare a meal without . . .?	Pouvez-vous préparer un repas sans . . .?	poo·vey·voo prey·pa·rey un re·pa son . . .
eggs	œufs	eu
meat stock	bouillon gras	boo·yon gra

emergencies

Help!	Au secours!	o skoor
Call . . .!	Appelez . . .!	a·pley . . .
an ambulance	une ambulance	ewn om·bew·lons
the police	la police	la po·lees

Could you help me, please?
Est-ce que vous pourriez m'aider, s'il vous plaît? — es·ke voo poo·ryey mey·dey seel voo pley

Could I use the telephone?
Est-ce que je pourrais utiliser le téléphone? — es·ke zhe poo·rey ew·tee·lee·zey le tey·ley·fon

I'm lost.
Je suis perdu/perdue. m/f — zhe swee pair·dew

Where are the toilets?
Où sont les toilettes? — oo son ley twa·let

I've been assaulted.
J'ai été violenté/violentée. m/f — zhey ey·tey vyo·lon·tey

I've been raped.
J'ai été violé/violée. m/f — zhey ey·tey vyo·ley

I've lost my ... My ... was/were stolen.	J'ai perdu ... On m'a volé ...	zhey pair·dew ... on ma vo·ley ...
bags	mes valises	mey va·leez
credit card	ma carte de crédit	ma kart de krey·dee
handbag	mon sac à main	mon sak a mun
jewellery	mes bijoux	mey bee·zhoo
money	mon argent	mon ar·zhon
passport	mon passeport	mom pas·por
travellers cheques	mes chèques de voyage	mey shek de vwa·yazh
wallet	mon portefeuille	mom por·te·feu·ye
I want to contact my ...	Je veux contacter mon ...	zher veu kon·tak·tey mon ...
consulate	consulat	kon·sew·la
embassy	ambassade	om·ba·sad

medical needs

Where's the nearest ...?	Où y a t-il ... par ici?	oo ee a teel ... par ee·see
dentist	un dentiste	un don·teest
doctor	un médecin	un meyd·sun
hospital	un hôpital	u·no·pee·tal
pharmacist	une pharmacie	ewn far·ma·see

I need a doctor (who speaks English).

J'ai besoin d'un médecin   zhey be·zwun dun meyd·sun
. (qui parle anglais).   (kee parl ong·gley)

It hurts here.

J'ai une douleur ici.   zhey ewn doo·leur ee·see

I'm allergic to (penicillin).

Je suis allergique   zhe swee za·lair·zheek
à (la pénicilline).   a (la pey·nee·see·leen)

english–french dictionary

French nouns and adjectives in this dictionary have their gender indicated by ⓜ (masculine) or ⓕ (feminine). If it's a plural noun, you'll also see ⓟⓛ. Words are also marked as n (noun), a (adjective), v (verb), sg (singular), pl (plural), inf (informal) and pol (polite) where necessary.

A

accommodation *logement* ⓜ lozh·mon
adaptor *adaptateur* ⓜ a·dap·ta·teur
after *après* a·prey
airport *aéroport* ⓜ a·ey·ro·por
alcohol *alcool* ⓜ al·kol
all a *tout/toute* ⓕ too/toot
allergy *allergie* ⓕ a·lair·zhee
and *et* ey
ankle *cheville* ⓕ she·vee·ye
antibiotics *antibiotiques* ⓜ ⓟⓛ on·tee·byo·teek
anti-inflammatories *anti-inflammatoires* ⓜ ⓟⓛ un·tee·un·fla·ma·twar
arm *bras* ⓜ bra
aspirin *aspirine* ⓕ as·pee·reen
asthma *asthme* ⓜ as·meu
ATM *guichet automatique de banque* ⓜ gee·shey o·to·ma·teek de bonk

B

baby *bébé* ⓜ bey·bey
back (body) *dos* ⓜ do
backpack *sac à dos* ⓜ sak a do
bad *mauvais/mauvaise* ⓜ/ⓕ mo·vey/mo·veyz
baggage claim *retrait des bagages* ⓜ re·trey dey ba·gazh
bank *banque* ⓕ bonk
bathroom *salle de bain* ⓕ sal de bun
battery (car) *batterie* ⓕ bat·ree
battery (general) *pile* ⓕ peel
beautiful *beau/belle* ⓜ/ⓕ bo/bel
bed *lit* ⓜ lee
bee *abeille* ⓕ a·bey
beer *bière* ⓕ byair
before *avant* a·von
bicycle *vélo* ⓜ vey·lo
big *grand/grande* ⓜ/ⓕ gron/grond
blanket *couverture* ⓕ koo·vair·tewr
blood group *groupe sanguin* ⓜ groop song·gun

bottle *bouteille* ⓕ boo·tey
bottle opener *ouvre-bouteille* ⓜ oo·vre·boo·tey
boy *garçon* ⓜ gar·son
brakes (car) *freins* ⓜ frun
breakfast *petit déjeuner* ⓜ pe·tee dey·zheu·ney
bronchitis *bronchite* ⓕ bron·sheet

C

café *café* ⓜ ka·fey
cancel *annuler* a·new·ley
can opener *ouvre-boîte* ⓜ oo·vre·bwat
cash *argent* ⓜ ar·zhon
cell phone *téléphone portable* ⓜ tey·ley·fon por·ta·ble
centre *centre* ⓜ son·tre
cheap *bon marché* ⓜ & ⓕ bon mar·shey
check (bill) *addition* ⓕ la·dee·syon
check-in *enregistrement* ⓜ on·re·zhee·stre·mon
chest *poitrine* ⓕ pwa·treen
child *enfant* ⓜ & ⓕ on·fon
cigarette *cigarette* ⓕ see·ga·ret
city *ville* ⓕ veel
clean a *propre* ⓜ & ⓕ pro·pre
closed *fermé/fermée* ⓜ/ⓕ fair·mey
codeine *codéine* ⓕ ko·dey·een
cold a *froid/froide* ⓜ/ⓕ frwa/frwad
collect call *appel en PCV* ⓜ a·pel on pey·sey·vey
condom *préservatif* ⓜ prey·zair·va·teef
constipation *constipation* ⓕ kon·stee·pa·syon
contact lenses *verres de contact* ⓜ ⓟⓛ vair de kon·takt
cough *toux* ⓕ too
currency exchange *taux de change* ⓜ to de shonzh
customs (immigration) *douane* ⓕ dwan

D

dairy products *produits laitiers* ⓜ ⓟⓛ pro·dwee ley·tyey
dangerous *dangereux/dangereuse* ⓜ/ⓕ don·zhreu/don·zhreuz
day *date de naissance* ⓕ dat de ney·sons
diaper *couche* ⓕ koosh

diarrhoea *diarrhée* ⓕ dya-rey
dinner *dîner* ⓜ dee-ney
dirty *sale* ⓜ&ⓕ sal
disabled *handicapé/handicapée* ⓜ/ⓕ on-dee-ka-pey
double bed *grand lit* ⓜ gron lee
drink *boisson* ⓕ bwa-son
drivers licence *permis de conduire* ⓜ
   pair-mee de kon-dweer
drug (illicit) *drogue* ⓕ drog

E

ear *oreille* ⓕ o-rey
east *est* ⓜ est
economy class *classe touriste* ⓕ klas too-reest
elevator *ascenseur* ⓜ a-son-seur
email *e-mail* ⓜ ey-mel
English (language) *anglais* ⓜ ong-gley
exchange rate *taux de change* ⓜ to de shonzh
exit *sortie* ⓕ sor-tee
expensive *cher/chère* ⓜ/ⓕ shair
eye *œil* ⓜ eu-ye

F

fast *rapide* ⓜ&ⓕ ra-peed
fever *fièvre* ⓕ fyev-re
finger *doigt* ⓜ dwa
first-aid kit *trousse à pharmacie* ⓕ troos a far-ma-see
first class *première classe* ⓕ pre-myair klas
fish *poisson* ⓜ pwa-son
food *nourriture* ⓕ noo-ree-tewr
foot *pied* ⓜ pyey
fork *fourchette* ⓕ foor-shet
free (of charge) *gratuit/gratuite* ⓜ/ⓕ
   gra-twee/gra-tweet
fruit *fruit* ⓜ frwee
funny *drôle* ⓜ&ⓕ drol

G

gift *cadeau* ⓜ ka-do
girl *fille* ⓕ fee-ye
glasses *lunettes* ⓕ pl lew-net
gluten *gluten* ⓜ glew-ten
good *bon/bonne* ⓜ/ⓕ bon
gram *gramme* ⓜ gram
guide *guide* ⓜ geed

H

hand *main* ⓕ mun
happy *heureux/heureuse* ⓜ/ⓕ eu-reu/eu-reuz
have *avoir* a-vwar
he *il* eel
head *tête* ⓕ tet
headache *mal à la tête* ⓜ mal a la tet
heart *cœur* ⓜ keur
heart condition *maladie de cœur* ⓕ ma-la-dee de keur
heat *chaleur* ⓕ sha-leur
here *ici* ee-see
high *haut/haute* ⓜ/ⓕ o/ot
highway *autoroute* ⓕ o-to-root
homosexual n *homosexuel/homosexuelle* ⓜ/ⓕ
   o-mo-sek-swel
hot *chaud/chaude* ⓜ/ⓕ sho/shod
(be) hungry *avoir faim* a-vwar fum

I

I *je* zhe
identification (card) *carte d'identité* ⓕ
   kart dee-don-tee-tey
ill *malade* ⓜ&ⓕ ma-lad
important *important/importante* ⓜ/ⓕ
   um-por-ton/um-por-tont
internet *Internet* ⓜ un-tair-net
interpreter *interprète* ⓜ&ⓕ un-tair-pret

K

key *clé* ⓕ kley
kilogram *kilogramme* ⓜ kee-lo-gram
kitchen *cuisine* ⓕ kwee-zeen
knife *couteau* ⓜ koo-to

L

laundry (place) *blanchisserie* ⓕ blon-shees-ree
lawyer *avocat/avocate* ⓜ/ⓕ a-vo-ka/a-vo-kat
left-luggage office *consigne* ⓕ kon-see-nye
leg *jambe* ⓕ zhomb
lesbian n *lesbienne* ⓕ les-byen
less *moins* mwun
letter (mail) *lettre* ⓕ le-trer
like v *aimer* ey-mey
lost-property office *bureau des objets trouvés* ⓜ
   bew-ro dey zob-zhey troo-vey

love v *aimer* ey-mey
lunch *déjeuner* ⓜ dey-zheu-ney

M

man *homme* ⓜ om
matches *allumettes* ⓕ pl a-lew-met
meat *viande* ⓕ vyond
medicine *médecine* ⓕ med-seen
message *message* ⓜ mey-sazh
mobile phone *téléphone portable* ⓜ tey-ley-fon por-ta-ble
month *mois* ⓜ mwa
morning *matin* ⓜ ma-tun
motorcycle *moto* ⓕ mo-to
mouth *bouche* ⓕ boosh
movie *film* ⓜ feelm
MSG *glutamate de sodium* ⓜ glew-ta-mat de so-dyom
museum *musée* ⓕ mew-zey
music *musique* ⓕ mew-zeek

N

name *nom* ⓜ nom
napkin *serviette* ⓕ sair-vyet
nappy *couche* ⓕ koosh
national park *parc national* ⓜ park na-syo-nal
nausea *nausée* ⓕ no-zey
neck *cou* ⓜ koo
new *nouveau/nouvelle* ⓜ/ⓕ noo-vo/noo-vel
news ⓕ pl *les nouvelles* ley noo-vel
newspaper *journal* ⓜ zhoor-nal
night *nuit* ⓕ nwee
nightclub *boîte* ⓕ bwat
noisy *bruyant/bruyante* ⓜ/ⓕ brew-yon/brew-yont
nonsmoking *non-fumeur* non-few-meur
north *nord* ⓜ nor
nose *nez* ⓜ ney
now *maintenant* mun-te-non
number *numéro* ⓜ new-mey-ro

O

oil *huile* ⓕ weel
OK *bien* byun
old *vieux/vieille* ⓜ/ⓕ vyeu/vyey
open a *ouvert/ouverte* ⓜ/ⓕ oo-vair/oo-vairt
outside *dehors* de-or

P

package *paquet* ⓜ pa-key
pain *douleur* ⓕ doo-leur
paper *papier* ⓜ pa-pyey
park (car) v *garer (une voiture)* ga-rey (ewn vwa-tewr)
passport *passeport* ⓜ pas-por
pay *payer* pey-yey
pen *stylo* ⓜ stee-lo
petrol *essence* ⓕ ey-sons
pharmacy *pharmacie* ⓕ far-ma-see
plate *assiette* ⓕ a-syet
postcard *carte postale* ⓕ kart pos-tal
post office *bureau de poste* ⓜ bew-ro de post
pregnant *enceinte* on-sunt

R

rain n *pluie* ⓕ plwee
razor *rasoir* ⓜ ra-zwar
registered mail *en recommandé* on re-ko-mon-dey
rent v *louer* loo-ey
repair v *réparer* rey-pa-rey
reservation *réservation* ⓕ rey-zair-va-syon
restaurant *restaurant* ⓜ res-to-ron
return v *revenir* rev-neer
road *route* ⓕ root
room *chambre* ⓕ shom-bre

S

sad *triste* treest
safe a *sans danger* ⓜ&ⓕ son don-zhey
sanitary napkin *serviette hygiénique* ⓕ
    sair-vyet ee-zhyey-neek
seafood *fruits de mer* ⓜ frwee de mair
seat *place* ⓕ plas
send *envoyer* on-vwa-yey
sex *sexe* ⓜ seks
shampoo *shampooing* ⓜ shom-pwung
share (a dorm) *partager* par-ta-zhey
shaving cream *mousse à raser* ⓕ moos a ra-zey
she *elle* el
sheet (bed) *drap* ⓜ dra
shirt *chemise* ⓕ she-meez
shoes *chaussures* ⓕ pl sho-sewr
shop *magasin* ⓜ ma-ga-zun
shower *douche* ⓕ doosh
skin *peau* ⓕ po

skirt *jupe* ① zhewp
sleep v *dormir* dor-meer
small *petit/petite* ⓜ/① pe-tee/pe-teet
smoke (cigarettes) v *fumer* few-mey
soap *savon* ⓜ sa-von
some *quelques* kel-ke
soon *bientôt* byun-to
sore throat *mal à la gorge* ⓜ mal a la gorzh
south *sud* ⓜ sewd
souvenir shop *magasin de souvenirs* ⓜ
    ma-ga-zun de soov-neer
speak *parler* par-ley
spoon *cuillère* ① kwee-yair
stamp *timbre* ⓜ tum-bre
stand-by ticket *billet stand-by* ⓜ bee-yey stond-bai
station (train) *gare* ① gar
stomach *estomac* ⓜ es-to-ma
stop v *arrêter* a-rey-tey
stop (bus) *arrêt* ⓜ a-rey
street *rue* ① rew
student *étudiant/étudiante* ⓜ/①
    ey-tew-dyon/ey-tew-dyont
sunscreen *écran solaire* ⓜ ey-kron so-lair
swim v *nager* na-zhey

T

tampons *tampons* ⓜ pl tom-pon
teeth *dents* ① don
telephone n *téléphone* tey-ley-fon
television *télé(vision)* ① tey-ley(vee-zyon)
temperature (weather) *température* ① tom-pey-ra-tewr
that (one) *cela* se-la
they *ils/elles* ⓜ/① eel/el
(be) thirsty *avoir soif* a-vwar swaf
this (one) *ceci* se-see
throat *gorge* ① gorzh
ticket *billet* bee-yey
time *temps* ⓜ tom
tired *fatigué/fatiguée* ⓜ/① fa-tee-gey
tissues *mouchoirs en papier* ⓜ pl moo-shwar om pa-pyey
today *aujourd'hui* o-zhoor-dwee
toilet *toilettes* ① pl twa-let
tonight *ce soir* se swar
toothache *mal aux dents* ⓜ mal o don
toothbrush *brosse à dents* ① bros a don

toothpaste *dentifrice* ⓜ don-tee-frees
torch (flashlight) *lampe de poche* ① lomp de posh
tourist office *office de tourisme* ⓜ o-fees de too-rees-me
towel *serviette* ① sair-vyet
travel agency *agence de voyage* ① a-zhons de vwa-yazh
travellers cheque *chèque de voyage* ⓜ shek de vwa-yazh
trousers *pantalon* ⓜ pon-ta-lon
twin beds *lits jumeaux* ⓜ pl dey lee zhew-mo
tyre *pneu* ⓜ pneu

V

vacant *libre* ⓜ&① lee-bre
vegetable *légume* ⓜ ley-gewm
vegetarian a *végétarien/végétarienne* ⓜ/①
    vey-zhey-ta-ryun/vey-zhey-ta-ryen
visa *visa* ⓜ vee-za

W

waiter *serveur/serveuse* ⓜ/① sair-veur/sair-veurz
walk v *marcher* mar-shey
wallet *portefeuille* ⓜ por-te-feu-ye
warm a *chaud/chaude* ⓜ/① sho/shod
wash (something) *laver* la-vey
watch *montre* ① mon-tre
water *eau* ① o
we *nous* noo
west *ouest* ⓜ west
wheelchair *fauteuil roulant* ⓜ fo-teu-ye roo-lon
when *quand* kon
where *où* oo
who *qui* kee
why *pourquoi* poor-kwa
window *fenêtre* ① fe-ney-tre
wine *vin* ① vun
with *avec* a-vek
without *sans* son
woman *femme* ① fam
write *écrire* ey-kreer

Y

you sg inf *tu* tew
you sg pol *vous* voo
you pl *vous* voo

Hausa

pronunciation

Vowels		Consonants	
Symbol	**English sound**	**Symbol**	**English sound**
a	run	b	bed
aa	father	b'	strong b with air sucked inward
ai	aisle	ch	cheat
aw	law	d	dog
ay	say	d'	strong d with air sucked inward
e	bet	g	go
ey	as in 'bet', but longer	h	hat
ee	see	j	jar
i	hit	k	kit
o	pot	k'	strong k
oo	zoo	l	lot
ow	now	m	man
u	put	n	not
'	like the pause in 'uh-oh' (comes before a vowel)	p	pet
		r	run
		s	sun
		sh	shot
		t	top
		ts'	as in 'lets', but spat out
		w	win
		y	yes
		y'	spat out y
		z	zero

In this chapter, the Hausa pronunciation is given in purple after each phrase. Each syllable is separated by a dot. For example:

Na gode. naa gaw·dey

Hausa's glottalised consonants, simplified here as b', d', k', ts' and y', are made by tightening and releasing the space between the vocal cords when you pronounce the sound. The b' and d' sounds have an extra twist – instead of breathing out, you breathe in.

introduction

According to some scholars, the name 'Hausa' is derived from a phrase meaning 'to climb/ride the bull'. As one of the lingua francas of West Africa, Hausa (*Hausa* how·sa) is spoken by around 60 million people. For two-thirds of these, Hausa is their first language. Most native speakers live in northern Nigeria and southern Niger, where Hausa is one of the national languages. There's a small community of native speakers in the Blue Nile area of Sudan, and it's also spoken in parts of Benin, Cameroon, and Ghana. Hausa is one of the Chadic languages (in the Afro-Asiatic language family), which came from the southern shores of Lake Chad in present-day northeastern Nigeria and northern Cameroon, and gradually migrated westward over the centuries. In the past, Hausa was written in *ajami*, a modified form of Arabic script, but since the early 19th century it has also been written in many areas with a slightly modified Roman alphabet. This alphabet, called *boko*, is now the official written form.

 hausa (native language)    **hausa** (generally understood)

language difficulties

Do you speak English?	*Kana/Kina jin turanci?* m/f	ka·naa/ki·naa jin too·ran·chee
Do you understand?	*Ka/Kin gane?* m/f	kaa/kin gaa·ney
I understand.	*Na gane.*	naa gaa·ney
I don't understand.	*Ban gane ba.*	ban gaa·ney ba
Could you please ...?	*Za ka/ki iya...?* m/f	zaa ka/ki i·ya ...
repeat that	*maimaita wannan*	mai·mai·ta wan·nan
speak more slowly	*yi magana sannu-sannu*	yi ma·ga·naa san·nu·san·nu
write it down	*rubuta wannan*	ru·boo·ta wan·nan

time, dates & numbers

What time is it?	*K'arfe nawa ne?*	k'ar·fey na·wa ney
It's one o'clock.	*K'arfe d'aya ne.*	k'ar·fey d'a·ya ney
It's (two) o'clock.	*K'arfe (biyu) ne.*	k'ar·fey (bi·yu) ney
Quarter past (one).	*K'arfe (d'aya) da kwata.*	k'ar·fey (d'a·ya) da kwa·taa
Half past (one).	*K'arfe (d'aya) da rabi.*	k'ar·fey (d'a·ya) da ra·bee
Quarter to (eight).	*(K'arfe takwas) ba kwata.*	(k'ar·fey tak·was) baa kwa·taa
At what time ...?	*K'arfe nawa ...?*	k'ar·fey na·wa ...
At ...	*A ...*	a ...
It's (15 December).	*Yau (sha biyar ga watan Disamba).*	yow (shaa bi·yar ga wa·tan di·sam·ba)
yesterday	*jiya*	ji·ya
today	*yau*	yow
tomorrow	*gobe*	gaw·be
Monday	*Littinin*	lit·ti·nin
Tuesday	*Talata*	ta·laa·taa
Wednesday	*Laraba*	laa·ra·baa
Thursday	*Alhamis*	al·ha·mis
Friday	*Juma'a*	ju·ma·'aa
Saturday	*Asabar*	a·sa·bar
Sunday	*Lahadi*	la·ha·di

numbers

0	*sifiri*	si·fi·ree	15	*(goma) sha biyar*	(gaw·ma) shaa bi·yar
1	*d'aya*	d'a·ya	16	*(goma) sha shida*	(gaw·ma) shaa shi·da
2	*biyu*	bi·yu	17	*(goma)*	(gaw·ma)
3	*uku*	u·ku		*sha bakwai*	shaa bak·wai
4	*hud'u*	hu·d'u	18	*(goma)*	(gaw·ma)
5	*biyar*	bi·yar		*sha takwas*	shaa tak·was
6	*shida*	shi·da	19	*(goma) sha tara*	(gaw·ma) shaa ta·ra
7	*bakwai*	bak·wai	20	*ashirin*	a·shi·rin
8	*takwas*	tak·was	21	*ashirin da d'aya*	a·shi·rin da d'a·ya
9	*tara*	ta·ra	22	*ashirin da biyu*	a·shi·rin da bi·yu
10	*goma*	gaw·ma	30	*talatin*	ta·laa·tin
11	*(goma)*	(gaw·ma)	40	*arba'in*	ar·ba·'in
	sha d'aya	shaa d'a·ya	50	*hamsin*	ham·sin
12	*(goma)*	(gaw·ma)	60	*sittin*	sit·tin
	sha biyu	shaa bi·yu	70	*saba'in*	sa·ba·'in
13	*(goma)*	(gaw·ma)	80	*tamanin*	ta·maa·nin
	sha uku	shaa u·ku	90	*tasa'in*	ta·sa·'in
14	*(goma)*	(gaw·ma)	100	*d'ari*	d'a·ree
	sha hud'u	shaa hu·d'u	1000	*dubu*	du·boo

border crossing

I'm here ...	*Na zo nan ...*	naa zaw nan ...
in transit	*don ya*	don yaa
	da zango	da zan·goo
on business	*don yin kasuwanci*	don yin ka·su·wan·chee
on holiday	*don yi hutu*	don yi hoo·too
I'm here for ...	*Zan yi ... a nan.*	zan yi ... a nan
(10) days	*kwana (goma)*	kwaa·naa (gaw·ma)
(three) weeks	*mako (uku)*	maa·kaw (u·ku)
(two) months	*wata (biyu)*	waa·taa (bi·yu)

I'm going to (Zaria).
Za ni (Zazzau).   zaa ni (zaz·zow)

I'm staying at the (Daula Hotel).
Ina zaune a (Daula Hotel).   i·naa zow·ne a (dow·la haw·tel)

tickets

One ... ticket (to Zinder), please.	*Tikitin ... guda d'aya (zuwa Zandar), don Allah.*	ti·ki·tin ... gu·daa d'a·ya (zu·waa zan·dar) don al·laa
one-way	*zuwa*	zu·waa
return	*zuwa da dawowa*	zu·waa da daa·waw·waa

I'd like to ... my ticket, please.	*Ina son in ... tikitina, don Allah.*	i·naa son in ... ti·ki·ti·naa don al·laa
cancel	*soke*	saw·kye
change	*canja*	chan·ja
collect	*karb'i*	kar·b'i

I'd like a smoking/nonsmoking seat, please.
Ina son abin zama ga masu/ marasa shan taba, don Allah. — i·naa son a·bin za·maa ga maa·su/ ma·ra·saa shan taa·baa don al·laa

Is there a toilet?
Akwai ban d'aki? — a·kwai ban d'aa·kee

Is there air conditioning?
Akwai na'urar sanyaya d'aki? — a·kwai naa·'oo·rar san·ya·ya d'aa·kee

How long does the trip take?
Tafiyar za ta dad'e? — ta·fi·yar zaa ta da·d'ee

Is it a direct route?
Wannan ce hanya kai tsaye? — wan·nan chey han·yaa kai ts'a·ye

transport

Where does flight (BA527) arrive/depart?
A ina jirgin sama (BA 527) zai sauka/tashi? — a i·naa jir·gin sa·ma (bi ei faiv too se·ven) zai sow·kaa/taa·shi

How long will it be delayed?
Minti nawa zai makara? — min·tee na·wa zai ma·ka·ra

Is this the ... (to Maiduguri)?	*Wannan ... (zuwa Maiduguri) ne/ce?* m/f	wan·nan ... (zu·waa mai·du·gu·ri) ney/chey m/f
boat	*jirgin ruwa* m	jir·gin ru·waa
bus	*mota* f	maw·taa
plane	*jirgin sama* m	jir·gin sa·ma
train	*jirgin k'asa* m	jir·gin k'a·saa

How much is it to …?
Nawa ne kud'in zuwa …?   na·wa ney ku·d'in zu·waa …

Please take me to (this address).
Ka/Ki d'auke ni zuwa (wurin mai   ka/ki d'ow·key ni zu·waa (wu·ree mai
lambar wannan adireshi), don Allah. m/f   lam·bar wan·nan a·di·rey·shee) don al·laa

I'd like to hire a …   *Ina son in yi hayar …*   i·naa son in yi ha·yar …
(with air conditioning).   *(tare da AC).*   (taa·re da ai·si)
    car   *mota*   maw·taa
    4WD   *mota mai juyawa*   maw·taa mai joo·yaa·waa
        da k'afa hud'u   da k'a·faa hu·d'u

How much is it for (three) days/weeks?
Nawa ne kud'in na   na·wa ney ku·d'in na
kwana/mako (uku)?   kwaa·naa/maa·kaw (u·ku)

directions

Where's the   *Ina … (mafi kusa)?*   i·naa … (ma·fee ku·sa)
(nearest) …?
    internet café   *internet cafe*   in·tey·net ka·fey
    market   *kasuwa*   kaa·su·waa

Is this the road to (Lagos)?
Wannan hanya zuwa (Ikko) ce?   wan·nan han·ya zu·waa (ik·ko) chey

Can you show me (on the map)?
Za ka/ki iya nuna mini   za ka/ki i·ya noo·naa mi·ni
(a taswira)? m/f   (a tas·wi·raa)

What's the address?
Mene ne adireshin?   mey·ney ney a·di·rey·shin

How far is it?
Mil nawa ne?   mil na·wa ney

How do I get there?
Ina ne hanyar zuwa can?   i·naa ney han·yar zu·waa chan

Turn left/right.
Yi hagu/dama.   yi ha·gu/daa·ma

It's ...	Ga shi/ta ... m/f	ga shi/ta ...
behind ...	bayan ...	baa·yan ...
in front of ...	gaban ...	ga·ban ...
near (to ...)	kusa (da ...)	ku·sa (da ...)
next to ...	daf da ...	daf da ...
on the corner	a kwana	a kwa·naa
opposite ...	daura da ...	dow·ra da ...
straight ahead	mik'e sosai	mee·k'ey so·sai
there	can	chan

accommodation

Where's a ...?	Ina ... yake?	i·naa ... yak·yey
camping ground	wurin da aka kafa	wu·rin da a·ka ka·fa
	tanti-tanti	tan·ti·tan·ti
guesthouse	gidan saukar bak'i	gi·dan sow·kar baa·k'ee
hotel	hotal	haw·tal
youth hostel	makwancin matasa	ma·kwan·chin ma·taa·saa

Can you recommend somewhere (cheap/good)?

Za ka/ki iya gaya mini ina za a   zaa ka/ki i·ya gaa·yaa mi·ni i·naa za a
sami wani wuri (mai araha/kyau)? m/f   saa·mi wa·ni wu·ree (mai a·ra·haa/kyow)

I'd like to book a room, please.

Ina son a kama mini d'aki,   i·naa son a kaa·maa mi·ni d'aa·kee
don Allah.   don al·laa

I have a reservation.

An kama mini d'aki a nan.   an kaa·maa mi·ni d'aa·kee a nan

Do you have	Kana/Kina da	ka·naa/ki·naa da
a ... room?	d'aki ...? m/f	d'aa·kee ...
single	ga mutum d'aya	ga mu·tum d'a·ya
double	ga mutane biyu	ga mu·taa·ney bi·yu
twin	biyu wad'anda	bi·yu wa·d'an·da
	aka had'a su	a·ka ha·d'a su

How much is	Nawa ne kud'in	na·wa ney ku·d'in
it per ...?	... d'aya?	... d'a·ya
night	kwana	kwaa·naa
person	mutum	mu·tum

I'd like to stay for (two) nights.
Ina son in yi kwana (biyu) a nan. i·naa son in yi kwaa·naa (bi·yu) a nan

What time is check-out?
Yaushe zan fita daga d'aki? yow·she zan fi·ta da·ga d'aa·kee

Am I allowed to camp here?
Za a bar ni in d'an zauna a nan? zaa a bar ni in d'an zow·naa a nan

banking & communications

Note that in Nigeria, unless you have a Nigerian bank account, it will be difficult to do any of the following things, except for changing money.

I'd like to ...	*Ina son in ...*	i·naa son in ...
arrange a transfer	*aika da kud'i*	ai·kaa da ku·d'ee
cash a cheque	*chanja cek na banki*	chan·ja chek na ban·kee
	zuwa kud'i	zu·waa ku·d'ee
change a travellers cheque	*canja cek*	chan·ja chek
	zuwa kud'i	zu·waa ku·d'ee
change money	*canja kud'i*	chan·ja ku·d'ee
withdraw money	*karb'i kud'i*	kar·b'i ku·d'ee

I want to ...	*Ina son ...*	i·naa son ...
to call (Singapore)	*buga waya zuwa (Singapur)*	bu·ga wa·yaa zu·waa (sin·ga·pur)
reverse the charges	*mutumin da zan*	mu·tu·min da zan
	buga masa waya	bu·ga ma·sa wa·yaa
	ya biya kud'in waya	ya bi·ya ku·d'in wa·yaa
use a printer	*yin amfani da printer*	yin am·faa·nee da prin·ter
use the internet	*yin amfani da internet*	yin am·faa·nee da in·tey·net

How much is it per hour?
Nawa ne kud'in wannan don na·wa ney ku·d'in wan·nan don
tsawon awa d'aya? ts'aa·won a·waa d'a·ya

How much does a (three-minute) call cost?
Nawa ne kud'in buga waya na·wa ney ku·d'in bu·ga wa·yaa
(wanda ya yi minti uku)? (wan·da ya yi min·tee u·ku)

(30 naira) per minute/hour.
(Naira talatin) don tsawon (nai·ra ta·laa·tin) don ts'aa·won
minti/awa d'aya. min·tee/a·waa d'a·ya

tours

When's the next ...?	*Yaushe za a yi ...?*	yow·she zaa a yi ...
day trip	*tafiya ta kwana d'aya*	ta·fi·yaa ta kwaa·naa d'a·ya
tour	*zagaye*	zaa·ga yey
Is ... included?	*Akwai ... a kud'in nan?*	ak·wai ... a ku·d'in nan
accommodation	*masauki*	ma·sow·kee
the admission charge	*tikitocin shiga*	ti·ki·taw·chin shi·ga
	wasu wurare	wa·su wu·raa·rey
food	*abinci*	a·bin·chi
transport	*sufuri*	su·fu·ree

How long is the tour?
Awa nawa za a yi zagayen?   a·wa na·wa zaa a yi zaa·ga·yen

What time should we be back?
K'arfe nawa za a koma?   k'ar·fey na·wa zaa a kaw·maa

shopping

I'm looking for ...
Ina neman ...   i·naa ne·man ...

I need film for this camera.
Ina son fim na wannan kyamara.   i·naa son fim na wan·nan kya·ma·ra

Can I listen to this?
Zan iya sauraron wannan?   zan i·ya sow·raa·ron wan·nan

Can I have my ... repaired?
Za ka/ki iya gyara mini ...? m/f   zaa ka/ki i·ya gya·raa mi·ni ...

When will it be ready?
Yaushe zan samu?   yow·she zan saa·moo

How much is it?
Kud'insa nawa ne?   ku·d'in·sa na·wa ney

Can you write down the price?
Za ka/ki iya rubuta mini nawa   zaa ka/ki i·ya ru·boo·taa mi·ni na·wa
ne kud'insa? m/f   ney ku·d'in·sa

What's your lowest price?
Mene ne kud'i na gaskiya?   mey·ney ney ku·d'ee na gas·ki·yaa

I'll give you (five) naira.
Zan ba ka/ki Naira (biyar). m/f — zan baa ka/ki nai·raa (bi·yar)

There's a mistake in the bill.
Akwai kuskure a bil. — a·kwai kus·ku·rey a bil

It's faulty.
An yi kuskure. — an yi kus·ku·rey

I'd like a refund, please.
Ina son a dawo mini da kud'ina, don Allah. — i·naa son a daa·waw mi·ni da ku·d'ee·naa don al·laa

I'd like a receipt, please.
Ba ni rasid'i, don Allah. — baa ni raa·si·d'ee don al·laa

Could you …?	*Kana/Kina iya …?* m/f	ka·naa/ki·naa i·ya …
burn a CD from	*sa abubuwa daga*	sa a·boo·bu·waa da·ga
my memory card	*katin nan zuwa faifai*	kaa·tin nan zu·waa fai·fai
develop this	*wanke wannan*	wan·kye wa·nan
film	*fim*	fim

making conversation

Hello.	*Sannu.*	san·nu
Good night.	*Sai da safe.*	say da saa·fe
Goodbye.	*Sai wani lokaci.*	say wa·ni law·ka·chee
Mr	*Malam*	maa·lam
Mrs/Ms/Miss	*Malama*	maa·la·maa

How are you?
Kana/Kina lafiya? m/f — ka·naa/ki·naa laa·fi·yaa

Fine, and you?
Lafiya lau, kai/ke fa? m/f — laa·fi·yaa low kai/kye fa

What's your name?
Ina sunanka/sunanki? m/f — i·naa soo·nan·ka/soo·nan·ki

My name's …
Sunana … — soo·naa·naa …

I'm pleased to meet you.
Na ji murnar saduwa da kai/ke. m/f — na ji mur·nar saa·du·waa da kai/kye

This is my ...	Wannan ... nawa/tawa. m/f	wan·nan ... naa·wa/taa·wa
boyfriend	saurayi	sow·ra·yee
daughter	y'a	y'aa
father	mahaifi	ma·hai·fee
friend	aboki m	a·baw·kee
girlfriend	budurwa	bu·dur·waa
husband	miji	mi·jee
mother	mahaifiya	ma·hai·fi·yaa
son	d'a	d'aa
wife	mata	maa·taa

Here's my ...	Ga ... nawa/tawa. m/f	gaa ... naa·wa/taa·wa
What's your ...?	Mene ne ...	mey·ney ney ...
address	adireshi(-nka/-nki m/f) m	a·di·rey·shi(·nka/·nki)
email address	adireshi(-nka/-nki m/f)	a·di·rey·shi(·nka/·nki)
	na i-mel m	na i·mel
phone number	lambar waya(-rka/-rki m/f) m	lam·bar wa·ya(·rka/·rki)

Where are you from?	Daga ina ka/kika fito? m/f	da·ga i·naa ka/ki·ka fi·taw

I'm from ...	Na fito daga ...	naa fi·taw da·ga ...
Australia	Ostareliya	os·ta·rey·li·ya
Canada	Kyanada	kya·na·da
New Zealand	New Zeland	nyu zi·lan
the UK	Ingila	in·gi·la
the USA	Amirka	a·mir·ka

I'm married.	Ina da miji/mata. m/f	i·naa da mi·jee/maa·taa
I'm not married.	Ba ni da miji/mata. m/f	baa ni da mi·jee/maa·taa
Can I take a photo (of you)?	Zan iya d'aukar hoto(-nka/-nki)? m/f	zan i·ya d'ow·kar haw·to(·nka/·nki)

eating out

Can you recommend a ...?	Za ka/ki iya gaya mini ... mai kyau? m/f	zaa ka/ki i·ya ga·yaa mi·ni ... mai kyow
bar	wurin shan giya	wu·rin shan gi·yaa
place to eat	wurin cin abinci	wu·rin chin a·bin·chi
dish	abinci	a·bin·chi

I'd like …, please.	*Ina son …, don Allah.*	i·naa son … don al·laa
the bill	*bil*	bil
the menu	*takardar bayyanin abinci*	ta·kar·dar bay·ya·nin a·bin·chi
a table for (two)	*tebur ga mutane (biyu)*	tey·bur ga mu·taa·ney (bi·yu)
that dish	*wannan abinci*	wan·nan a·bin·chi
Do you have vegetarian food?	*Kana/Kina da abinci maras nama?* m/f	ka·naa/ki·naa da a·bin·chi maa·ras naa·maa
Could you prepare a meal without …?	*Kana/Kina iya yin abinci ba tare da … ba?* m/f	ka·naa/ki·naa i·ya yin a·bin·chi baa taa·re da … ba
eggs	*k'wai*	k'wai
meat stock	*nama*	naa·maa
(cup of) coffee …	*kofi (guda d'aya) …*	kaw·fee (gu·daa d'a·ya) …
(cup of) tea …	*shayi (guda d'aya) …*	shaa·yi (gu·daa d'a·ya) …
with milk	*da madara*	da ma·da·raa
without sugar	*ba sukari*	baa su·ka·ree
(boiled) water	*ruwa(-n da aka tafasa)*	ru·wa(·n da a·ka ta·fa·saa)

emergencies

Help!	*Taimake ni!*	tai·ma·kyey ni
Call …!	*Kirawo …!*	ki·raa·waw …
an ambulance	*motar d'aukar maras lafiya*	moo·tar d'ow·kar maa·ras laa·fi·yaa
a doctor	*likita*	li·ki·taa
the police	*'yan sanda*	'yan san·daa

Could you help me, please?
Kana iya ka taimake ni, don Alla. m — ka·naa i·ya ka tai·ma·kyey ni don al·laa
Kina iya ki taimake ni, don Alla. f — ki·naa i·ya ki tai·ma·kyey ni don al·laa

I'm lost.
Na manta hanya. — naa man·ta han·yaa

Where are the toilets?
Ina ban d'aki yake? — i·naa ban d'aa·kee yak·yey

I want to report an offence.
Ina son in sanar da ku wani laifi. — i·na son in sa·nar da koo wa·ni lai·fee

I have insurance.
Ina da inshora. — i·naa da in·shaw·raa

I want to contact my consulate/embassy.
Ina son in buga waya zuwa — i·naa son in bu·ga wa·yaa zu·waa
ofishin jakadanci kasarmu. — aw·fi·shin ja·kaa·dan·chee ka·sar·mu

I've been ...
	An yi mini ...	an yi mi·ni ...
assaulted	*farmaki*	far·ma·kee
raped	*fyad'e*	fyaa·d'ey
robbed	*sata*	saa·taa

My ... was/were stolen.
	An sace mini ...	an saa·chey mi·ni ...
bags	*kaya*	kaa·yaa
credit card	*katin adashin banki*	kaa·tin a·daa·shin ban·kee
jewellery	*kayan ado*	kaa·yan a·daw
money	*kud'i*	ku·d'ee
passport	*fasfo*	fas·faw
travellers cheques	*cek*	chek
wallet	*alabe*	a·la·bey

medical needs

Where's the nearest ...?
	Ina ne/ce ...	i·naa ney/chey ...
	mafi kusa? m/f	ma·fee ku·sa
dentist	*likitan hak'ori* m	li·ki·tan ha·k'aw·ree
doctor	*likita* m	li·ki·ta
hospital	*asibiti* f	a·si·bi·ti
pharmacist	*kantin magani* m	kan·tin maa·ga·nee

I need a doctor (who speaks English).
Ina bukatar likita — i·naa bu·kaa·tar li·ki·ta
(wanda yake jin Turanci). — (wan·da yak·yey jin too·ran·chee)

Could I see a female doctor?
Zan iya ganin likita mace? — zan i·ya ga·nin li·ki·ta ma·che

It hurts here.
Na ji ciwo a nan. — naa ji chee·waw a nan

I'm allergic to (penicillin).
An hana ni yin amfani — an ha·naa ni yin am·faa·nee
da (penisilin). — da (pe·ni·si·lin)

english–hausa dictionary

Hausa nouns in this dictionary have their gender marked with ⓜ (masculine) or ⓕ (feminine). If it's a plural noun, you'll also see pl. Note that some adjectives have only one form for both genders. Words are also marked as n (noun), a (adjective), v (verb), sg (singular) and pl (plural) where necessary.

A

accommodation *masauki* ⓜ ma-sow-kee
adaptor *macanjin wuta* ⓜ ma-chan-jin wu-taa
after *bayan* baa-yan
airport *filin jirgin sama* ⓜ fee-lin jir-gin sa-ma
alcohol *barasa* ⓕ baa-raa-saa
all *duk* duk
and *da* da
ankle *idon k'afa* ⓜ i-don k'a-fa
arm *hannu* ⓜ han-noo
asthma *ciwon asma* ⓜ chi-won as-maa

B

baby *jariri* ⓜ jaa-ree-ree
back (body) *baya* ⓜ baa-yaa
backpack *jakar baya* ⓕ ja-kar baa-yaa
bad *maras kyau* ma-ras kyow
bank *banki* ⓜ ban-kee
bathroom *ban d'aki* ⓜ ban d'aa-kee
battery *batir* ⓜ baa-tir
beautiful *mai kyau* mai kyow
bed *gado* ⓜ ga-daw
beer *giya* ⓕ gi-yaa
bees *zuma* ⓜ zu-maa
before *kafin* kaa-fin
bicycle *keke* ⓜ kyey-kyey
big *babba/manya* ⓜ/ⓕ bab-ba/man-yaa
blanket *bargo* ⓜ bar-gaw
blood group *irin jini* ⓜ i-rin ji-nee
bottle *kwalaba* ⓕ kwa-la-baa
bottle opener *mabud'in kwalaba* ⓜ ma-boo-d'in kwa-la-baa
boy *yaro* ⓜ yaa-raw
brakes (car) *birki* ⓜ bir-kee
breakfast *karin kumallo* ⓜ ka-rin ku-mal-law
bronchitis *mashak'o* ⓜ maa-shaa-k'aw

C

cancel *soke* saw-key
can opener *mabud'in gwangwani* ⓜ ma-boo-d'in gwan-gwa-nee
cash *kud'i* ⓜ ku-d'ee
cell phone *salula* ⓕ sa-loo-laa
centre *tsakiya* ⓕ ts'a-ki-yaa
cheap *mai araha* mai a-ra-haa
check (bill) *lissafi* ⓜ lis-saa-fee
chest *k'irji* ⓜ k'ir-jee
child *yaro* ⓜ yaa-raw
cigarette *taba* ⓕ taa-baa
city *birni* ⓜ bir-nee
clean a *mai tsabta* mai ts'ab-taa
closed a *rufe* a ru-fe
cold a *mai sanyi* mai san-yee
condom *roba* ⓕ raw-baa
constipation *kumburin ciki* ⓜ kum-bu-rin chi-kee
cough *tari* ⓜ taa-ree
currency exchange *canjin kud'i* ⓜ chan-jin ku-d'ee
customs (immigration) *kwastan* ⓜ kwas-tan

D

dangerous *mai had'ari* mai ha-d'a-ree
date (time) *kwanan wata* ⓜ kwaa-nan wa-taa
day (24 hours) *kwana* ⓜ kwaa-naa
daytime *rana* ⓕ raa-naa
diaper *banten jinjiri* ⓜ ban-ten jin-ji-ree
diarrhoea *gudawa* ⓕ gu-daa-waa
dinner *abincin dare* ⓜ a-bin-chin da-re
dirty *mai daud'a* mai dow-d'aa
disabled *nak'asashe* na-k'a-sash-shey
double bed *gado ga mutane biyu* ⓜ ga-daw ga mu-taa-ney bi-yu
drink *abin sha* ⓜ a-bin sha
drivers licence *lasin tuk'i* ⓜ laa-sin too-k'ee
drug (illicit) *mugun k'waya* ⓕ moo-gun k'waa-yaa

E

ear *kunne* ⓜ kun·ney
east *gabas* ⓕ ga·bas
economy class *sikinkila* ⓕ si·kin·ki·la
elevator *lifta* ⓕ lif·taa
email *wasik'ar i-mel* ⓜ wa·see·k'ar ee·mel
English (language) *Turanci* ⓕ too·ran·chee
exchange rate *k'arfin kud'i* ⓜ k'ar·fin ku·d'ee
exit *mafita* ⓕ ma·fi·taa
expensive *mai tsada* mai ts'aa·daa
eye *ido* ⓜ i·daw

F

fast *mai sauri* mai sow·ree
fever *zazzab'i* ⓜ zaz·za·b'ee
finger *yatsa* ⓕ yaa·ts'aa
first class *faskila* fas·ki·la
fish *kifi* ⓜ kee·fee
food *abinci* a·bin·chi
foot *k'afa* ⓕ k'a·faa
fork *cokali mai yatsu* ⓜ chaw·ka·lee mai yaa·ts'oo
free (of charge) *a kyauta* a kyow·taa
fruit *'ya'yan itace* pl y'a·y'an i·taa·chey
funny *mai ban dariya* mai ban daa·ri·yaa

G

game park *wurin shak'atawa* ⓜ wu·rin shaa·k'a·ta·waa
gift *kyauta* ⓕ kyow·taa
girl *yarinya* ⓕ yaa·rin·yaa
glass *kofi* ⓜ kaw·fee
glasses *tabarau* ⓜ ta·baa·row
good *mai kyau* mai kyow
guide n *ja-gora* ⓜ jaa·gaw·ra

H

hand *hannu* ⓜ han·noo
happy *mai farin ciki* mai fa·rin chi·kee
he *shi* shee
head *kai* ⓜ kai
headache *ciwon kai* ⓜ chee·won kai
heart *zuciya* ⓕ zoo·chi·yaa
heart condition *halin zuciya* ⓜ haa·lin zoo·chi·yaa
heat *zafi* ⓜ zaa·fee
here *nan* nan

high *dogo/doguwa* ⓜ/ⓕ daw·gaw/daw·gu·waa
highway *babbar hanya* ⓕ bab·bar han·yaa
homosexual n *d'an daudu* ⓜ d'an dow·du
hot *mai zafi* mai zaa·fee
hungry *mai jin yunwa* mai jin yun·waa

I

I *ni* nee
identification (card) *katin shaida* ⓕ kaa·tin shai·daa
ill *maras lafiya* ma·ras laa·fi·yaa
important *muhimmi/muhimmiya* ⓜ/ⓕ mu·him·mee/mu·him·mi·yaa
interpreter *mai fassara* ⓜ mai fas·sa·raa

K

key *makulli* ⓜ ma·kul·lee
kilogram *kilo* ⓜ ki·law
kitchen (modern) *kicin* ⓜ ki·chin
kitchen (traditional) *madafa* ⓕ ma·da·faa
knife *wuk'a* ⓕ wu·k'aa

L

laundry (place) *mawanka* ⓕ ma·wan·kaa
lawyer *lauya* ⓜ low·yaa
leg *k'afa* ⓕ k'a·faa
lesbian n *y'ar mad'igo* ⓕ y'ar maa·d'i·gaw
less (do less) v *rage* rag·yey
letter (mail) *wasik'a* ⓕ wa·see·k'aa
like v *so* so
love v *so* so
lunch *abincin rana* ⓜ a·bin·chin raa·naa

M

man *mutum* ⓜ mu·tum
matches *ashana* ⓕ a·shaa·naa
meat *nama* ⓜ naa·maa
medicine *magani* ⓜ maa·ga·nee
message *sak'o* ⓜ saa·k'aw
mobile phone *salula* ⓕ sa·loo·laa
month *wata* ⓜ waa·taa
morning *safiya* saa·fi·yaa
(in the) morning *safe* saa·fe
motorcycle *babur* ⓜ baa·bur
motorcycle taxi *acaba* ⓕ a·cha·baa

mouth *baki* ⓜ baa-kee
movie *fim* ⓜ fim
museum *gidan kayan tarihi* ⓜ
gi-dan kaa-yan taa-ree-hee
music *kad'e-kad'e* pl ka-d'ey-k'a-dey

N

name *suna* ⓜ soo-naa
napkin *takardar goge hannu* ⓕ ta-kar-dar gaw-ge
han-noo
nappy *banten jinjiri* ⓜ ban-ten jin-ji-ree
national park *gandun daji* ⓜ gan-dun daa-jee
nausea *tashin zuciya* ⓜ taa-shin zoo-chi-yaa
neck *wuya* ⓕ wu-yaa
new *sabo/sabuwa* ⓜ/ⓕ saa-baw/saa-bu-waa
news *labari* ⓜ laa-baa-ree
newspaper *jarida* ⓕ ja-ree-daa
night *dare* da-rey
nightclub *kulob* ku-lob
noisy *mai k'ara* mai k'a-raa
nonsmoking *ga marasa shan taba*
ga ma-ra-saa shan taa-baa
north *arewa* ⓕ a-rey-wa
nose *hanci* ⓜ han-chee
now *yanzu* yan-zu
number *lamba* ⓕ lam-baa
nuts *gyad'a* ⓜ gya-d'aa

O

oil (engine) *man inji* ⓜ man in-jee
OK *shi ke nan* shee kyey nan
old *tsoho/tsohuwa* ⓜ/ⓕ ts'aw-haw/ts'aw-hu-waa
open a *a bude* a boo-de
outside *waje* wa-je

P

package *k'unshi* ⓜ k'un-shee
pain *ciwo* ⓜ chee-waw
palace *fad'a* ⓕ faa-d'a
paper *takarda* ⓕ ta-kar-daa
park (car) v *ajiye* a-ji-ye
passport *fasfo* ⓜ fas-fo
pay v *biya* bi-yaa
pen *biro* ⓜ bee-raw
petrol *man fetur* ⓜ man fey-tur

pharmacy *kantin magani* ⓜ kan-tin maa-ga-nee
plate *faranti* ⓕ fa-ran-tee
postcard *katin gaisuwa* ⓜ kaa-tin gai-su-waa
post office *gidan waya* ⓜ gi-dan wa-yaa
pregnant *mai juna biyu* mai joo-naa bi-yu

Q

quiet *mai shiru* mai shi-roo

R

rain *ruwan sama* ⓜ ru-wan sa-ma
razor (modern) *reza* ⓕ rey-zaa
razor (traditional) *aska* ⓕ as-kaa
registered mail *wasik'a ta rajista* ⓕ
wa-see-k'a ta ra-jis-taa
rent v *yi hayar* yi ha-yar
repair v *gyara* gyaa-raa
reservation (room) *kama d'aki* kaa-ma d'a-kee
restaurant *gidan cin abinci* ⓜ gi-dan chin a-bin-chi
return v *koma* kaw-maa
road *hanya* ⓕ han-yaa
room *d'aki* ⓜ d'a-kee

S

sad *mai bak'in ciki* mai ba-k'in chi-kee
safe (not dangerous) a *mai lafiya* mai laa-fi-yaa
safe (reliable) a *mai aminci* mai a-min-chee
seafood *abinci daga teku* a-bin-chi da-ga tey-ku
seat *abin zama* ⓜ a-bin za-maa
send *aika da* ai-kaa da
sex (gender) *jinsi* ⓜ jin-see
sex (intercourse) *jima'i* ⓜ ji-maa-'ee
shampoo *shamfu* ⓜ sham-fu
shaving cream *sabulu na aski* saa-bu-lu na as-kee
she *ita* i-ta
sheet (bed) *zanen gado* za-nen ga-daw
shirt (modern) *taguwa* ⓕ ta-gu-waa
shirt (long traditional) *riga* ⓕ ree-gaa
shoes *takalma* taa-kal-maa
shop *kanti* ⓕ kan-tee
shower *shawa* ⓕ shaa-waa
skin *fata* ⓕ faa-taa
skirt (modern) *siket* ⓜ si-ket
skirt (traditional) *zane* ⓜ za-ney
sleep v *yi barci* yi bar-chee

small *k'arami/k'arama* ⓜ/ⓕ k'a·ra·mee/k'a·ra·maa
soap *sabulu* ⓜ saa·bu·loo
some *kad'an* ka·d'an
soon *an jima* an ji·maa
sore throat *miki* ⓜ mee·kee
south *kudu* ⓜ ku·du
speak *yi magana* yi ma·ga·naa
spoon *cokali* ⓜ chaw·ka·lee
stamp *kan sarki* ⓜ kan sar·kee
station (train) *tasha(-r jirgin k'asa)* ⓕ
  ta·sha(-r jir·gin k'a·saa)
stomach *ciki* ⓜ chi·kee
stop v *tsaya* ts'a·yaa
stop (bus) *tasha(-r mota)* ⓕ ta·sha(-r mo·taa)
street (in general) *hanya* ⓕ han·yaa
street (paved only) *titi* ⓜ tee·tee
student *d'alibi/d'aliba* ⓜ/ⓕ d'aa·li·bee/d'aa·li·baa
swim v *yi iyo* yi i·yaw

T

teeth *hak'ora* pl ha·k'aw·raa
telephone *waya* ⓕ wa·yaa
television *talabijin* ⓕ ta·la·bi·jin
temperature (weather) *yanayi* ⓜ ya·na·yee
tent *tanti* ⓜ tan·tee
that (one) *wancan/waccan* ⓜ/ⓕ
  wan·chan/wach·chan
they *su* soo
thirsty *mai jin k'ishirwa* mai jin k'i·shir·waa
this (one) *wannan* ⓜ&ⓕ wan·nan
throat *mak'ogwaro* ⓜ ma·k'aw·gwa·raw
ticket *tikiti* ⓜ ti·ki·ti
time *lokaci* ⓜ law·ka·chee
tired *mai gajiya* mai ga·ji·yaa
tissues *takardun share majina* pl ta·kar·dun shaa·re
  maa·ji·naa
today *yau* yow
toilet *ban d'aki* ⓜ ban d'aa·kee
tonight *yau da dare* yow da da·re
toothache *ciwon hak'ora* ⓜ chi·won ha·k'aw·raa
toothbrush *buroshin goge baki* ⓜ
  bu·raw·shin gaw·gye baa·kee
toothpaste *man goge hak'ora* ⓜ
  man gaw·ge ha·k'aw·raa

torch (flashlight) *tocilan* ⓕ taw·chi·lan
towel *tawul* ⓜ taa·wul
translate *fassara* fas·sa·raa
travellers cheque *cek* ⓜ chek
trousers *wando* ⓜ wan·daw
tyre *taya* ⓕ taa·yaa

U

underwear (underpants) *kamfai* ⓜ kam·fai
urgent *na/ta gaggawa* ⓜ/ⓕ na/ta gag·gaa·waa

V

vacant *wanda ba kome a wurin*
  wan·da baa kaw·mey a wu·rin
vegetarian a *ga wanda ba ya cin nama*
  ga wan·da ba baa yaa chin naa·maa

W

waiter *sabis* ⓜ&ⓕ saa·bis
walk v *yi yawo* yi yaa·waw
wallet *alabe* ⓕ a·la·bey
warm a *mai d'umi* mai d'u·mee
wash (something) *wanke* wan·kyey
watch *kallo* ⓜ kal·law
water *ruwa* ⓜ ru·waa
we *mu* moo
west *yamma* ⓕ yam·ma
wheelchair *keken gurgu* ⓜ key·ken gur·goo
when *yaushe* yow·shey
where *ina* i·naa
who *wane ne* waa·ney ney
why *saboda me* sa·baw·da mey
window *taga* ⓕ taa·gaa
wine *giya* ⓕ gi·yaa
wine (palm) *bammi* ⓜ bam·mee
with *tare da* taa·re da
without *ba tare da . . . ba* baa taa·re da . . . ba
woman *mace* ⓕ ma·che
write *rubuta* ru·boo·taa

Y

you sg *kai/ke* ⓜ/ⓕ kai/kyey
you pl *ku* koo

Malagasy

pronunciation

Vowels		Consonants	
Symbol	**English sound**	**Symbol**	**English sound**
aa	f**a**ther	b	**b**ed
ai	**ai**sle	d	**d**og
e	b**e**t	dz	a**dz**e
i	h**i**t	f	**f**un
o	p**o**t	g	**g**o
ow	n**ow**	h	**h**at
u	p**u**t	k	**k**it
		l	**l**ot
		m	**m**an
		n	**n**ot
		ng	ri**ng**
		p	**p**et
		r	**r**un
		s	**s**un
		t	**t**op
		v	**v**ery
		w	**w**in
		y	**y**es
		z	**z**ero

In this chapter, the Malagasy pronunciation is given in pink after each phrase.

The pronunciation of Malagasy words is not always obvious from their written form. Unstressed syllables can be elided (dropped) and words may be pronounced in different ways depending on where they fall in a sentence. If you follow the pink pronunciation guides you can't go wrong, however.

Each syllable is separated by a dot, and the syllable stressed in each word is italicised.

For example:

Misaotra.   mi-*sotr*

introduction

As the official language of Madagascar, Malagasy (*malagasy* maa·*laa*·gaas) has around 25 million speakers. Malagasy belongs to the Malayo-Polynesian branch of the Austronesian language family and is unrelated to its neighbouring African languages. Its closest relative is the little-known Ma'anyan, a language from southern Borneo, with which it shares over 90 per cent of its vocabulary. This close relationship exists because Madagascar was first settled by Indonesians from southern Borneo. Over the centuries, the language has also been influenced by English and French – first in the 19th century by British and French missionaries, and later as a result of colonisation by the French in the first half of the 20th century. With proverbs like 'If a tree is good to be used for making a boat, it is because it grew on good soil' (*Ny hazo no vanon-ko lakana, dia ny tany naniriany no tsara* ni *haa*·zu nu va·nun·*ku laa*·kaa·naa de ni *taa*·ni naa·ni·*ri*·ni nu tsaar), Madagascar's language is just as colourful and fascinating as its wildlife, landscapes and people.

▬ **malagasy** (native language)

language difficulties

Do you speak English?	*Miteny angilisy ve ianao?*	mi·*ten* aan·gi·*lis* ve *i*·aa·now
Do you understand?	*Azonao ve?*	*aa*·zu·now ve
I (don't) understand.	*(Tsy) Azoko.*	(tsi) *aa*·zuk
Could you please …?	*Mba afaka … azafady?*	mbaa *aa*·faak … aa·zaa·*faad*
repeat that	*averinao ve izany*	aa·*ve*·ri·now ve *i*·zaan
speak more	*miteny miadana*	mi·*ten* mi·*aa*·daan
slowly	*kokoa ve ianao*	ku·*ku* ve *i*·aa·now
write it down	*soratanao ve izany*	su·raa·*taa*·now ve *i*·zaan

time, dates & numbers

What time is it?	*Amin'ny firy izao?*	aa·min·*ni*·fi *ri*·zow
It's one o'clock.	*Amin'ny iray ora izao.*	aa·min·*ni* rai ur *i*·zow
It's (two) o'clock.	*Amin'ny (roa) izao.*	aa·min·*ni* (ru) *i*·zow
Quarter past (one).	*(Iray) sy fahefany.*	(rai) si faa·*he*·faan
Half past (one).	*(Iray) sy sasany.*	(rai) si *saa*·saan
Quarter to (eight).	*(Valo) latsaka fahefany.*	(vaal) *laat*·saa·kaa faa·*he*·faan
At what time …?	*Amin'ny firy …?*	aa·min·*ni* fir …
At …	*Amin'ny …*	aa·min·*ni* …
It's (15 December).	*(Dimy ambinifolo Desambra) androany.*	(dim *aam*·bin·*ful* de·*saam*·braa) aan·*dru*·aan
yesterday	*omaly*	*u*·maal
today	*androany*	aan·*dru*·aan
tomorrow	*rahampitso*	raa·haam·*pits*
Monday	*Alatsinainy*	aa·laat·*si*·nain
Tuesday	*Talata*	*taa*·laat
Wednesday	*Alarobia*	aa·laa·*ru*·bi
Thursday	*Alakamisy*	aa·laa·*kaa*·mis
Friday	*Zomà*	zu·*maa*
Saturday	*Asabotsy*	aa·saa·*buts*
Sunday	*Alahady*	aa·laa·*haad*

0	*aotra*	*ow*·traa	16	*enina*	*e*·ni·	
1	*isa/iray*	*i*·saa/*i*·rai		*ambinifolo*	*naam*·bin·*ful*	
2	*roa*	ru	17	*fito*	fi·tu·	
3	*telo*	tel		*ambinifolo*	*aam*·bin·*ful*	
4	*efatra*	e·faatr	18	*valo*	vaa·lu·	
5	*dimy*	dim		*ambinifolo*	*aam*·bin·*ful*	
6	*enina*	*e*·nin	19	*sivy ambinifolo*	si·vi·*aam*·bin·*ful*	
7	*fito*	fit	20	*roapolo*	ru·aa·*pul*	
8	*valo*	vaal	21	*iraika*	*i*·rai·	
9	*sivy*	siv		*ambiroampolo*	*kaam*·bi·ro·*pu*	
10	*folo*	ful	22	*roa*	ru	
11	*iraika*	*i*·rai·		*ambiroampolo*	*aam*·bi·ro·*pul*	
	ambinifolo	*kaam*·bin·*ful*	30	*telopolo*	te·lu·*pul*	
12	*roa*	ru	40	*efapolo*	e·faa·*pul*	
	ambinifolo	*aam*·bin·*ful*	50	*dimampolo*	di·maam·*pul*	
13	*telo*	tel	60	*enimpolo*	e·ni·*pul*	
	ambinifolo	*aam*·bin·*ful*	70	*fitopolo*	fi·tu·*pul*	
14	*efatra*	e·faa·*traam*·	80	*valopolo*	vaa·lu·*pul*	
	ambinifolo	bin·*ful*	90	*sivifolo*	si·vi·*ful*	
15	*dmy*	dim	100	*zato*	zaat	
	iambinifolo	*aam*·bin·*ful*	1000	*arivo*	*aa*·riv	

border crossing

I'm here ...	... *aho no eto.*	... ow nu et
in transit	*Mandalo fotsiny*	maan·*daa*·lu *fut*·sin
on business	*Manao raharaha*	maa·*now* raa·haa·*raa*
on holiday	*Miala sasatra*	mi·*aa*·laa *saa*·saatr

I'm here for ...	... *aho no eto.*	... ow nu et
(10) days	*(Folo) andro*	(ful) aandr
(three) weeks	*(Telo) herinandro*	(tel) he·*ri*·naandr
(two) months	*(Roa) volana*	(ru) *vu*·laan

I'm going to (Mahajanga).
Ho any (Mahajanga) aho.   ho aan (maa·haa·*dzaang*) ow

I'm staying at (the Zahamotel).
Mipetraka ao amin'ny (Zahamotel) aho.   mi·*pe*·traa·kow aa·min·*ni* (zaa·*mo*·tel) ow

tickets

A ... ticket	Tapakila ... iray	taa-paa-*kil* ... *i*-rai
(to Toliary), please.	(mankany Toliary), azafady.	(*maa*-kaan tu-*li*-aar) aa-zaa-*faad*
one-way	mandroso	maan-drus
return	miverina	mi-*ve*-rin

I'd like to ... my	Mba te ... ny tapakilako	mbaa te ... ni taa-paa-*ki*-laa-ku
ticket, please.	aho, azafady.	ow aa-zaa-*faad*
cancel	hanafoana	haa-naa-*fo*-naa
change	hanolo	*haa*-nul
collect	haka	*haa*-kaa

I'd like a ...	Toerana ho an'ny ...	tu-*e*-raa-naa u *aan*-ni ...
seat, please.	no mba tiako, azafady.	nu mbaa *ti*-ku aa-zaa-*faad*
nonsmoking	tsy mifoka sigara	tsi mi-*fuk* si-gaar
smoking	mifoka	mi-*fuk*

Is there a toilet/air conditioning?
Misy efitra fidiovan/kilimatizera ve?   *mi*-si e-fi-traa fi-di-*u*-vaan/kli-*maa*-ti-zer ve

How long does the trip take?
Hafiriana ny dia?   haa-fi-*ri*-naa ni di

Is it a direct route?
Tsy mijanojanona ve?   tsi mi-dzaa-nu-*dzaa*-nu-naa ve

transport

Where does the (Air Madagascar) flight arrive/depart?
Aiza ny sidina (Air Madagascar)   *ai*-zaa ni *si*-di-naa (air maa-daa-*gaa*-si-kaar)
no tonga/miainga?   nu *tun*-gaa/mi-*ain*-gaa

How long will it be delayed?
Hafiriana ny fahatarany?   haa-fi-*ri*-naa ni faa-haa-*taa*-raan

Is this the ...	Ity ve ny ... mankany	i-*ti* ve ni ... maa-*kaan*
to (Toamasina)?	(Toamasina)?	(to-*maa*-sin)?
boat	sambo	saamb
bus	aotobisy	o-*to*-bis
plane	roaplanina	ro-plaan
train	lamasinina	laa-*maa*-sin

How much is it to ...?
  Ohatrinona ny ...?   o·*trin*·naa ni ...

Please take me to (this address).
  Mba ento any amin'   mbaa *en*·tu aa·ni aa·min
  (ityadiresy ity) aho azafady.   (tiaa·di·*res* ti) ow aa·zaa·*faad*

I'd like to hire a car/4WD (with air conditioning).
  Mba te hanarama fiara/4x4   mbaa te haa·naa·*raa*·maa fi·aar/kaat·*kaat*·raa
  (misy kilimatizera) aho azafady.   (mis kli·*maa*·ti·zer) ow aa·zaa·*faad*

How much is it for (three) days/weeks?
  Ohatrinona ny (telo)   o·*trin*·naa ni (*te*·lu)
  andro/herinandro?   *aan*·dru/he·ri·*naan*·dru

directions

Where's the	*Aiza ny ...*	ai·zaa ni ...
(nearest) ...?	*(akaiky indrindra)?*	(aa·*kaik* in·*drin*·draa)
internet café	*sibera*	si·ber
market	*tsena*	tsen

Is this the road to (Antsirabe)?
  Ity ve ny lalana mankany (Antsirabe)?   i·ti ve ni *laa*·laan maa·*kaan* (aan·tsi·raa·*be*)

Can you show me (on the map)?
  Afaka asehonao ahy   aa·*faak* aa·se·u·*now* waa
  (eoamin'ny sarintany) ve?   (e·uaa·min·*ni* saa·rin·*taan*) ve

What's the address?
  Inona ny adiresy?   i·nu·naa ni aa·di·*res*

How far is it?
  Hafiriana avy eto?   haa·fi·ri·naa *aa*·vi et

How do I get there?
  Ahoana no lalako mankany?   ow·o·naa nu *laa*·laa·ku *maa*·kaan

Turn left/right.
  Mivilia ankavia/ankavanana.   mi·vi·*li* aan·kaa·*vi*/aan·kaa·*vaa*·naan

It's ...	... ilay izy.	... i·lai iz
behind ...	Ao ambadiky ny ...	ow aam·baa·di·ki ni ...
in front of ...	Manoloana ny ...	maa·nu·lo·naa ni ...
near (to ...)	Akaiky ny	aa·kai·ki ni
next to ...	Manaraka ny	maa·naa·raa·kaa ni
on the corner	Eo an-jorony	e·waan·dzu·run
opposite ...	Mifanatrika ...	mi·faa·naa·trik ...
straight ahead	Mandeha mahitsy	maan·de maa·hits
there	Eo	e·u

accommodation

Where's a ...?	Aiza no misy ...?	ai·zaa nu mis ...
camping ground	toerana filasiana	tu·e·raan fi·laa·si·naa
guesthouse	tranom-bahiny	traa·num·baa·hin
hotel	hôtely	o·tel
youth hostel	fandraisana Tanora	faan·drai·saa·naa taa·nur

Can you recommend somewhere cheap/good?
Afaka manoro ahy toerana aa·faa·kaa maa·nur waa tu·e·raa·naa
mora/tsara ve ianao? mu·raa/tsaa·raa ve i·aa·now

I'd like to book a room, please.
Mba te hamandrika efitra mbaa te haa·maan·dri·kaa e·fi·traa
iray aho, azafady. rai ow aa·zaa·faad

I have a reservation.
Manana famandrihana iray aho. maa·naa·naa faa·maan·dri·haa·naa rai ow

Do you have	Misy ... ve ato aminao	mis ... ve aat·waa·mi·now
a ... room?	efitra iray ...?	e·fi·traa i·rai ...
single	ho an'olon-tokana	waa·nu·lun·dru
double	misy fandriana lehibe	mis faan·dri·naa le·hi·be
twin	misy fandriana kely	mis faan·dri·naa kel

How much is it per night/person?
Ohatrinona isan' alina/olona? o·trin·i·saan aa·lin/u·lun

I'd like to stay for (two) nights.
Mba saika hipetraka (roa) alina aho. mbaa sai·kaa i·pe·traa·kaa (ru) aa·li·now

What time is check-out?
  Amin'ny firy no   aa·min·*ni* fir nu
  fara-famerenana lakile?   faa·raa·faa·me·*re*·naa·naa laa·ki·*le*

Am I allowed to camp here?
  Mahazo milasy eto ve aho?   maa·*haa*·zu mi·*laas* e·tu ve *ow*

banking & communications

I'd like to ...	*Mba te ... aho azafady.*	mbaa te ... ow aa·zaa·*faad*
arrange a transfer	*hikarakara*	hi·kaa·*raa*·kaar
	famindram-bola	faa·min·*draam*·bul
cash a cheque	*hanakalo seky*	haa·naa·*kaa*·lu *se*·ki
change a travellers	*hanakalo seky de*	haa·naa·*kaa*·lu *se*·ki de
cheque	*voiazy*	vo·*yaa*·zi
change money	*hanakalo vola*	haa·naa·*kaa*·lu *vu*·laa
withdraw money	*hisintona vola*	hi·*sin*·tu·naa *vu*·laa

I want to ...	*Te ... aho.*	te ... ow
buy a phonecard	*hividy karatra*	*hi*·vid kaa·*raa*·traa
	telefaonina	te·le·*fon*
call (Singapore)	*hiantso an'l*	hi·*aan*·tsu aa·ni
	(Singapore)	(sin·gaa·*pur*)
reverse the	*hanafaona ny*	haa·naa·*fo*·naa ni
charges	*sarany*	*saa*·raa·ni
use the intenet	*hampiasa emprimanty*	haam·pi·*aas* em·pri·*maan*·ti
use a printer	*hijery enterinety*	hi·*dze*·ri en·*ter*·net

How much is it per hour?
  Ohatrinona ny adiny iray?   o·*trin*·naa ni *aa*·din rai

How much does a (three-minute) call cost?
  Ohatrinona ny miantso (telo minitra)?   o·*trin*·naa ni mi·*aant*·su (tel mi·*ni*·traa)

(One ariary) per minute.
  (Ariary) ny iray minitra.   (aa·ri·aar) ni *i*·rai mi·*ni*·traa

tours

When's the	*Rahoviana ny*	row·*vi*·naa ni
next ...?	*... manaraka?*	... maa·*naa*·raa·kaa
day trip	*dia atoandro*	di aa·*tu*·aan·dru
tour	*toro*	tur

Is ... included?	Ao antiny ve ...?	ow aa·*naa*·ti·ni ve ...
accommodation	ny toerana ipetrahana	ni tu·e·raa·ni·*pe*·traa·haan
the admission charge	ny vidim-pidirana	ni vi·dim·pi·*di*·raan
food	sakafo	*saa*·kaaf
transport	fitaterana	fi·taa·*te*·raan

How long is the tour?
Hafiriana ny toro?   haa·fi·*ri*·naa ni tur

What time should we be back?
Amin'ny firy isika no   aa·min·*ni* fi·ri·si·kaa nu
tokony ho tafaverina?   *tu*·kun nu taa·faa·*ve*·rin

shopping

I'm looking for ...
Mitady ... aho.   mi·*taa*·di ... ow

I need film for this camera.
Mila pelikiola ho an'ity   *mi*·laa pe·*li*·ki·ul waa·ni·*ti*
fakantsary ity aho.   faa·*kaan*·tsaa·ri·*ti* ow

Can I listen to this?
Azoko henoina ve ity?   aa·zuk we·*nu*·naa ve i·*ti*

Can I have my ... repaired?
Afaka amboarina ve ny ... -ko?   aa·faa·kaamb·*waa*·rin ve ni ... ·ku

When will it be ready?
Rahoviana no vita?   row·*vi*·naa nu *vi*·taa

How much is it?
Ohatrinona?   o·*trin*

Can you write down the price?
Mba afaka soratanao ve ny vidiny?   mbaa aa·faa·kaa su·raa·*taa*·now ve ni *vi*·din

What's your lowest price?
Ohatrinona ny vidiny farany?   o·*trin*·naa ni *vi*·din faa·raan

I'll give you (five) ariary.
Omeko Ariary (dimy) ianao.   u·*me*·ku aa·ri·aa·ri (*di*·mi) *aa*·now

There's a mistake in the bill.
Miso diso ny fakitiora. mis *di*·su ni faak·*tu*·raa

It's faulty.
Tsy marina io. tsi maa·ri·*ni*·u

I'd like a receipt, please.
Mba mila resiò aho, azafady. mbaa *mi*·laa re·si·u ow aa·zaa·*faad*

Do you accept ...?	*Mandray ... ve ianao?*	maan·*drai* ... ve *i*·aa·now
credit cards	*karatra kiredy*	*kaa*·raa·traa kre·*di*
travellers cheques	*seky de voiazy*	se·ki de vo·*yaa*·zi

Could you ...?	*Mba afaka ... ve ianao azafady?*	mbaa·*aa*·faak ... ve *i*·aa·now aa·zaa·*faad*
burn a CD from my memory card	*mameno CD avy amin'ny oridinaterako*	maa·*me*·nu se·de *aa*·vi aa·min·ni o·ri·di·naa·*te*·raa·ku
develop this film	*manasa ity pelikiola ity*	maa·*naa*·saa i·*ti* pe·*li*·ki·ul i·*ti*

making conversation

Hello.	*Manao ahoana.*	maa·*now* aa·hon
Good night.	*Tafandria mandry.*	taa·faan·*dri maan*·dri
Goodbye.	*Veloma.*	ve·*lum*

Mr	*Ingahy*	in·*gaa*
Mrs	*Ramatoa*	raa·maa·*tu*
Ms/Miss	*Ramatoakely*	raa·maa·*tu*·kel

How are you?
Manao ahoana ianao? maa·*now* aa·ho·*ni*·aa·now

Fine, and you?
Tsara, ary ianao? tsaar aa·ri·*aa*·now

What's your name?
Iza no anaranao? *i*·zaa nu aa·*naa*·raa·now

My name's ...
... no anarako. ... nu aa·*naa*·raa·ku

I'm pleased to meet you.
Faly mahafantatra anao. *faa*·li *maa*·faan·taa·traa now

This is my ...	Izy no ...ko.	i·zi nu ...ku
boyfriend	sakaiza-	saa·kai·zaa·
brother (man/ woman saying)	rahalahi-/ anadahi-	raa·laa·hi·/ aa·naa·daa·hi·
daughter	zanaka vavi-	zaa·naa·kaa vaa·vi·
father	rai-	rai·
friend	nama-	naa·maa·
girlfriend	sakaiza-	saa·kai·zaa·
husband	vadi-	vaa·di·
mother	reni-	re·ni·
sister (man/ woman saying)	anabavi-/ rahavavi-	aa·naa·baa·vi·/ raa·vaa·vi·
son	zanaka lahi-	zaa·naa·kaa laa·hi·
wife	vadi-	vaa·di·

Here's my ...	Ity ny ...ko.	i·ti ni ...ku
What's your ...?	Inona ny ...nao?	i·nu·naa ni ...now
address	adiresi-	aa·di·re·si·
email address	adiresy maila-	aa·di·res mai·laa·
phone number	numerao telefaoni-	nu·me·row te·le·fon·

Where are you from?	Avy aiza ianao?	aa·vi ai·zaa i·aa·now

I'm from ...	Avy any ... aho.	aa·vi aa·ni ... ow
Australia	Aositralia	os·traa·li
Canada	Kanadà	kaa·naa·daa
New Zealand	Niò Zelandy	ni·u ze·laan·di
the UK	Angiletera	aan·gle·ter
the USA	Amerika	aa·me·rik

I'm (not) married.	(Tsy) Manam-bady aho.	(tsi) maa·naam·baa·di ow
Can I take a photo (of you)?	Afaka maka sary (anao) ve aho?	aa·faa·kaa maa·kaa saa·ri (aa·now) ve ow

eating out

Can you recommend a ...?	Afaka manoro ahy ... tsara ve ianao?	aa·faa·kaa maa·nur waa ... tsaar ve i·aa·now
bar	bara	baa·raa
dish	sakafo	saa·kaaf
place to eat	toerana	tu·e·raan
	hisakafoanana	i·saa·kaa·fu·aa·naan

I'd like ..., please.	Mba mila ..., azafady.	mbaa *mi*·laa ... aa·zaa·*faad*
the bill	ny fakitiora	ni faak·ti·*ur*
the menu	ny lisitra sakafo	ni *lis*·traa *saa*·kaaf
a table for (two)	latabatra ho an' (olon-droa)	laa·*taa*·baa·traa waan (u·lun·*dru*)
that dish	iny sakafo iny	in saa·*kaa*·fu in

| Do you have vegetarian food? | Manana sakafo tsy misy hena ve ianareo? | maa·naa·naa *saa*·kaaf tsi mis he·naa ve i·aa·naa·*re*·u |

Could you prepare a meal without ...?	Mba afaka manao sakafo tsy misy ... ve ianareo?	mbaa aa·faak maa·*now saa*·kaaf tsi mis ... ve i·aa·*naa*·re·u
eggs	atody	aa·*tud*
meat stock	hena	he·naa

(cup of) coffee ...	kafe (iray kaopy) ...	kaa·*fe* (i·*rai* kop) ...
(cup of) tea ...	dite (iray kaopy) ...	di·*te* (i·*rai* kop) ...
with milk	misy ronono	mis *ru*·nun
without sugar	tsy misy siramamy	tsi mis si·*raa*·maam

| (boiled) water | rano (mangotraka) | *raa*·nu (maan·*gu*·traak) |

emergencies

| Help! | Vonjeo! | vun·*dze*·u |
| I'm lost. | Very aho. | ve·ri ow |

Call ...!	Antsoy ny ...!	aant·*su*·i ni ...
an ambulance	ambilansy	aam·*bi*·laans
a doctor	dokotera	duk·*ter*
the police	polisy	po·*lis*

Could you help me, please?
Mba ampio kely aho, azafady?   mbaa aam·*pi*·u kel ow aa·zaa·*faad*

Where are the toilets?
Aiza ny trano fivoahana?   *ai*·zaa ni *traa*·nu fi·vu·*aa*·haan

I want to report an offence.
Mba te hitatitra heloka iray aho.   mbaa te hi·*taa*·ti·traa he·lu·ki rai ow

I have insurance.
Manana fiantohana aho.   maa·naa·naa fi·aan·*tu*·haa·now

I want to contact my consulate/embassy.
Te hanatona ny masoivohonay aho.   te haa-*naa*-tu-naa ni maa-su-i-*vu*-aa-nai ow

I've been ...	*Nisy ... aho.*	nis ... ow
assaulted	*nanafika*	naa-*naa*-fik
raped	*nanolana*	naa-*nu*-laan
robbed	*nangalatra*	naan-*gaa*-laa-traa

I've lost my ...	*Very ny ...ko.*	*ve*-ri ni ...ku
My ... was/were	*Nisy nangalatra*	nis naan-*gaa*-laa-traa
stolen.	*ny ...ko.*	ni ...ku
bags	*haro-*	*haa*-ru-
handbag	*paoketra-*	po-*ke*-traa-
jewellery	*firava-*	fi-*raa*-vaa-
money	*vola-*	*vu*-laa-
passport	*pasipaoro-*	paa-si-*por*-
travellers cheques	*seki-*	*se*-ki-
wallet	*paoketra keli-*	po-*ke*-traa *kel*-

medical needs

Where's the	*Aiza ny ...*	*ai*-zaa ni ...
nearest ...?	*akaiky indrindra?*	aa-*kaik* in-*drin*-draa
dentist	*mpanao nify*	paa-*now* nif
doctor	*dokotera*	duk-*ter*
hospital	*hôpitaly*	ho-pi-*taal*
pharmacist	*fivarotam-panafody*	fi-vaa-*ru*-taam-paa-naa-fud

I need a doctor (who speaks English).
Mba mila dokotera   mbaa *mi*-laa duk-te-*raa*
(miteny Angilisy) aho.   (*mi*-ten aan-gi-*lis*) ow

Could I see a female doctor?
Mba afaka manatona dokotera   mbaa *aa*-faa-kaa maa-*naa*-tu-naa duk-te-*raa*
vavy ve aho azafady?   vaav ve ow aa-zaa-*faad*

It hurts here.
Marary eto.   maa-*raa*-ri et

I'm allergic to (penicillin).
Tys mahazaka (penisilina) aho.   tsi maa-haa-*zaa*-kaa (pe-*ni*-si-lin) ow

english–malagasy dictionary

In this dictionary, words are marked as n (noun), a (adjective), v (verb), ⓜ (masculine), ① (feminine), sg (singular) and pl (plural) where necessary.

A

accommodation *toerana ipetrahana* tu-e-raa-ni-pe-traa-haan
adaptor *adapitera* aa-*daa*-pi-ter
after *aoriana* ow-ri-naa
airport *tobi-piaramanidina* tu-bi-pi-aa-raa-maa-*ni*-din
alcohol *alikaola* aa-li-*ko*-laa
all *rehetra* re-*he*-traa
allergy *tsy fahazakana* tsi faa-haa-*zaa*-kaan
and *ary* aa-ri
ankle *kitrokely* ki-*tru*-kel
antibiotics *antibiôtika* aan-ti-bi-*o*-ti-kaa
anti-inflammatories *tsy mampivonto* tsi maam-pi-*vun*-tu
arm *sandry* saan-dri
aspirin *asipirinina* aa-si-*pi*-rin
asthma *asima* aas-maa

B

baby *zazakely* zaa-zaa-*ke*-li
back (body) *lamosina* laa-*mu*-si-naa
backpack *kitapo fibaby* ki-*taa*-pu fi-baab
bad *ratsy* raats
baggage claim *fijerena entana* fi-dze-*re*-naa *en*-taan
bank *banky* baan-ki
bathroom *efitra fandroana* e-fi-traa faan-*dru*-aan
battery *pila* pil
beautiful *tsara tarehy* tsaa-raa *taa*-re
bed *fandriana* faan-*drin*
beer *labiera* laa-*bi*-er
bees *tantely* taan-tel
before *mialoha* mi-aa-*lu*
bicycle *bisikileta* bis-ki-*le*-taa
big *ngeza* nge-zaa
blanket *firakotra* fi-*raa*-ku-traa
blood group *sokajin-drà* so-kaad-zin-*draa*
bottle *tavoahangy* taa-vu-*haan*-gi
bottle opener *famohana tavoahangy* faa-mu-*haa*-naa taa-vu-*haan*-gi
boy *lahy* laa
brakes (car) *fire* fre
breakfast *sakafo maraina* saa-kaaf maa-*rai*-naa
bronchitis *koha-davareny* ku-haa-daa-*vaa*-ren

C

café *kafe* kaa-*fe*
cancel *foanana* fu-*aa*-naa-naa
can opener *famohana kapoaka* faa-mu-*haa*-naa *kaa*-pok
cash n *lelavola* le-laa-vu-laa
cell phone *paoritabila* por-*taa*-bi-laa
centre n *ivo* i-vu
cheap *moravidy* mu-*raa*-vid
check (bill) *seky* se-ki
check-in n *tomboka fidirana* tum-bu-kaa fi-*di*-raan
chest *tratra* traa-traa
child *ankizy* aan-kiz
cigarette *sigara* si-*gaa*-raa
city *tanàn-dehibe* taa-*naan*-de-hi-be
clean a *madio* maa-di-u
closed *mihidy* mi-*hid*
codeine *kaodehinina* ko-de-in
cold a *mangatsiaka* maan-gaa-*tsik*
condom *kapoty* kaa-po-ti
constipation *fitohanana* fi-to-*haa*-naa-naa
contact lenses *solomaso* su-lu-*maa*-su
cough n *kohaka* ku-haak
currency exchange *fanakalozana devizy* faa-naa-kaa-*lu*-zaa-naa de-*viz*
customs (immigration) *ladoany* laa-*du*-aan

D

dairy products *ronono* ru-*nun*
dangerous *mampidi-doza* maam-*pi*-di-duz
date (time) n *daty* daa-ti
day *andro* aan-dru
diaper *tatin-jazz* taa-tind-*zaa*-zaa
diarrhoea *mivalana* mi-vaa-laan
dinner *sakafo hariva* saa-*kaa*-fu aa-*ri*-vaa
dirty *maloto* maa-lut
disabled *kilemaina* ki-le-*mai*-naa
double bed *fandriana lehibe* faan-*dri*-naa *le*-hi-be
drink n *zava-pisotro* zaa-vaa-*pi*-su-tru
drivers licence *perimia* per-*mi*
drug (illicit) *zava-mahadomelina* zaa-vaa-maa-*du*-mel

E

ear *sofina* su-fi-naa
east *atsinanana* aat-si-*naa*-naan
economy class *kilasy faharoa* ki-*laa*-si faa-haa-ru
elevator *asansera* aa-*saan*-ser
email n *mailaka* mai-laak
English (language) *angilisy* aan-gi-*lis*
exchange rate *vidy takalo* vi-di taa-*kaa*-lu
exit n *fivoahana* fi-vu-aa-haan
expensive *lafo* laa-fu
eye *maso* maa-su

F

fast a *haingana* hain-gaa-naa
fever *tazo* taa-zu
finger *rantsan-tanana* raant-saan-*taa*-naan
first-aid kit *fanafody vonjy taitra*
  faa-naa-*fu*-di vund-zi-*tai*-traa
first class *kilasy voalohany* ki-*laa*-si vu-aa-*lu*-haan
fish n *trondro* trun-dru
food *sakafo* saa-*kaaf*
foot *tongotra* tun-*gu*-traa
fork *forisety* fu-ri-se-ti
free (of charge) *maimaimpoana* mai-mai-*po*-naa
fruit *voankazo* vu-aan-*kaaz*
funny *mampiomehy* maam-pi-u-*me*

G

game park *kianjan-dalao* ki-aand-zaan-*daa*-low
gift *fanomezana* faa-nu-*me*-zaan
girl *vehivavy* ve-*hi*-vaav
glass (drinking) *vera* ve-raa
glasses *solomaso* su-lu-maas
gluten *gilotenina* glu-*ten*
good *tsara* tsaa-raa
gram *girama* graa-maa
guide n *mpitarika* pi-*taa*-ri-kaa

H

hand *tanana* taa-naa-naa
happy *faly* faa-li
have *manana* maa-naa-naa
he *izy* iz
head *loha* lu

headache *aretina an-doha* aa-re-tin-aan-*du*
heart *fò* fu
heart condition *toe-pò* tu-e-*pu*
heat n *hafanana* haa-*faa*-naan
here *eto* e-tu
high *avo* aa-vu
highway *lalambe* laa-*laam*-be
homosexual n&a *sarindahy/sarimbavy* ⚣ / ⚢
  saa-rim-*daa*/saa-rim-*baa*-vi
hot *mahamay* maa-mai
hungry *noana* no-naa

I

I *aho* ow
identification (card) *kara-panondro* kaa-raa-*paa*-nun-dru
ill *marary* maa-*raa*-ri
important *zava-dehibe* zaa-vaa-de-hi-*be*
internet *enterinety* en-ter-net
interpreter *mpandika teny* paan-*di*-kaa *te*-ni

J

job *asa* aa-saa

K

key *lakile* laa-ki-le
kilogram *kilao* ki-*low*
kitchen *lakozia* laa-ku-zi
knife *antsy* aant-si

L

laundry (place) *fanasan-damba* faa-naa-saan-*daam*-baa
lawyer *mpisolo vava* mpi-su-lu vaa-*vaa*
left-luggage office *birao mpitahiry entana*
  bi-row pi-taa-hi-ri en-taa-naa
leg *ranjo* raand-zu
lesbian n&a *sarindahy* saa-rin-*daa*
less *kely kokoa* ke-li ku-*ko*
letter (mail) *taratasy* taa-*raa*-taas
like v *tia* ti
lost-property office *biraon' entana very*
  bi-row-ni-en-taa-naa-ve-ri
love v *tia* ti
lunch *sakafo atoandro* saa-*kaaf* waa-tu-*aan*-dru

M

man *lehilahy* le-hi-*laa*
matches *afokasoka* aa-fu-*kaa*-su-kaa
meat *hena* he-naa
medicine *fanafody* faa-naa-*fu*-di
message *hafatra* haa-faa-traa
mobile phone *paoritabila* por-*taa*-bi-laa
month *volana* vu-laa-naa
morning *maraina* maa-*rai*-naa
motorcycle *môtô* mo-*to*
mouth *vava* vaa-vaa
movie *sarimihetsika* saa-ri-mi-*het*-si-kaa
MSG *MSG* em-es-dze
museum *trano firaketana* traan fi-raa-*ke*-taan
music *mozika* mu-*zik*

N

name n *anarana* aa-*naa*-raan
napkin *serivietan-databatra*
     se-ri-vi-e-taan-daa-*taa*-baa-traa
nappy *te hatory* te haa-*tu*-ri
national park *parika nasiônaly* paar-kaa naa-si-o-*naa*-li
nausea *malohilohy* maa-*lo*-hi-*lo*-hi
neck *hatoka* haa-*tu*-kaa
new *vaovao* vow-*vow*
news *vaovao* vow-*vow*
newspaper *gazety* gaa-ze-ti
night *alina* aa-li-naa
nightclub *toeram-pandihizana* tu-e-raam-paan-di-*hi*-zaana
noisy *mitabataba* mi-taa-baa-*taa*-baa
nonsmoking *tsy mifoka sigara* tsi mi-*fu*-kaa si-*gaa*-raa
north *avaratra* aa-*vaa*-raa-traa
nose *orona* u-ru-naa
now *izao* i-zow
number *isa* i-saa
nuts *voanjo* vu-*aan*-dzu

O

oil (engine) *menaka* me-naa-kaa
OK *mety* me-ti
old *antitra* aan-ti-traa
open a *mivoha* mi-*vu*
outside *ivelany* i-*ve*-laa-ni

P

package *entana* en-taa-naa
pain *fanaintainana* faa-nain-*tai*-naa-naa

palace *rova* ru-vaa
paper *taratasy* taa-raa-taas
park (car) v *fijanonana* fid-zaa-*nu*-naan
passport *pasipaoro* paa-si-*po*-ru
pay v *karama* *kaa*-raa-maa
pen *penina* pen
petrol *lasantsy* laa-*saant*-si
pharmacy *farimasia* faa-ri-*maa*-si
plate *lovia* lu-*vi*
postcard *karatra paositaly* kaa-raa-traa pos-*taa*-li
post office *paositra* po-si-traa
pregnant *bevohoka* be-vu-*kaa*

Q

quiet *mangiangiana* maan-gin-*gi*-naa

R

rain n *orana* u-raan
razor *hareza* haa-rez
registered mail *taratasy rekômande*
     taa-raa-*taas* re-ko-maan-*de*
rent v *hofany* hu-faan
repair v *mamboatra* maam-*bo*-traa
reservation *famandrihana* faa-maan-*dri*-haan
restaurant *hôtely fisakafoana* o-*te*-li fi-saa-kaa-*fu*-aa-naa
return v *miverina* mi-*ve*-ri-naa
road *lalana* *laa*-laa-naa
room *efitra* e-fi-traa

S

sad *malahelo* maa-laa-*he*-lu
safe a *milamina* mi-*laa*-mi-naa
sanitary napkin *serivieta fidiovana*
     se-ri-*vi*-e-taa fi-di-*u*-vaa-naa
seafood *hazan-drano* haa-zaan-*draa*-nu
seat *fitoerana* fi-tu-e-raan
send *mandefa* maan-*def*
sex *vavy na lahy* vaa-vi naa *laa*
shampoo *fanasam-bolo* faa-naa-saam-*bu*-lu
share (a dorm, etc) *mizara* mi-*zaa*-raa
shaving cream *kirema fiharatana* krem fi-haa-*raa*-taan
she *izy* iz
sheet (bed) *lambam-pandriana* laam-baam-paan-*dri*-naa
shirt *lobaka* lu-baa-kaa
shoes *kiraro* ki-*raa*-ru

shop n *fivarotana* fi-vaa-*ru*-taan
shower n *fandroana* faan-*dru*-naa
skin *hoditra* hu-di-traa
skirt *zipo* zi-po
sleep v *matory* maa-*tu*-ri
small *kely* ke-li
smoke (cigarettes) v *mifoka* mi-*fu*-kaa
soap *savony* saa-*vu*-ni
some *sasany* saa-saan
soon *atoato* aa-tu-*aa*-tu
sore throat *aretin-tenda* aa-re-tin-*ten*-daa
south *atsimo* aat-*si*-mu
souvenir shop *fivarotana fahatsiarovana*
fi-vaa-*ru*-taan faa-tsi-aa-*ru*-vaan
speak *miteny* mi-ten
spoon *sotro* su-tru
stamp *hajia* haad-zi
stand-by ticket *tapakila ho an'ny lisitra miandry*
taa-*paa*-kil waan-ni-*li*-si-traa mi-aan-dri
station (train) *gara* gaa-raa
stomach *vavony* vaa-vu-ni
stop v *mijanona* mid-*zaa*-nu-naa
stop (bus) n *fijanonana* fid-zaa-nu-naan
street *arabe* aa-raa-be
student *mpianatra* pi-*aa*-naa-traa
sunscreen *aro-masoandro* aa-ru-maa-su-*aan*-dru
swim v *milomano* mi-*lu*-maan

T

tampons *servieta hyjienika* se-ri-*vi*-e-taa hi-dzi-e-*ni*-kaa
teeth *nify* nif
telephone n *telefaonina* te-*le*-fon
television *televiziona* te-le-*vi*-zi-on
temperature (weather) *hafanana* haa-*faa*-naan
tent *lay* lai
that (one) *iny* i-ni
they *zareo* zaa-*re*-u
thirsty *mangetaheta* maan-*ge*-taa-*he*-taa
this (one) *ity* i-ti
throat *tenda* ten-daa
ticket *tapakila* taa-*paa*-kil
time *fotoana* fu-ton
tired *vizana* vi-zaan
tissues *mosoara* mu-*swaa*-raa
today *androany* aan-*dru*-aan
toilet *toerana fivoahana* tu-e-raan fi-*vu*-aa-haan
tonight *rahalina* raa-*haa*-li-naa
toothache *areti-nify* aa-re-ti-nif
toothbrush *borosinify* bu-*ru*-si-nif
toothpaste *dantifirisy* daan-ti-fris

torch (flashlight) *lampy de paosy* laam-pi de pos
tourist office *biraon'ny vahiny* bi-row-ni *vaa*-hin
towel *serivieta* se-ri-*vi*-e-taa
translate *mandika teny* maan-*di*-kaa ten
travel agency *birao mpandrindra dia*
bi-row *paan*-drin-draa di
travellers cheque *seky de voiazy* se-ki de *vo*-yaa-zi
trousers *pataloha* paa-taa-lu
twin beds *fandriana kely* faan-*dri*-naa kel
tyre *kodiarana* ku-di-aa-raan

U

underwear *atin 'akanjo* aa-ti-naa-*kaan*-dzu
urgent *maika* mai-kaa

V

vacant *malalaka* maa-*laa*-laa-kaa
vegetarian a *tsy misy hena* tsi mis *he*-naa
visa *vizà* vi-zaa

W

waiter *mpandroso sakafo* paan-*dru*-su *saa*-kaaf
walk v *mandeha tongotra* maan-de *tun*-gu-traa
wallet *paoketra kely* *po*-ke-traa kel
warm a *mafana* maa-faan
wash (something) *manasa* maa-naas
watch n *famataranandro* faa-maa-taa-*raa*-naan-dru
water *rano* raa-nu
we (including person addressed) *isika* i-sik
we (excluding person addressed) *izahay* i-*zaa*-hai
weekend *faran'ny herinandro* faa-raan-ni he-*ri*-naan-dru
west *andrefana* aan-*dre*-faan
wheelchair *sezan'ny kilemaina* se-zaan-ni ki-*le*-mai-naa
when *oviana* o-*vi*-naa
where *aiza* ai-zaa
who *iza* i-zaa
why *nahoana* naa-hon
window *varavarankely* vaa-raa-*vaa*-raan-kel
wine *divay* di-vai
with *miaraka amin'ny* mi-aa-raa-*kaa*-min-ni
without *tsy misy* tsi mis
woman *vehivavy* ve-*hi*-vaav
write *manoratra* maa-nu-*raa*-traa

Y

you sg *ianao* i-aa-now
you pl *ianareo* i-aa-naa-*re*-u

Portuguese

pronunciation

Vowels		Consonants	
Symbol	**English sound**	**Symbol**	**English sound**
a	run	b	bed
aa	father	d	dog
ai	aisle	f	fun
ay	say	g	go
e	bet	k	kit
ee	see	l	lot
o	pot	ly	million
oh	note	m	man
oo	zoo	n	not
ow	now	ng	ring (indicates the preceding vowel is nasal)
oy	boy		
		ny	canyon
		p	pet
		r	like 'tt' in 'butter' said fast
		rr	run (throaty)
		s	sun
		sh	shot
		t	top
		v	very
		w	win
		y	yes
		z	zero
		zh	pleasure

In this chapter, the Portuguese pronunciation is given in red after each word or phrase.

Each syllable is separated by a dot, and the syllable stressed in each word is italicised.

For example:
Olá. o-laa

language difficulties

Do you speak English?	*Fala inglês?*	*faa·la eeng·glesh*
Do you understand?	*Entende?*	*eng·teng·de*
I (don't) understand.	*(Não) Entendo.*	*(nowng) eng·teng·doo*
Could you please ...?	*Podia ..., por favor?*	*poo·dee·a ... poor fa·vor*
repeat that	*repetir isto*	*rre·pe·teer eesh·too*
speak more slowly	*falar mais devagar*	*fa·laar maish de·va·gaar*
write it down	*escrever isso*	*shkre·ver ee·soo*

time, dates & numbers

What time is it?	*Que horas são?*	*kee o·rash sowng*
It's one o'clock.	*É uma hora.*	*e oo·ma o·ra*
It's (ten) o'clock.	*São (dez) horas.*	*sowng (desh) o·rash*
Quarter past (ten).	*(Dez) e quinze.*	*(desh) e keeng·ze*
Half past (ten).	*(Dez) e meia.*	*(desh) e may·a*
Quarter to (eleven).	*Quinze para as (onze).*	*keeng·ze pa·ra ash (ong·ze)*
At what time ...?	*A que horas ...?*	*a ke o·rash ...*
At ...	*À ...*	*aa ...*
It's (18 October).	*Hoje é dia (dezoito de Outubro).*	*o·zhe e dee·a (de·zoy·too de oh·too·broo)*
Monday	*segunda-feira*	*se·goong·da·fay·ra*
Tuesday	*terça-feira*	*ter·sa·fay·ra*
Wednesday	*quarta-feira*	*kwaar·ta·fay·ra*
Thursday	*quinta-feira*	*keeng·ta·fay·ra*
Friday	*sexta-feira*	*saysh·ta·fay·ra*
Saturday	*sábado*	*saa·ba·doo*
Sunday	*domingo*	*doo·meeng·goo*
yesterday	*ontem*	*ong·teng*
today	*hoje*	*o·zhe*
tomorrow	*amanhã*	*aa·ma·nyang*

numbers

0	*zero*	ze·roo	16	*dezasseis*	de·za·saysh
1	*um*	oong	17	*dezassete*	de·za·se·te
2	*dois*	doysh	18	*dezoito*	de·zoy·too
3	*três*	tresh	19	*dezanove*	de·za·no·ve
4	*quatro*	kwaa·troo	20	*vinte*	veeng·te
5	*cinco*	seeng·koo	21	*vinte e um*	veeng·te e oong
6	*seis*	saysh	22	*vinte e dois*	veeng·te e doysh
7	*sete*	se·te	30	*trinta*	treeng·ta
8	*oito*	oy·too	40	*quarenta*	kwa·reng·ta
9	*nove*	no·ve	50	*cinquenta*	seeng·kweng·ta
10	*dez*	desh	60	*sessenta*	se·seng·ta
11	*onze*	ong·ze	70	*setenta*	se·teng·ta
12	*doze*	do·ze	80	*oitenta*	oy·teng·ta
13	*treze*	tre·ze	90	*noventa*	no·veng·ta
14	*catorze*	ka·tor·ze	100	*cem*	seng
15	*quinze*	keeng·ze	1000	*mil*	meel

border crossing

I'm here ...
Estou ...
shtoh ...

   in transit
em trânsito
eng *trang*·zee·too

   on business
em negócios
eng ne·*go*·syoosh

   on holiday
de férias
de *fe*·ree·ash

I'm here for ...
Vou ficar por ...
voh fee·*kaar* poor ...

   (10) days
(dez) dias
(desh) *dee*·ash

   (three) weeks
(três) semanas
(tresh) se·*ma*·nash

   (two) months
(dois) meses
(doysh) *me*·zesh

I'm going to (Maputo).
Vou para (Maputo).
voh *pa*·ra (ma·*poo*·to)

I'm staying at the (Panorama Hotel).
Estou no (Hotel Panorama).
shtoh noo (o·*tel* pa·no·*ra*·ma)

tickets

One ... ticket (to Sofala), please.	Um bilhete de ... (para Sofala), por favor.	oong bee-*lye*-te de ... (pra so-*faa*-laa) poor fa-*vor*
one-way	ida	ee-da
return	ida e volta	ee-da ee vol-ta

Is there ...?	Tem ...?	teng ...
air conditioning	ar condicionado	aar kong-dee-syoo-*naa*-doo
a toilet	casa de banho	*kaa*-za de ba-nyoo

I'd like a ... seat, please.	Queria um lugar ... por favor.	ke-*ree*-a oong loo-*gaar* ... poor fa-*vor*
nonsmoking	de não fumadores	de nowng foo-ma-*do*-resh
smoking	para fumadores	pra foo-ma-*do*-resh

transport

Is this the ... to (Luanda)?	Este é o ... para (Luanda)?	esh-te e oo ... pra (*lwan*-da)
boat	barco	*baar*-koo
bus	autocarro	ow-to-*kaa*-rroo
train	comboio	kong-*boy*-oo

| How much is it to ...? |
| Quanto custa até ao ...? | kwang-too *koosh*-ta a-*te* ow ... |

| Please take me to (this address). |
| Leve-me para (este endereço), por favor. | *le*-ve-me *pa*-ra (esh-te eng-de-*re*-soo) poor fa-*vor* |

I'd like to hire a ...	Queria alugar ...	ke-*ree*-a a-loo-*gaar* ...
car (with air conditioning)	um carro (com ar condicionado)	oong *kaa*-rroo (kong aar kong-dee-syoo-*naa*-doo)
4WD	4WD	*kwaa*-troo poor *kwaa*-troo

directions

Where's the nearest ...?	Onde é o ... mais perto?	ong·de e oo ... maish per·to
internet café	café da internet	ka·fe da eeng·ter·net
market	mercado	mer·kaa·doo
It's ...	É...	e ...
behind ...	atrás de ...	a·traash de ...
in front of ...	em frente de ...	eng freng·te de ...
near (to ...)	perto (de ...)	per·too (de ...)
next to ...	ao lado de ...	ow laa·doo de ...
on the corner	na esquina	na shkee·na
opposite ...	do lado oposto ...	doo laa·doo oo·posh·too ...
straight ahead	em frente	eng freng·te
there	lá	laa

accommodation

I'd like to book a room, please.
Eu queria fazer uma   e·oo ke·ree·a fa·zer oo·ma
reserva, por favor.   rre·zer·va poor fa·vor

I'd like to stay for (three) nights.
Para (três) noites.   pa·ra (tresh) noy·tesh

Do you have a ... room?	Tem um quarto ...?	teng oong kwaar·too ...
single	de solteiro	de sol·tay·roo
double	de casal	de ka·zaal
twin	duplo	doo·ploo
How much is it per ...?	Quanto custa por ...?	kwang·too koosh·ta poor ...
night	noite	noy·te
person	pessoa	pe·so·a

banking & communications

I'd like to ...	Queria ...	ke-*ree*-a ...
change a travellers cheque	trocar traveller cheque	troo-*kaar* tra-ve-ler shek
change money	trocar dinheiro	troo-*kaar* dee-*nyay*-roo
get internet access	ter acesso à internet	ter a-*se*-soo aa eeng-ter-*net*
withdraw money	levantar dinheiro	le-vang-*taar* dee-*nyay*-roo

shopping

I'm looking for ...
Estou à procura de ... shtoh aa proo-*koo*-ra de ...

How much is it?
Quanto custa? kwang-too *koosh*-ta

Can you write down the price?
Pode escrever o preço? po-de shkre-*ver* oo *pre*-soo

Do you accept ...?	Aceitam ...?	a-*say*-tang ...
credit cards	cartão de crédito	kar-*towng* de *kre*-dee-too
travellers cheques	travellers cheques	tra-ve-ler *she*-kesh

making conversation

Hello.	Olá.	o-*laa*
Good night.	Boa noite.	bo-a *noy*-te
Goodbye.	Adeus.	a-*de*-oosh
Mr	Senhor	se-*nyor*
Mrs	Senhora	se-*nyo*-ra
Ms	Menina	me-*nee*-na
How are you?	Como está?	*ko*-moo shtaa
Fine. And you?	Bem, e você?	beng e vo-*se*
What's your name?	Qual é o seu nome?	kwaal e oo *se*-oo *no*-me
My name's ...	O meu nome é ...	oo *me*-oo *no*-me e ...
I'm pleased to meet you.	Prazer em conhecê-lo/ conhecê-la. m/f	pra-*zer* eng koo-nye-*se*-lo/ koo-nye-*se*-la

This is my ...	Este é o meu ... m	esh-te e oo me-oo ...
	Esta é a minha ... f	esh-ta e a mee-nya ...
boyfriend	namorado	na-moo-raa-doo
daughter	filha	fee-lya
friend	amigo/a m/f	a-mee-goo/ga
girlfriend	namorada	na-moo-raa-da
husband	marido	ma-ree-doo
partner (intimate)	companheiro/a m/f	kong-pa-nyay-roo/a
son	filho	fee-lyoo
wife	esposa	shpo-za
I'm ...	Eu sou ...	e-oo soh ...
married	casado/a m/f	ka-zaa-doo/a
single	solteiro/a m/f	sol-tay-roo/a

Where are you from?	De onde é?	dong-de e
I'm from ...	Eu sou ...	e-oo soh ...
Australia	da Austrália	da owsh-traa-lya
Canada	do Canadá	doo ka-na-daa
New Zealand	da Nova Zelândia	da no-va ze-lang-dya
the UK	do Reino Unido	doo ray-noo oo-nee-doo
the USA	dos Estados Unidos	doosh shtaa-doosh oo-nee-doosh
Here's my ...	Aqui está o meu ...	a-kee shtaa oo me-oo ...
What's your ...?	Qual é o seu ...?	kwaal e oo se-oo ...
address	endereço	eng-de-re-soo
email address	email	ee-mayl
phone number	número de telefone	noo-me-roo de te-le-fo-ne
Can I take a photo (of you)?	Posso(-lhe) tirar uma fotografia?	po-soo(-lye) tee-raar oo-ma foo-too-graa-fee-a

eating out

I'd like …, please.	Queria …, por favor.	ke·ree·a … poor fa·vor
the bill	a conta	a kong·ta
the menu	um menu	oong me·noo
a table for (five)	uma mesa para (cinco)	oo·ma me·za pa·ra (seeng·koo)
that dish	aquele prato	a·ke·le praa·too

Do you have vegetarian food?	Tem comida vegetariana?	teng koo·mee·da ve·zhe·ta·ree·aa·na

Could you prepare a meal without …?	Pode preparar sem …?	po·de pre·pa·raar seng …
eggs	ovos	o·voosh
meat stock	caldo de carne	kaal·doo de kaar·ne

emergencies

Help!	Socorro!	soo·ko·rroo

Call …!	Chame …!	shaa·me …
an ambulance	uma ambulância	oo·ma ang·boo·lang·sya
the police	a polícia	a poo·lee·sya

Could you help me, please?
Pode ajudar, por favor? po·de a·zhoo·daar poor fa·vor

Can I use the telephone?
Posso usar o seu telefone? po·soo oo·zaar oo se·oo te·le·fo·ne

I'm lost.
Estou perdido/a. m/f shtoh per·dee·doo/a

Where are the toilets?
Onde é a casa de banho? ong·de e a kaa·za de ba·nyoo

I've been assaulted.
Eu fui agredido/a. m/f e·oo fwee a·gre·dee·doo/a

I've been raped.
Eu fui violado/a. m/f e·oo fwee vee·oo·laa·doo/a

I've lost my ...	Eu perdi ...	e·oo per·dee ...
My ... was/were stolen.	Roubaram ...	rroh·baa·rang ...
bags	os meus sacos	oosh me·oosh saa·koosh
credit card	o meu cartão de crédito	oo me·oo kar·towng de kre·dee·too
handbag	a minha bolsa	a mee·nya bol·sa
jewellery	as minhas jóias	ash mee·nyash zhoy·ash
money	o meu dinheiro	oo me·oo dee·nyay·roo
passport	o meu passaporte	oo me·oo paa·sa·por·te
travellers cheques	os meus travellers cheques	oosh me·oosh tra·ve·ler she·kesh
wallet	a minha carteira	a mee·nya kar·tay·ra
I want to contact my ...	Eu quero contactar com ...	e·oo ke·roo kong·tak·taar kong ...
embassy	a minha embaixada	a mee·nya eng·bai·shaa·da
consulate	o meu consulado	oo me·oo kong·soo·laa·doo

medical needs

Where's the nearest ...?	Qual é ... mais perto?	kwaal e ... maish per·too
dentist	o dentista	oo deng·teesh·ta
doctor	o médico m	oo me·dee·koo
	a médica f	a me·dee·ka
hospital	o hospital	oo osh·pee·taal
pharmacist	a farmácia	a far·maa·sya

I need a doctor (who speaks English).
Eu preciso de um médico (que fale inglês).
e·oo pre·see·zoo de oong me·dee·koo (que faa·le eeng·glesh)

It hurts here.
Dói-me aqui.
doy·me a·kee

I'm allergic to (penicillin).
Eu sou alérgico/a a (penicilina). m/f
e·oo soh a·ler·zhee·koo/a a (pe·nee·see·lee·na)

english–portuguese dictionary

Portuguese nouns and adjectives in this dictionary have their gender indicated with ⓜ (masculine) and ⓕ (feminine). If it's a plural noun, you'll see pl too. Words are also marked as v (verb), n (noun), a (adjective), pl (plural), sg (singular), inf (informal) and pol (polite) where necessary.

A

accommodation *hospedagem* ⓕ osh-pe-*daa*-zheng
after *depois* de-*poysh*
airport *aeroporto* ⓜ a-e-ro-*por*-too
alcohol *alcoól* ⓜ al-ko-ol
all a *todo/a* ⓜ/ⓕ to-doo/a
allergy *alergia* ⓕ a-ler-*zhee*-a
and e e
ankle *tornozelo* ⓜ toor-noo-*ze*-loo
antibiotics *antibióticos* ⓜ pl ang-tee-bee-*o*-tee-koosh
arm *braço* ⓜ *braa*-soo
aspirin *aspirina* ⓕ ash-pee-*ree*-na
asthma *asma* ⓕ *ash*-ma
ATM *caixa automático* ⓜ *kai*-sha ow-too-*maa*-tee-koo

B

baby *bebé* ⓜ&ⓕ be-*be*
back (body) *costas* ⓕ pl *kosh*-tash
backpack *mochila* ⓕ moo-*shee*-la
bad *mau/má* ⓜ/ⓕ ma-oo/maa
baggage claim *balcão de bagagens* ⓜ
  bal-*kowng* de ba-*gaa*-zhengsh
bank *banco* ⓜ *bang*-koo
bathroom *casa de banho* ⓕ *kaa*-za de ba-*nyoo*
battery *pilha* ⓕ *pee*-lya
beautiful *bonito/a* ⓜ/ⓕ boo-*nee*-too/a
bed *cama* ⓕ *ka*-ma
bee *abelha* ⓕ a-*be*-lya
beer *cerveja* ⓕ ser-*ve*-zha
before *antes* *ang*-tesh
bicycle *bicicleta* ⓕ bee-see-*kle*-ta
big *grande* ⓜ&ⓕ *grang*-de
blanket *cobertor* ⓜ koo-ber-*tor*
blood group *grupo sanguíneo* ⓜ
  groo-poo sang-*gwee*-nee-oo
bottle *garrafa* ⓕ ga-*rraa*-fa
bottle opener *saca-rolhas* ⓜ *saa*-ka-*rro*-lyash
boy *menino* ⓜ me-*nee*-noo
brake (car) *travão* ⓜ tra-*vowng*
breakfast *pequeno almoço* ⓜ pe-*ke*-noo aal-*mo*-soo

C

cancel *cancelar* kang-se-*laar*
can opener *abre latas* ⓜ *aa*-bre *laa*-tash
cash *dinheiro* ⓜ dee-*nyay*-roo
cell phone *telemóvel* ⓜ te-le-*mo*-vel
centre *centro* ⓜ *seng*-troo
cheap *barato/a* ⓜ/ⓕ ba-*raa*-too/a
check (bill) *conta* ⓕ *kong*-ta
chest *peito* ⓜ *pay*-too
child *criança* ⓜ&ⓕ kree-*ang*-sa
cigarette *cigarro* ⓜ see-*gaa*-roo
city *cidade* ⓕ see-*daa*-de
clean a *limpo/a* ⓜ/ⓕ *leeng*-poo/a
closed *fechado/a* ⓜ/ⓕ fe-*shaa*-doo/a
cold a *frio/a* ⓜ/ⓕ *free*-oo/a
collect call *ligação a cobrar* ⓕ
  lee-ga-*sowng* a koo-*braar*
condom *preservativo* ⓜ pre-zer-va-*tee*-voo
constipation *prisão de ventre* ⓕ
  pree-*zowng* de *ven*-tre
contact lenses *lentes de contacto* ⓜ pl
  leng-tesh de kong-*taak*-too
cough *tosse* ⓕ *to*-se
currency exchange *câmbio* ⓜ *kang*-byoo
customs (immigration) *alfândega* ⓕ aal-*fang*-de-ga

D

dairy products *produtos lácteos* ⓜ pl
  pro-*doo*-toosh *laak*-tee-oosh
dangerous *perigoso/a* ⓜ/ⓕ pe-ree-*go*-zoo/a
day *dia* ⓜ *dee*-a
diaper *fralda* ⓕ *fraal*-da
diarrhoea *diarreia* ⓕ dee-a-*rray*-a
dinner *jantar* ⓜ zhang-*taar*
dirty *sujo/a* ⓜ/ⓕ *soo*-zhoo/a
disabled *deficiente* de-fee-see-*eng*-te
double bed *cama de casal* ⓕ *ka*-ma de ka-*zaal*
drink *bebida* ⓕ be-*bee*-da
drivers licence *carta de condução* ⓕ
  kaar-ta de kong-doo-*sowng*
drug (illicit) *droga* ⓕ *dro*-ga

E

ear *orelha* ① o-re-lya
east *leste* lesh-te
economy class *classe económica* ①
  klaa-se ee-koo-no-mee-ka
elevator *elevador* ⑩ ee-le-va-dor
email *email* ⑩ ee-mayl
English (language) *inglês* ⑩ eeng-glesh
exchange rate *taxa de câmbio* ① taa-sha de kang-byoo
exit *saída* ① saa-ee-da
expensive *caro/a* ⑩/① kaa-roo/a

F

fast *rápido/a* ⑩/① rraa-pee-doo/a
fever *febre* ① fe-bre
finger *dedo* ⑩ de-doo
first-aid kit *estojo de primeiros socorros* ⑩
  shto-zhoo de pree-may-roosh so-ko-rroosh
first class *primeira classe* ① pree-may-ra klaa-se
fish *peixe* ⑩ pay-she
food *comida* ① koo-mee-da
foot *pé* ⑩ pe
fork *garfo* ⑩ gaar-foo
free (of charge) *grátis* graa-teesh
funny *engraçado/a* ⑩/① eng-gra-saa-doo/a

G

gift *presente* ⑩ pre-zeng-te
girl *menina* ① me-nee-na
glass (drinking) *copo* ⑩ ko-poo
glasses *óculos* ⑩ pl o-koo-loosh
gluten *glúten* ⑩ gloo-teng
good *bom/boa* ⑩/① bong/bo-a
gram *grama* ① graa-ma
guide n *guia* ⑩ gee-a

H

hand *mão* ① mowng
happy *feliz* ⑩&① fe-leesh
have *ter* ter
he *ele* e-le
head *cabeça* ① ka-be-sa
headache *dor de cabeça* ① dor de ka-be-sa
heart *coração* ⑩ koo-ra-sowng

heart condition *problema de coração* ⑩
  proo-ble-ma de koo-ra-sowng
heat *calor* ⑩ ka-lor
here *aqui* a-kee
high *alto/a* ⑩/① aal-too/aa
highway *autoestrada* ① ow-to-shtraa-da
homosexual n&a *homosexual* ⑩&①
  o-mo-sek-soo-aal
hot *quente* keng-te
hungry *faminto/a* ⑩/① fa-meeng-too/a

I

I *eu* e-oo
identification (card) *bilhete de identidade* ⑩
  bee-lye-te de ee-deng-tee-daa-de
ill *doente* ⑩&① doo-eng-te
important *importante* ⑩&① eeng-por-tang-te
Internet *internet* ① eeng-ter-net
interpreter *intérprete* ⑩&① eeng-ter-pre-te

K

key *chave* ① shaa-ve
kilogram *quilograma* ① kee-loo-graa-ma
kitchen *cozinha* ① koo-zee-nya
knife *faca* ① faa-ka

L

laundry (place) *lavandaria* ① la-vang-da-ree-a
lawyer *advogado/a* ⑩/① a-de-voo-gaa-doo/a
left-luggage office *perdidos e achados* ⑩ pl
  per-dee-doosh ee aa-shaa-doosh
leg *perna* ① per-na
lesbian n&a *lésbica* ① lezh-bee-ka
less *menos* me-noosh
letter (mail) *carta* ① kaar-ta
like v *gostar* goosh-taar
lost-property office *gabinete de perdidos e achados* ⑩
  gaa-bee-ne-te de per-dee-doosh ee a-shaa-doosh
love v *amar* a-maar
lunch *almoço* ⑩ aal-mo-soo

M

man *homem* ⑩ o-meng
matches *fósforos* ⑩ pl fosh-foo-roosh
meat *carne* ① kaar-ne
medicine *medicamentos* ⑩ pl me-dee-ka-meng-toosh

message *mensagem* ① meng-*saa*-zheng
mobile phone *telemóvel* ⓜ te-le-*mo*-vel
month *mês* ⓜ mesh
morning *manhã* ① ma-*nyang*
motorcycle *mota* ① *mo*-ta
mouth *boca* ① *bo*-ka
movie *filme* ⓜ *feel*-me
MSG *MSG* ⓜ e-me-e-se-*zhe*
museum *museu* ⓜ moo-*ze*-oo
music *música* ① *moo*-zee-ka

N

name *nome* ⓜ *no*-me
napkin *guardanapo* ⓜ gwar-da-*naa*-poo
nappy *fralda* ① *fraal*-da
national park *parque nacional* ⓜ
  paar-ke na-syoo-*naal*
nausea *náusea* ① *now*-zee-a
neck *pescoço* ⓜ pesh-*ko*-soo
new *novo/a* ⓜ/① *no*-voo/a
news *notícias* ① pl noo-*tee*-syash
newspaper *jornal* ⓜ zhor-*naal*
night *noite* ① *noy*-te
noisy *barulhento/a* ⓜ/① ba-roo-*lyeng*-too/a
nonsmoking *não-fumador* nowng-foo-ma-*dor*
north *norte* *nor*-te
nose *nariz* ⓜ na-*reesh*
now *agora* a-*go*-ra
number *número* ⓜ *noo*-me-roo
nuts *oleaginosas* ① pl o-lee-a-zhee-*no*-zash

O

oil (engine) *petróleo* ⓜ pe-*tro*-lyoo
OK *bem* beng
old *velho/a* ⓜ/① *ve*-lyoo/a
open a *aberto/a* ⓜ/① a-*ber*-too/a
outside *fora* *fo*-ra

P

package *embrulho* ⓜ eng-*broo*-lyoo
pain *dor* ① dor
paper *papel* ⓜ pa-*pel*
park (car) v *estacionar* shta-syoo-*naar*
passport *passaporte* ⓜ paa-sa-*por*-te
pay *pagar* pa-*gaar*
pen *caneta* ① ka-*ne*-ta
petrol *gasolina* ① ga-zoo-*lee*-na

pharmacy *farmácia* ① far-*maa*-sya
plate *prato* ① *praa*-too
postcard *postal* ⓜ poosh-*taal*
post office *correio* ⓜ koo-*rray*-oo
pregnant *grávida* ① *graa*-vee-da

R

rain *chuva* ① *shoo*-va
razor *gilete* ① zhee-*le*-te
registered mail *correio registado* ⓜ
  koo-*rray*-oo re-zhee-*shtaa*-doo
rent v *alugar* a-loo-*gaar*
repair v *consertar* kong-ser-*taar*
reservation *reserva* ① rre-*zer*-va
restaurant *restaurante* ⓜ rresh-tow-*rang*-te
return v *voltar* vol-*taar*
road *estrada* ① *shtraa*-da
room *quarto* ⓜ *kwaar*-too

S

sad *triste* *treesh*-te
safe a *seguro/a* ⓜ/① se-*goo*-roo/a
sanitary napkin *penso higiénico* ⓜ
  peng-soo ee-zhee-e-nee-koo
seafood *marisco* ⓜ ma-*reesh*-koo
seat *assento* ⓜ a-*seng*-too
send *enviar* eng-vee-*aar*
sex *sexo* ⓜ *sek*-soo
shampoo *champô* ⓜ shang-*poo*
share (a dorm) *partilhar* par-tee-*lyaar*
shaving cream *creme de barbear* ⓜ
  kre-me de bar-bee-*aar*
she *ela* *e*-la
sheet (bed) *lençol* ⓜ leng-*sol*
shirt *camisa* ① ka-*mee*-za
shoes *sapatos* ⓜ pl sa-*paa*-toosh
shop n *loja* ① *lo*-zha
shower n *chuveiro* ⓜ shoo-*vay*-roo
skin *pele* ① *pe*-le
skirt *saia* ① *sai*-a
sleep v *dormir* door-*meer*
small *pequeno/a* ⓜ/① pe-*ke*-noo/a
smoke (cigarettes) v *fumar* foo-*maar*
soap *sabonete* ⓜ sa-boo-*ne*-te
some *uns/umas* ⓜ/① pl oongsh/*oo*-mash
soon *em breve* eng *bre*-ve
sore throat *dores de garganta* ① pl
  do-resh de gar-*gang*-ta

south *sul* sool
souvenir shop *loja de lembranças* ①
 lo-zha de leng-*brang*-sash
speak *falar* fa-*laar*
spoon *colher* ① koo-*lyer*
stamp *selo* ⓜ *se*-loo
stand-by ticket *bilhete sem garantia* ⓜ
 bee-*lye*-te seng ga-rang-*tee*-a
station (train) *estação* ① shta-*sowng*
stomach *estômago* ⓜ *shto*-ma-goo
stop v *parar* pa-*raar*
stop (bus) *paragem* ① pa-*raa*-zheng
street *rua* ① *rroo*-a
student *estudante* ⓜ&① shtoo-*dang*-te
sunscreen *protecção anti-solar* ①
 proo-te-*sowng* ang-tee-soo-*laar*
swim v *nadar* na-*daar*

T

tampons *tampões* ⓜ pl tang-*powngsh*
teeth *dentes* ⓜ pl *deng*-tesh
telephone *telefone* ① te-le-*fo*-ne
television *televisão* ① te-le-vee-*zowng*
temperature (weather) *temperatura* ①
 teng-pe-ra-*too*-ra
tent *tenda* ① *teng*-da
that one *aquele/a* ⓜ/① a-*ke*-le/a
they *eles/elas* ⓜ/① *e*-lesh/e-lash
thirsty *sedento/a* ⓜ/① se-*deng*-too/a
this one *este/a* ⓜ/① *esh*-te/a
throat *garganta* ① gar-*gang*-ta
ticket *bilhete* ⓜ bee-*lye*-te
time *tempo* ⓜ *teng*-poo
tired *cansado/a* ⓜ/① kang-*saa*-doo/a
tissues *lenços de papel* ⓜ pl *leng*-soosh de pa-*pel*
today *hoje* o-zhe
toilet *casa de banho* ① *kaa*-za de ba-*nyoo*
tonight *hoje à noite* o-zhe aa *noy*-te
toothache *dor de dentes* ① dor de *deng*-tesh
toothbrush *escova de dentes* ① *shko*-va de *deng*-tesh
toothpaste *pasta de dentes* ① *paash*-ta de *deng*-tesh
torch (flashlight) *lanterna eléctrica* ①
 lang-*ter*-na ee-*le*-tree-ka
tourist office *escritório de turismo* ⓜ
 shkree-*to*-ryoo de too-*reezh*-moo
towel *toalha* ① *twaa*-lya
translate *traduzir* tra-doo-*zeer*

travel agency *agência de viagens* ①
 a-*zheng*-sya de vee-*aa*-zhengsh
travellers cheque *travellers cheque* ⓜ *tra*-ve-ler shek
trousers *calças* ① pl *kaal*-sash
twin beds *camas gémeas* ① pl *ka*-mash zhe-me-ash
tyre *pneu* ⓜ pe-*ne*-oo

U

underwear *roupa interior* ① rroh-pa eeng-te-ree-*or*
urgent *urgente* ⓜ&① oor-*zheng*-te

V

vacant *vago/a* ⓜ/① *vaa*-goo/a
vegetable *legume* ⓜ le-*goo*-me
vegetarian a *vegetariano/a* ⓜ/① ve-zhe-ta-ree-*a*-noo/a
visa *visto* ① *veesh*-too

W

waiter *criado/a de mesa* ⓜ/① kree-*aa*-doo/a de *me*-za
walk v *caminhar* ka-mee-*nyaar*
wallet *carteira* ① kar-*tay*-ra
warm a *morno/a* ⓜ/① *mor*-noo/a
wash (something) *lavar* la-*vaar*
watch *relógio* ⓜ rre-lo-*zhyoo*
water *água* ① *aa*-gwa
we *nós* nosh
weekend *fim-de-semana* ⓜ feeng-de-se-*ma*-na
west *oeste* o-*esh*-te
wheelchair *cadeira de rodas* ① ka-*day*-ra de *rro*-dash
when *quando* *kwang*-doo
where *onde* *ong*-de
who *quem* keng
why *porquê* poor-*ke*
window *janela* ① zha-*ne*-la
wine *vinho* ⓜ *vee*-nyoo
with *com* kong
without *sem* seng
woman *mulher* ① moo-*lyer*
write *escrever* shkre-*ver*

Y

you inf sg/pl *tu/vocês* too/vo-*sesh*
you pol sg/pl *você/vós* vo-*se*/vosh

Shona

Vowels		Consonants	
Symbol	**English sound**	**Symbol**	**English sound**
aa	**father**	b	**b**ed
e	b**e**t	b'	strong b with air sucked inward
ee	s**ee**	ch	**ch**eat
o	p**o**t	d	**d**og
oo	z**oo**	d'	strong d with air sucked inward
		dz	a**dz**e
		f	**f**un
		g	**g**o
		h	**h**at
		j	**j**ar
		k	**k**it
		m	**m**an
		n	**n**ot
		ng	ri**ng**
		ny	ca**ny**on
		p	**p**et
		r	**r**un (trilled)
		s	**s**un
		sh	**sh**ot
		t	**t**op
		ts	le**ts**
		v	**v**ery
		w	**w**in
		y	**y**es
		z	**z**ero
		zh	plea**s**ure

In this chapter,
the Shona pronunciation
is given in orange after each phrase.

Each syllable is separated
by a dot. For example:

Mazviita.   maa·zvee·ta

Shona's glottalised consonants,
simplified as b' and d'
in our pronunciation guide,
are made by tightening and releasing
the space between the vocal cords
when you pronounce them.
Both sounds are 'implosive' – instead of
breathing out to make the sound, you
breathe in.

introduction

'Saunter', 'stroll', 'amble', 'march': a few of the English variations on 'walk'. Shona (*ChiShona* chee·sho·na) beats English hands down in this department, though – what about 'walk with buttocks shaking' (*mbwembwera* mbwe·mbwe·raa), 'walk squelchingly through mud' (*chakwaira* chaa·kwaa·ee·raa), 'walk with a stick' (*donzva* d'o·nzvaa), 'walk a long way' (*panha* paa·nhaa) or 'walk in a very short dress' (*pushuka* poo·shoo·kaa)? And that's just a sample of the more than 200 words Shona has for this everyday activity. Shona, a member of the Bantu language family, is spoken by about 11 million people, mainly in the southern African countries of Mozambique, Botswana and Zambia, in addition to a large number in the diaspora. The vast majority of speakers, however, are in Zimbabwe: the three official languages are English, Shona and Ndebele, but Shona is spoken by about 70 per cent of the population. The language has a flourishing literary culture, including novels, short stories, plays and journalism, and an enormous output of poetry – in fact, due to the metaphorical nature of the language, it's as though every Shona speaker is a poet.

■ **shona** (native language) ▢ **shona** (generally understood)

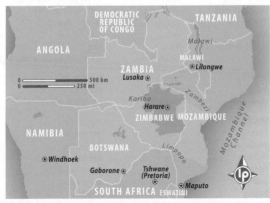

language difficulties

Do you speak English?	*Munotaura chiNgezi here?*	moo·no·taa·oo·raa chee·nge·zee he·re
Do you understand?	*Munonzvisisa here?*	moo·no·nzvee·see·saa he·re
I understand.	*Ndinonzvisisa.*	ndee·no·nzvee·see·saa
I don't understand.	*Handinzvisisi.*	haa·ndee·nzvee·see·see
Could you please ...?	*Munga ... wo here?*	moo·ngaa ... wo he·re
repeat that	*dzokorora izvozvo*	dzo·ko·ro·raa i·zvo·zvo
speak more slowly	*taurisa zvinyoronyoro*	taa·oo·ree·saa zvee·nyo·ro·nyo·ro
write it down	*zvinyorei pasi*	zvee·nyo·re·ee paa·see

time, dates & numbers

In time and date expressions, Shona uses English-style numbers.

What time is it?	*Inguvai?*	ee·ngoo·vaa·ee
It's (two) o'clock.	*I(tu) kiroko.*	ee·(too) kee·ro·ko
Quarter past (one).	*Kota pasiti (hwani).*	ko·taa paa·see·tee (hwaa·nee)
Half past (one).	*Hafu pasiti (hwani).*	haa·foo paa·see·tee (hwaa·nee)
Quarter to (eight).	*Kota tu(eyiti).*	ko·taa too·(e·yee·tee)
At what time ...?	*Nenguvai ...?*	ne·ngoo·vaa·ee ...
At ...	*Na ...*	naa ...
It's (15 December).	*Ndi (15 Dhisemba).*	ndee (fee·fee·tee·nee dee·se·mbaa)
yesterday	*nezuro*	ne·zoo·ro
today	*nhasi*	nhaa·see
tomorrow	*mangwana*	maa·ngwaa·naa
Monday	*Muvhuro*	moo·vhoo·ro
Tuesday	*Chipiri*	chee·pee·ree
Wednesday	*Chitatu*	chee·taa·too
Thursday	*China*	chee·naa
Friday	*Chishanu*	chee·shaa·noo
Saturday	*Mugovera*	mu·go·ve·raa
Sunday	*Svondo*	svo·ndo

numbers

0	*ziro*	zee·ro	20	*makumi*	ma·koo·mee	
1	*-mwe*	-mwe		*maviri*	maa·vee·ree	
2	*-viri*	-vee·ree	21	*makumi*	ma·koo·mee	
3	*-tatu*	-taa·too		*maviri*	maa·vee·ree	
4	*-na*	-naa		*neimwe*	ne·ee·mwe	
5	*-shanu*	-shaa·noo	22	*makumi*	ma·koo·mee	
6	*-tanhatu*	-taa·nhaa·too		*maviri*	maa·vee·ree	
7	*-nomwe*	-no·mwe		*nembiri*	ne·mbee·ree	
8	*-sere*	-se·re	30	*makumi*	maa·koo·mee	
9	*-pfumbamwe*	-pfoo·mbaa·mwe		*matatu*	maa·taa·too	
10	*gumi*	goo·mee	40	*makumi*	maa·koo·mee	
11	*gumi neimwe*	goo·mee ne·ee·mwe		*mana*	maa·naa	
12	*gumi*	goo·mee	50	*makumi*	maa·koo·mee	
	nembiri	ne·mbee·ree		*mashanu*	maa·shaa·noo	
13	*gumi*	goo·mee	60	*makumi*	maa·koo·mee	
	nenhatu	ne·nhaa·too		*matanhatu*	maa·taa·nhaa·too	
14	*gumi nena*	goo·mee ne·naa	70	*makumi*	maa·koo·mee	
15	*gumineshanu*	goo·mee·ne·shaa·noo		*manomwe*	maa·no·mwe	
16	*gumi*	goo·mee	80	*makumi*	maa·koo·mee	
	nenhanhatu	ne·nhaa·nhaa·too		*masere*	maa·se·re	
17	*gumi*	goo·mee	90	*makumi*	maa·koo·mee	
	nenomwe	ne·no·mwe		*mapfu-*	maa·pfoo-	
18	*gumi nesere*	goo·mee ne·se·re		*mbamwe*	mbaa·mwe	
19	*gumi nepfu-*	goo·mee ne·pfoo-	100	*zana*	zaa·naa	
	mbamwe	mbaa·mwe	1000	*chiuru*	chee·oo·roo	

border crossing

I'm here ...	*Ndiri muno ...*	ndee·ree moo·no ...
in transit	*patiranziti*	paa·tee·ra·nzee·tee
on business	*nezve bhizinesi*	ne·zve bee·zee·ne·see
on holiday	*pahorodhi*	paa·ho·ro·dee
I'm here for ...	*Ndiri muno kwe ...*	ndee·ree moo·no kwe ...
(10) days	*mazuva (gumi)*	maa·zoo·vaa (goo·mee)
(three) weeks	*mavhiki (matatu)*	maa·vhee·kee (maa·ta·too)
(two) months	*mwedzi (miviri)*	mwe·dzee (mee·vee·ree)

I'm going to (Gweru).
Ndiri kuenda ku (Gweru).
ndee·ree koo·e·ndaa koo (gwe·roo)

I'm staying at the (Midland Hotel).
Ndiri kugara pa (Midland Hotera).
ndee·ree koo·gaa·raa paa (mee·dlaand ho·te·raa)

tickets

One ... ticket (to Bulawayo), please.	*Ndinodawo tiketi rimwe ... (roku Bhuruwayo).*	ndee·no·daa·wo tee·ke·tee ree·mwe ... (ro·koo boo·roo·waa·yo)
one-way	*rehwaniweyi*	re·hwaa·nee·we·yee
return	*rokuenda ndichidzoka*	ro·koo·e·ndaa ndee·chee·dzo·kaa
I'd like to ... my ticket, please.	*Ndinodawo ku ... tiketi rangu.*	ndee·no·daa·wo koo ... tee·ke·tee raa·ngoo
cancel	*kanzura*	kaa·nzoo·raa
change	*chinja*	chee·njaa
collect	*korekita*	ko·re·kee·ta
Is there a ...?	*Pane ... here?*	paa·ne ... he·re
toilet	*chimbudzi*	che·mboo·dzee
air conditioning	*eya kondishina*	e·yaa ko·ndee·shee·naa

I'd like a smoking/nonsmoking seat, please.
Ndingadawo pasiti panoputirwa/ pasingaputirwi.
ndee·ngaa·daa·wo paa·see·tee paa·no·poo·tee·rwaa/ paa·see·ngaa·poo·tee·rwee

How long does the trip take?
Pane mufambo wakadii?
paa·ne moo·faa·mbo waa·kaa·dee·ee

Is it a direct route?
Iyi ndiyo nzira inonanga ikoko here?
ee·yee ndee·yo nzee·raa ee·no·naa·ngaa ee·ko·ko he·re

transport

Where does the flight (to Victoria Falls) arrive/depart?
Ndege ye (kuVictoria Falls)   nde-ge ye (koo-vee-kee-to-ree-yaa fols)
inosvikira/inosimukira   ee-no-svee-kee-raa/ee-no-see-moo-kee-raa
kupi?   koo-pee

How long will it be delayed?
Ichanonoka zvakadii?   ee-chaa-no-no-kaa zva-kaa-d'ee-ee

Is this the bus to (Chivhu)?
Iri ndiro bhazi roku   ee-ree ndee-ro baa-zee ro-koo
(Chivhu) here?   (chee-vhoo) he-re

Is this the train to (Mutare)?
Ichi ndicho chitima chokwa   ee-che ndee-cho chee-tee-maa cho-kwaa
(Mutare) here?   (moo-taa-re) he-re

How much is it to …?
Kunoita marii kuenda ku …?   koo-no-ee-taa maa-ree-ee koo-e-ndaa koo …

Please take me to (this address).
Nditakureiwo kuenda   ndee-taa-koo-re-ee-wo koo-e-ndaa
ku (adhiresi iyi).   koo (aa-dee-re-see ee-yee)

I'd like to hire a …   *Ndinoda kuhaya …*   ndee-no-d'a koo-haa-yaa …
(with air conditioning).   *(ine eya kondishina).*   (ee-ne e-ya ko-ndee-shee-naa)
   car   *motokari*   mo-to-kaa-ree
   4WD   *ye fohwiri*   ye fo-hwee-ree
     dhiraivhi   dee-raa-ee-vhe

How much is it for (three) days/weeks?
Inoita marii kwemazuva/   ee-no-ee-taa maa-ree-ee kwe-maa-zoo-vaa/
mavhiki (matatu)?   maa-vhee-kee (maa-taa-too)

directions

Where's the (nearest) internet café?
Ko indaneti kafe   ko ee-ndaa-ne-tee kaa-fe
(iri pedyo pedyo) iri kupi?   (ee-ree pe-jgo pe-jgo) ee-ree koo-pee

Where's the (nearest) market?
Ko musika (uri pedyo pedyo)   ko moo-see-kaa (oo-ree pe-jgo pe-jgo)
uri kupi?   oo-ree koo-pee

Is this the road to (Mozambique)?

*Uyu ndiwo mugwagwa woku
(Mozambiki) here?*

oo·yoo ndee·wo moo·gwaa·gwaa wo·koo
(mo·zaa·mbee·kee) he·re

Can you show me (on the map)?

*Munganditaridzawo
(pamepu) here?*

moo·ngaa·ndee·taa·ree·dzaa·wo
(paa·me·poo) he·re

What's the address?	*Kero yacho ndiyani?*	ke·ro yaa·cho ndee·yaa·nee
How far is it?	*Kure zvakadii?*	koo·re zvaa·kaa·d'ee·ee
How do I get there?	*Ndinosvikako sei?*	ndee·no·svee·kaa·ko se·ee
Turn left/right.	*Konera kuruboshwe/ kurudyi.*	ko·ne·raa koo·roo·bo·shwe/ koo·roo·jgee

It's ...	*Iri ...*	ee·ree ...
behind ...	*seri ...*	se·ree ...
in front of ...	*mberi kwe ...*	mbe·ree kwe
near (to ...)	*pedyo (ne ...)*	pe·jgo (ne ...)
next to ...	*padivi pe ...*	pa·d'ee·vee pe ...
on the corner	*pakona*	paa·ko·naa
opposite ...	*pakatarisana ne ...*	paa·kaa·taa·ree·saa·naa ne ...
straight ahead	*nanga mberi*	naa·nga mbe·ree
there	*apo*	aa·po

accommodation

Where's a ...?	*Ndokupi ...?*	ndo·koo·pee ...
camping ground	*kunokembwa*	koo·no·ke·mbwaa
guesthouse	*kuimba yavaenzi*	koo·ee·mbaa yaa·vaa·e·nzee
hotel	*kuhotera*	koo·ho·te·raa
youth hostel	*kuhositeri*	koo·ho·see·te·ree

Can you recommend somewhere cheap/good?

*Ungarekomenda kumwe
kwakachipa/kwakanaka?*

oo·ngaa·re·ko·me·ndaa koo·mwe
kwaa·kaa·chee·paa/kwaa·kaa·naa·kaa

I'd like to book a room, please.

*Ndinokumbirawo
kubhuka rumu.*

ndee·no·koo·mbee·raa·wo
koo·boo·kaa roo·moo

I have a reservation.

Ndakarizevha.

ndaa·kaa·ree·ze·vha

Do you have a ... room?	*Mune rumu* *... here?*	moo·ne roo·moo ... he·re
single	*yomunhu mumwe*	yo·moo·nhoo moo·mwe
double	*yavanhu vaviri*	yaa·vaa·nhoo vaa·vee·ree
twin	*ine mibhedha miviri*	ee·ne mee·be·daa mee·vee·ree

How much is it per (night/person)?
Imarii pa(zuva/munhu)?   ee·maa·ree·ee paa·(zoo·vaa/moo·nhoo)

I'd like to stay for (two) nights.
Ndingada kugara   ndee·ngaa·daa koo·gaa·raa
kweusiku (huviri).   kwe·oo·see·koo (hoo·vee·ree)

What time is check-out?
Cheki auti iriko nenguvai?   che·kee aa·oo·tee ee·ree·ko ne·ngoo·vaa·ee

Am I allowed to camp here?
Ndinobvumirwa kukemba   ndee·no·bvoo·mee·rwaa koo·ke·mbaa
panohere?   paa·no·he·re

banking & communications

I'd like to ...	*Ndinoda ku-...*	ndee·no·daa koo·-...
arrange a transfer	*ronga zvetiranzifeya*	ro·ngaa zve·tee·raa·nzee·fe·yaa
cash a cheque	*kesha cheki*	ke·shaa che·kee
change a travellers cheque	*chinja macheki okufambisa*	chee·njaa maa·che·kee o·koo·faa·mbee·saa
change money	*chinja mari*	chee·njaa maa·ree
withdraw money	*dhirowa mari*	dee·ro·waa maa·ree

I want to ...	*Ndinoda ku-...*	ndee·no·daa koo·-...
buy a phonecard	*tenga kadhi refoni*	te·ngaa kaa·dee re·fo·nee
call (Singapore)	*fonera (kuSingapo)*	fo·ne·raa (koo·see·ngaa·po)
reverse the charges	*rivhesa machaji*	ree·vhe·saa maa·chaa·jee
use a printer	*shandisai purinda*	shaa·ndee·saa·ee poo·ree·ndaa
use the internet	*shandisai indaneti*	shaa·ndee·saa·ee ee·ndaa·ne·tee

How much is it per hour?
Imarii paawa?   ee·maa·ree·ee paa·aa·waa

How much does a (three-minute) call cost?
Kufona kwe (maminitsi matatu)   koo·fo·naa kwe (maa·mee·nee·tsee maa·taa·too)
kunoita marii?   koo·no·ee·taa maa·ree·ee

(One dollar) per minute/hour.
(Dhora rimwe) paminiti/paawa.   (do·raa ree·mwe) paa·mee·nee·tee/paa·aa·waa

tours

When's the next ...?	Ko ... rini?	ko ... ree·nee
day trip	rwendo rwanhasi	rwe·ndo rwaa·nhaa·see
	runotevera ruriko	roo·no·te·ve·raa roo·re·ko
tour	tuwa inotevera	too·waa ee·no·te·ve·raa
	iriko	ee·ree·ko
Is ... included?	Ko ...·kasanganiswa	ko ...·kaa·saa·ngaa·nee·swaa
	here?	he·re
accommodation	pokurara pa	po·koo·raa·raa paa
the admission	mari yokupindisa	maa·ree yo·koo·pee·ndee·saa
charge	ya	yaa
food	mari yokudya ya	maa·ree yo·koo·jgaa yaa·
transport	mari yokufambisa	maa·ree yo·koo·faa·mbee·saa
	ya	yaa

How long is the tour?
Tuwa ichatora nguva yakadii?   too·waa ee·chaa·to·raa ngoo·vaa yaa·kaa·d'ee·ee

What time should we be back?
Tinofanira kudzoka nenguvaii?   tee·no·faa·nee·raa koo·dzo·kaa ne·ngoo·vaa·ee·ee

shopping

I'm looking for ...
Ndiri kutsvaga ...   ndee·ree koo·tsvaa·gaa ...

I need film for this camera.
Ndinoda firimu rekamera iyi.   ndee·no·da fee·ree·moo re·kaa·me·raa ee·yee

Can I listen to this?
Ndingateererawo kune
izvi here?   ndee·ngaa·te·e·re·raa·wo koo·nee
ee·zvee he·re

Can I have my ... repaired?
Ndingagadzirirwa ...
yangu here?   ndee·ngaa·gaa·dzee·ree·rwaa ...
yaa·ngoo he·re

When will it be ready?
Inenge yapera rinhi?   ee·ne·nge yaa·pe·raa ree·nee

How much is it?
Inoita marii?   ee·o·ee·taa maa·ree·ee

Can you write down the price?
Unganyora mutengo
wacho pasi here?   oo·ngaa·nyo·raa moo·te·ngo
waa·cho paa·see he·re

What's your lowest price?
Mutengo wakachipisa ndoupi? moo·te·ngo waa·kaa·chee·pee·saa ndo·oo·pee

I'll give you (five) dollars.
Ndinokupai madhora (mashanu). ndee·no·koo·paa·ee maa·do·raa (maa·shaa·noo)

There's a mistake in the bill.
Pane chakanganiswa pabhiri. pa·ne chaa·kaa·ngaa·nee·swaa paa·bee·ree

It's faulty.
Rakanyangara. raa·kaa·nyaa·ngaa·raa

I'd like a receipt/refund, please.
Ndinodawo risiti/rifandi. ndee·no·daa·wo ree·see·tee/ree·faa·ndee

Do you accept ...?	*Munobvuma ... here?*	moo·no·bvoo·maa ... he·re
credit cards	*makiredhiti kadzi*	maa·kee·re·dee·tee kaa·dzee
debit cards	*madhebhiti kadzi*	ma·de·bee·tee ka·dzee
travellers cheques	*macheki*	maa·che·kee
	okufambisa	oo·koo·faa·mbee·saa

Could you ...?	*Munga ... here?*	moo·nga ... he·re
burn a CD from	*pisa CD kubva*	pee·sa see·dee koo·bvaa
my memory card	*mumemori*	moo·me·mo·ree
	kadhi rangu	kaa·dee raa·ngoo
develop this film	*dhivheropai*	dee·vhe·ro·pa·ee
	firimu iri	fee·ree·moo ee·ree

making conversation

Hello.	*Mhoroi.*	mho·ro·ee
Good night.	*Rarai zvakanaka.*	raa·raa·ee zvaa·kaa·naa·kaa
Goodbye.	*Tichaonana.*	tee·chaa·o·naa·naa
Mr	*Va-*	vaa-
Mrs	*Mai*	maa·ee
Ms/Miss	*Muzvare*	moo·zvaa·re
How are you?	*Makadii?*	maa·kaa·d'ee·ee
Fine, and you?	*Ndiripo makadiiwo?*	ndee·ree·po maa·kaa·d'ee·ee·wo
What's your name?	*Zita renyu ndiani?*	zee·taa re·nyoo ndee·aa·nee
My name's ...	*Zita rangu ndinonzi ...*	zee·taa raa·ngoo ndee·no·nzee ...
I'm pleased to	*Ndinofara*	ndee·no·faa·raa
meet you.	*kukuzivai.*	koo·koo·zee·vaa·ee

This is my ...

boyfriend	*Uyu mukomana wangu.*	oo·yoo moo·ko·maa·naa waa·ngoo
daughter	*Uyu mwanasikana wangu.*	oo·yoo mwaa·naa·see·kaa·naa waa·ngoo
father	*Ava ndi-baba vangu.*	aa·vaa ndee·b'aa·b'aa vaa·ngoo
friend	*Iyi ishamwari yangu.*	ee·yee ee·shaa·mwaa·ree yaa·ngoo
girlfriend	*Uyu musikana wangu.*	oo·yoo moo·see·kaa·naa waa·ngoo
husband	*Uyu murume wangu.*	oo·yoo moo·roo·me waa·ngoo
mother	*Ava ndi-amai vangu.*	aa·vaa ndee·aa·maa·ee vaa·ngoo
sibling (of the opposite sex)	*Iyi ihanzvadzi yangu.*	ee·yee ee·haa·nzvaa·dzee yaa·ngoo
sibling (elder of the same sex)	*Uyu mukoma wangu.*	oo·yoo moo·ko·maa waa·ngoo
sibling (younger of the same sex)	*Uyu munin'ina wangu.*	oo·yoo moo·nee·ngee·naa waa·ngoo
son	*Uyu mwanakomana wangu.*	oo·yoo mwaa·naa·ko·maa·naa waa·ngoo
wife	*Ava vadzimai vangu.*	aa·vaa vaa·dzee·maa·ee vaa·ngoo

Here's my ...	*Heyi ... yangu.*	he·yee ... yaa·ngoo
What's your ...?	*Ko ... yenyu ndiani?*	ko ... ye·nyoo ndee·aa·nee
(email) address	*(imeiri) adhiresi*	(ee·me·ree) a·dee·re·see
phone number	*nhamba yefoni*	nhaa·mbaa ye·fo·nee

Where are you from?	*Munobva kupi?*	moo·no·bvaa koo·pee

I'm from ...	*Ndinobva ku ...*	ndee·no·bvaa koo ...
Australia	*Ositireriya*	o·see·tee·re·ree·yaa
Canada	*Kanadha*	kaa·naa·daa
New Zealand	*Nyuzirandi*	nyoo·zee·raa·ndee

I'm married. m	*Ndakaroora.*	ndaa·kaa·ro·o·raa
I'm married. f	*Ndakaroorwa.*	ndaa·kaa·ro·o·rwaa
I'm not married. m	*Handina kuroora.*	haa·ndee·naa koo·ro·o·raa
I'm not married. f	*Handina kuroorwa.*	haa·ndee·naa koo·ro·o·rwaa
Can I take a photo (of you)?	*Ndingatora pikicha (inewe) here?*	ndee·ngaa·to·raa pee·kee·chaa (ee·ne·we) he·re

eating out

Can you recommend a ...?	Munga-rekomenda ... here?	moo·nga·re·ko·me·ndaa ... he·re
bar	bhawa	baa·waa
dish	chokudya	cho·koo·jgaa
place to eat	nzvimbo yokudyira	nzvee·mbo yo·koo·jgee·raa

I'd like ..., please.	Ndingadawo ...	ndee·ngaa·daa·wo ...
the bill	bhiri	bee·ree
the menu	minyu	mee·nyoo
a table for (two)	tebhuru ye (vaviri)	te·boo·roo ye (vaa·vee·ree)
that dish	chikafu icho	chee·kaa·foo ee·cho

Do you have vegetarian food?	Mune kudya kwechivhegiterieni here?	moo·ne koo·jga kwe·chee·vhe·gee·te·ree·e·nee he·re

Could you prepare a meal without ...?	Mungagadzira kudya kusina ... here?	moo·ngaa·gaa·dzee·raa koo·jga koo·see·naa ... he·re
eggs	mazai	maa·zaa·ee
meat stock	muto wenyama	mo·to we·nyaa·maa

(cup of) coffee/tea ...	(kapu ye-)kofi/tii ...	(kaa·poo ye·)ko·fee/tee·ee ...
with milk	ine mukaka	ee·ne moo·kaa·kaa
without sugar	isina shuga	ee·see·naa shoo·gaa

(boiled) water	mvura (yakavidzwa)	mvoo·raa (yaa·kaa·vee·dzwaa)

emergencies

Call ...!	Daidzai ...!	d'aa·ee·dzaa·ee ...
an ambulance	ambhurenzi	aam·boo·re·nzee
a doctor	dhokotera	do·ko·te·raa
the police	mapurisa	maa·poo·ree·saa

Could you help me, please?
Mungandibatsirawo here?   moo·ngaa·ndee·b'aa·tsee·raa·wo he·re

Where are the toilets?
Zvimbudzi zviri kupi?   zvee·mboo·dzee zvee·ree koo·pee

I want to report an offence.
Ndinoda kumhan'ara mhosva.   ndee·no·daa koo·mha·ngaa·raa mho·svaa

I have insurance.
Ndine ishuwarenzi.　　　　ndee·ne ee·shoo·waa·re·nzee

I want to contact my consulate/embassy.
Ndinoda kutaura neEmbasi　　ndee·no·d'aa koo·taa·oo·raa ne·e·mba·see
yangu.　　　　　　　　　yaa·ngoo

My bags were stolen.
Mabhegi angu abiwa.　　　maa·bhe·gee aa·ngoo aa·b'ee·waa

My passport was stolen.
Pasipoti rangu rabiwa.　　　paa·see·po·tee raa·ngoo raa·b'ee·waa

My wallet was stolen.
Chikwama changu chabiwa.　chee·kwaa·maa chaa·ngoo chaa·b'ee·waa

I've been assaulted. Ndarohwa.　　ndaa·roh·waa
I've been raped. Ndabatwa chibharo.　ndaa·baa·twaa chee·ba·ro
I've been robbed. Ndabirwa.　　ndaa·bee·rwaa

medical needs

Where's the nearest dentist?
Chiremba wemazino ari　　　chee·re·mbaa we·maa·zee·no aa·ree
pedyo pedyo ari kupi?　　　pe·jgo pe·jgo aa·ree koo·pee

Where's the nearest doctor?
Dhokotera ari pedyo　　　　do·ko·te·raa aa·ree pe·jgo
pedyo ari kupi?　　　　　　pe·jgo aa·ree koo·pee

Where's the nearest pharmacist?
Famasi iri pedyo pedyo iri kupi?　faa·maa·see ee·ree pe·jgo pe·jgo ee·ree koo·pee

I need a doctor (who speaks English).
Ndinoda dhokotera　　　　ndee·no·d'aa do·ke·te·raa
(anotaura chiNgezi).　　　　(aa·no·taa·oo·raa chee·nge·zee)

Could I see a female doctor?
Ndingaonawo dhokotera　　ndee·ngaa·o·naa·wo do·ko·te·raa
wechikadzi here?　　　　　we·chee·kaa·dzee he·re

It hurts here.
Panorwadza ndapapa.　　　paa·no·rwaa·dzaa ndaa·paa·paa

I'm allergic to (penicillin).
Muviri wangu unosema　　　moo·vee·ree waa·ngoo oo·no·se·maa
(penesirini).　　　　　　　(pe·ne·see·ree·nee)

english–shona dictionary

In this dictionary, words are marked as n (noun), a (adjective), v (verb), sg (singular), pl (plural), inf (informal) and pol (polite) where necessary.

A

accommodation *pokurara* po-koo-raa-raa
adaptor *adhaputa* aa-daa-poo-taa
after *musure* moo-soo-re
airport *nhandare yendege* nhaa-ndaa-re ye-nde-ge
alcohol *hwahwa* hwaa-hwaa
all -*ose* -o-se
allergy *rusemo* roo-se-mo
and *na-* naa-
ankle *ziso regumbo* zee-so re-goo-mbo
antibiotics *mapiritsi okudzivirira*
  maa-pee-ree-tsee o-koo-dzee-vee-ree-raa
arm *ruoko* roo-o-ko
asthma *asima* a-see-maa
ATM *ATM* ay-tee-em

B

baby *mucheche* moo-che-che
back (body) *musana* moo-saa-naa
backpack *nhava yokumusana*
  nhaa-vaa yo-koo-moo-saa-naa
bad -*ipa* -ee-paa
baggage claim *kunotorwa mabhegi*
  koo-no-to-rwaa maa-be-gee
bank *bhangi* baa-ngee
bathroom *imba yokugezera* ee-mbaa yo-koo-ge-ze-ra
battery *bhatiri* baa-tee-ree
beautiful *kunaka* koo-naa-kaa
bed *mubhedha* moo-be-daa
beer *doro* do-ro
bees *nyuchi* nyoo-chee
before *pasure* paa-soo-re
bicycle *bhasikoro* baa-see-ko-ro
big -*kuru* -koo-roo
blanket *jira* jee-raa
blood group *chikamu cheropa* chee-kaa-moo che-ro-paa
bottle *bhodhoro* bo-do-ro
bottle opener *chivhuro chebhodhoro*
  chee-vhoo-ro che-bo-do-ro
boy *mukomana* moo-ko-maa-naa
brakes (car) *mabhureki* maa-boo-re-kee
breakfast *bhurekifasi* boo-re-kee-faa-see
bronchitis *chirwere chemapapu*
  chee-rwe-re che-maa-paa-pu

C

café *kafe* kaa-fe
cancel *kanzura* kaa-nzoo-raa
can opener *chivhuro chegaba*
  chee-vhoo-ro che-gaa-b'aa
cash n *keshi* ke-shee
cell phone *serifoni* se-ree-fo-nee
centre n *pakati* paa-kaa-tee
cheap *chipa* chee-paa
check (bill) *cheki* che-kee
check-in n *pokuchekaini* po-koo-che-kaa-ee-nee
chest *chipfuva* chee-pfoo-vaa
child *mwana* mwaa-naa
cigarette *mudzanga* moo-dzaa-ngaa
city *guta* goo-taa
clean a *chena* che-naa
closed *vharwa* vhaa-rwaa
cold a -*tonhora* -to-nho-raa
collect call *rivhesi chaji* ree-ve-see chaa-jee
condom *kondomu* ko-ndo-moo
constipation *kupatirwa* koo-paa-tee-rwaa
contact lenses *makondakiti renzi*
  maa-ko-ndaa-kee-tee re-nzee
cough n -*kosora* -ko-so-raa
currency exchange *kuchinjiwa kwemari*
  koo-chee-njee-waa kwe-maa-ree
customs (immigration) *kupinda nokubuda*
  koo-pee-ndaa no-koo-b'oo-d'aa

D

dairy products *zvine mukaka* zvee-ne moo-ka-ka
dangerous -*ne ngozi* -ne ngo-zee
date (time) *musi we (nguva)* moo-see we (ngoo-vaa)
day *zuva* zoo-vaa
diaper *napukeni* naa-poo-ke-nee
diarrhoea *manyoka* maa-nyo-kaa
dinner *zvokudya* zo-koo-jgaa
dirty *tsvina* tsvee-naa
disabled *chikosha* chee-ko-shaa
double bed *mubhedha wevanhu vaviri*
  moo-be-daa we-vaa-nhoo vaa-vee-ree
drink n *chokunwa* cho-koo-nwaa
drivers licence *raisenzi yemotokari*
  raa-ee-se-nzee ye-mo-to-kaa-ree
drug (illicit) *dhiragi* dee-raa-gee

E

ear *nzeve* nze-ve
east *madokero* maa-do-ke-ro
economy class *mbhombhera* mbo-mbe-raa
elevator *rifuti* ree-foo-tee
email n *imeri* ee-me-ree
English (language) *chiNgezi* chee-nge-zee
exchange rate *reti yokochinja mari*
re-tee yo-ko-chee-njaa maa-ree
exit n *pokubuda napo* po-koo-b'oo-d'aa naa-po
expensive *-dhura* -doo-raa
eye *ziso* zee-so

F

fast *-kurumidza* -koo-roo-mee-dzaa
fever *hosha* ho-shaa
finger *munwe* moo-nwe
first-aid kit *bhokisi refesiti eidhi*
bo-kee-see re-fe-see-tee e-ee-dee
first class *kutopa* koo-to-paa
fish n *hove* ho-ve
food *kudya* koo-jgaa
foot *tsoka* tso-kaa
fork *foroko* fo-ro-kaa
free (of charge) *mahara* ma-haa-raa
fruit *muchero* moo-che-ro
funny *-setsa* -se-tsaa

G

game park *gemupaki* maa-ge-moo-paa-kee
gift *chipo* chee-po
girl *musikana* moo-see-kaa-naa
glass (drinking) *girazi* gee-raa-zee
glasses *magirazi* ma-gee-raa-zee
gluten *-rembuka* -re-mboo-kaa
good *-naka* -na-kaa
gram *giramu* gee-raa-moo
guide n *mutungamiriri* moo-too-ngaa-mee-ree-ree

H

hand *ruoko* roo-o-ko
happy *-fara* -faa-raa
have *-ne* -ne
he *a-* aa-
head *musoro* moo-so-ro
headache *kutemwa nemusoro* koo-te-mwaa ne-moo-so-ro
heart *moyo* mo-yo

heart condition *chirwere chemoyo* chee-rwe-re che-mo-yo
heat n *kudziya* koo-dzee-yaa
here *pano* paa-no
high *-refu* -re-foo
highway *mugwagwa* moo-gwaa-gwaa
homosexual n *ngochani* ngo-chaa-nee
homosexual a *hungochani* hoo-ngo-chaa-nee
hot *-pisa* -pee-saa
hungry *-ne nzara* -ne nzaa-raa

I

I *Ini* ee-nee
identification (card) *chitupa* chee-too-paa
ill *-rwara* -rwaa-raa
important *-kosha* -ko-shaa
internet *Indaneti* ee-ndaa-ne-tee
interpreter *muturikiri* moo-too-ree-kee-ree

K

key *kiyi* kee-yee
kilogram *kirogiramu* kee-ro-gee-raa-moo
kitchen *imba yokubikira* ee-mbaa yo-koo-b'ee-kee-raa
knife *banga* b'aa-ngaa

L

laundry (place) *imba yokuwachira*
ee-mbaa yo-koo-waa-chee-raa
lawyer *gweta* gwe-taa
left-luggage office *pahofisi panosiiwa nhumbi*
paa-ho-fee-see pa-no-see-ee-waa nhoo-mbee
leg *gumbo* goo-mbo
lesbian n *ngochani* ngo-chaa-nee
lesbian a *hungochani* hoo-ngo-chaa-nee
less *hafuka* haa-foo-ka
letter (mail) *tsamba* tsaa-mbaa
like v *-da* -d'aa
lost-property office
pahofisi panochengetedzwa zvakarasika
paa-hof-ee-see paa-no-che-nge-te-dzwa
zva-kaa-raa-see-kaa
love v *-da* -daa
lunch *ranji* raa-njee

M

man *murume* moo-roo-me
matches *machisi* maa-chee-see
meat *nyama* nyaa-maa

medicine *mushonga* moo-sho-ngaa
message *shoko* sho-ko
mobile phone *serifoni* se-ree-fo-nee
month *mwedzi* mwe-dzee
morning *mangwanani* ma-ngwaa-naa-nee
motorcycle *mudhudhudhu* moo-doo-doo-doo
mouth *muromo* moo-ro-mo
movie *firimu* fee-ree-moo
MSG *MSG* em-es-jee
museum *muziyamu* moo-zee-ya-moo
music *mumanzi* moo-maa-nzee

N

name n *zita* zee-taa
napkin *napukeni* naa-poo-ke-nee
nappy *mutambo* moo-taa-mbo
national park *neshinari paki* ne-shee-naa-ree paa-kee
nausea *chisvoto* chee-swo-to
neck *huro* hoo-ro
new *-tsva* -tsvaa
news *nhau* nha-oo
newspaper *bepanhau* be-paa-nha-oo
night *usiku* oo-see-koo
nightclub *naiti kirabhu* na-ee-tee kee-raa-bu
noisy *ruzha* roo-zha
nonsmoking *hapaputirwi fodya* haa-paa-poo-tee-rwee fo-jgaa
north *maodzanyemba* ma-o-dzaa-nye-mbaa
nose *mhino* m-hee-no
now *ikozvino* ee-ko-zvee-no
number *nhamba* nhaa-mbaa
nuts *nzungu* nzoo-ngoo

O

oil (engine) *oiri* o-ee-ree
OK *okeyi* o-ke-yee
old *tsaru* tsaa-roo
open a *vhurika* vhoo-ree-kaa
outside *panze* paa-nze

P

package *pakeji* paa-ke-jee
pain *chirwadzo* chee-rwaa-dzo
palace *dzimbabwe* dzee-mbaa-bwe
paper *bepa* b'e-paa
park (car) v *-paka* -paa-kaa
passport *pasipoti* paa-see-po-tee
pay *-bhadhara* -baa-daa-raa
pen *chinyoreso* chee-nyo-re-so

petrol *peturo* pe-tu-ro
pharmacy *famasi* faa-maa-see
plate *ndiro* ndee-ro
postcard *positikadhi* po-see-tee-kaa-dee
post office *hofisi yetsamba* ho-fee-see ye-tsaa-mbaa
pregnant *-ne nhumbu* -ne noo-mboo

R

rain n *mvura* mvoo-ra
registered mail *tsamba yaka rejisitiwa* tsaa-mbaa yaa-kaa re-jee-see-tee-waa
rent v *-renda* -re-ndaa
repair v *-gadzira* -gaa-dzee-raa
reservation *kurizevha* koo-ree-ze-vhaa
restaurant *resitorendi* re-see-to-re-ndee
return v *-dzoka* -dzo-kaa
road *mugwagwa* moo-gwaa-gwaa
room *imba* ee-mbaa

S

sad *-suruvara* -soo-roo-vaa-raa
safe a *banya* baa-nyaa
sanitary napkin *chidhende* chee-de-nde
seafood *chokudya chomumvura* cho-koo-jgaa cho-moo-mvoo-raa
seat *chigaro* chee-gaa-ro
send *-tuma* -too-maa
(have) sex *-svirana* -swee-raa-naa
shampoo *shambu* shaa-mboo
share (a dorm, etc) *kusheya* koo-she-yaa
shaving cream *kirimu yokushevha* kee-ree-moo yo-koo-she-vhaa
she a- aa-
sheet (bed) *shiti (bhedha)* shee-tee (be-daa)
shirt *hembe* he-mbe
shoes *shangu* shaa-ngoo
shop n *chitoro* chee-to-ro
shower n *shawa* shaa-waa
skin *ganda* gaa-ndaa
skirt *siketi* see-ke-tee
sleep v *-rara* -raa-raa
small *-diki* -d'ee-kee
smoke (cigarettes) v *-puta* -poo-taa
soap *sipo* see-po
some *-mwe* -mwe
soon *iko zvino* ee-ko zvee-no
sore throat *-karakata* -kaa-raa-kaa-taa
south *chamhembe* chaa-mhe-mbe
souvenir shop *chitoro chesuvheniya* chee-to-ro che-soo-vhe-nee-yaa

speak *-taura* -taa-oo-raa
spoon *chipunu* chee-poo-noo
stamp n *chitambi* chee-taa-mbee
station (train) *chiteshi chechitima*
  chee-te-shee che-chee-tee-maa
stomach *dumbu* d'oo-mboo
stop v *-mira* -mee-raa
stop (bus) n *chiteshi chebhazi* chee-te-shee che-baa-zee
street *mugwagwa* moo-gwaa-gwaa
student *mudzidzi* moo-dzee-dzee
sunscreen *mafuta okudzivirira zuva*
  maa-foo-taa o-koo-dzee-vee-ree-raa zoo-vaa
swim v *-shambira* -shaa-mbee-raa

T

tampons *matambuni* maa-taa-mboo-nee
teeth *mazino* maa-zee-no
telephone n *foni* fo-nee
television *terevhizhini* te-re-vhee-zhee-nee
temperature (weather) *temburicha* te-mboo-ree-chaa
tent *tende* te-nde
that (one) *icho* ee-cho
they (lit: people) *ivo* ee-vo
thirsty *-ne nyota* -ne nyo-taa
this (one) *ichi* ee-chee
throat *huro* hoo-ro
ticket *tikiti* tee-kee-tee
time *nguva* ngoo-vaa
tired *-neta* -ne-taa
tissues *matishu* maa-tee-shoo
today *nhasi* nhaa-see
toilet *chimbudzi* chee-mboo-dzee
tonight *usiku hwuno* oo-see-koo hwoo-no
toothache *kurwadza kwezino* koo-rwaa-dza kwe-zee-no
toothbrush *bhurashi remazino* boo-raa-shee re-maa-zee-no
toothpaste *mushonga wemazino*
  moo-sho-ngaa we-maa-zee-no
torch (flashlight) *tochi* to-chee
tourist office *hofisi yetuwarizimu*
  ho-fee-see ye-too-waa-ree-zee-moo
towel *tauro* taa-oo-ro
translate *-turikira* -too-ree-kee-raa
travel agency *tiraveri ajendi* tee-raa-ve-ree aa-je-ndee
travellers cheque *macheki okufambisa*
  maa-che-kee o-koo-faa-mbee-saa
trousers *mabhurukwa* maa-boo-roo-kwaa

twin beds *imba ine mibhedha miviri*
  ee-mba ee-ne mee-be-daa mee-vee-ree
tyre *taya* taa-yaa

U

underwear *nduwe* ndoo-we
urgent *kukurumidza* koo-koo-roo-mee-dzaa

V

vacant *pane nzvimbo* paa-ne nvee-mbo
vegetable n *muriwo* moo-ree-wo
vegetarian a *muvhejiteriyeni* moo-vhe-jee-te-ree-ye-nee
visa *vhiza* vhee-zaa

W

waiter *hweta* hwe-taa
walk v *-famba* -faa-mbaa
wallet *chikwama* chee-kwaa-maa
warm a *-dziya* -dzee-yaa
wash (something) *-geza* -ge-zaa
watch n *wachi* waa-chee
water *mvura* mvoo-raa
we *ti-* tee-
weekend *hwikendi* hwee-ke-ndee
west *madokero* maa-d'o-ke-ro
wheelchair *hwiricheya* hwee-ree-che-yaa
when *rini* ree-nee
where (at what place) *papi* paa-pee
where (in what place) *mupi* moo-pee
where (to where) *kupi* koo-pee
who *ani* aa-nee
why *sei* se-ee
window *hwindo* hwee-ndo
wine *waini* waa-ee-nee
with *ne-* ne-
without *-sina* -see-naa
woman *mukadzi* moo-kaa-dzee
write *nyora* nyo-raa

Y

you sg inf/pol *iwe/imi* ee-we/ee-mee
you pl inf&pol *imi* ee-mee

Swahili

pronunciation

Vowels		Consonants	
Symbol	English sound	Symbol	English sound
aa	father	b	bed
ee	see	ch	cheat
ey	as in 'bet', but longer	d	dog
oh	note	dh	that
oo	zoo	f	fun
		g	go
		h	hat
		j	jar
		k	kit
		l	lot
		m	man
		n	not
		ng	ring
		ny	canyon
		p	pet
		r	run (but softer, more like a light 'd')
		s	sun
		sh	shot
		t	top
		th	thin
		v	very
		w	win
		y	yes
		z	zero

In this chapter, the Swahili pronunciation is given in brown after each phrase.

Each syllable is separated by a dot, and the syllable stressed in each word is italicised.

For example:
Habari.   haa·*baa*·ree

KISWAHILI – pronunciation

146

SWAHILI
kiswahili

introduction

Swahili (*kiswahili* kee·swa·*hee*·lee) is one of the most widely spoken African languages, with an estimated 50 million-plus speakers throughout East Africa. Though it's the mother tongue of only about 4 to 5 million people, it's used as a second language or a lingua franca by speakers of many other African languages. Swahili is the national language of Tanzania and Kenya and is widely used in Uganda, Rwanda and Burundi, as well as in the eastern part of the Democratic Republic of Congo and on the Indian Ocean islands of Zanzibar and the Comoros. There are speakers of Swahili in the southern parts of Ethiopia and Somalia, the north of Mozambique and Zambia, and even on the northwestern coast of Madagascar. Swahili belongs to the Bantu group of languages from the Niger-Congo family and can be traced back to the first millenium AD. Standard Swahili developed from the urban dialect of Zanzibar City, dominant from precolonial times. Although there are many dialects of Swahili, you'll be understood if you stick to the standard coastal form, as used in this book.

 **swahili** (native language)   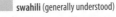 **swahili** (generally understood)

language difficulties

Do you speak (English)?	*Unasema (Kiingereza)?*	oo·naa·*sey*·maa (kee·een·gey·*rey*·zaa)
Do you understand?	*Unaelewa?*	oo·naa·ey·*ley*·waa
I understand.	*Naelewa.*	naa·ey·*ley*·waa
I don't understand.	*Sielewi.*	see·ey·*ley*·wee
Could you please ...?	*Tafadhali ...*	taa·faa·*dhaa*·lee ...
repeat that	*sema tena*	*sey*·maa *tey*·naa
speak more slowly	*sema pole pole*	*sey*·maa *poh*·ley *poh*·ley
write it down	*andika*	aan·*dee*·kaa

time, dates & numbers

What time is it?	*Ni saa ngapi?*	nee saa n·*gaa*·pee
It's one o'clock.	*Ni saa saba.*	nee saa *saa*·baa
It's (two) o'clock.	*Ni saa (nane).*	nee saa (*naa*·ne)
Quarter past (one).	*Ni saa (saba) na robo.*	nee saa (*saa*·baa) naa *roh*·boh
Half past (one).	*Ni saa (saba) na nusu.*	nee saa (*saa*·baa) naa *noo*·soo
Quarter to (ten).	*Ni saa (nne) kasarobo.*	nee saa (*n*·ney) kaa·saa·*roh*·boh
At what time ...?	*... saa ngapi?*	... saa n·*gaa*·pee
At ...	*Saa ...*	saa ...
It's (18 October).	*Ni (tarehe kumi na nane, mwezi wa kumi).* (lit: date eighteen, month tenth)	nee (taa·*rey*·hey *koo*·mee naa *naa*·ney *mwey*·zee waa *koo*·mee)

yesterday	*jana*	*jaa*·naa
today	*leo*	*ley*·oh
tomorrow	*kesho*	*key*·shoh
Monday	*Jumatatu*	joo·maa·*taa*·too
Tuesday	*Jumanne*	joo·maa·*n*·ney
Wednesday	*Jumatano*	joo·maa·*taa*·noh
Thursday	*Alhamisi*	aal·haa·*mee*·see
Friday	*Ijumaa*	ee·joo·*maa*
Saturday	*Jumamosi*	joo·maa·*moh*·see
Sunday	*Jumapili*	joo·maa·*pee*·lee

0	sifuri	see-*foo*-ree	17	kumi na saba	*koo*-mee naa *saa*-baa
1	moja	moh-jaa	18	kumi na nane	*koo*-mee naa *naa*-ney
2	mbili	m-*bee*-lee	19	kumi na tisa	*koo*-mee naa *tee*-saa
3	tatu	*taa*-too	20	ishirini	ee-shee-*ree*-nee
4	nne	n-*ney*	21	ishirini	ee-shee-*ree*-nee
5	tano	*taa*-noh		na moja	naa *moh*-jaa
6	sita	see-taa	22	ishirini	ee-shee-*ree*-nee
7	saba	*saa*-baa		na mbili	naa m-*bee*-lee
8	nane	*naa*-ney	30	thelathini	they-laa-*thee*-nee
9	tisa	*tee*-saa	40	arobaini	aa-roh-baa-*ee*-nee
10	kumi	*koo*-mee	50	hamsini	haam-*see*-nee
11	kumi na moja	*koo*-mee naa *moh*-jaa	60	sitini	see-*tee*-nee
12	kumi na mbili	*koo*-mee naa m-*bee*-lee	70	sabini	saa-*bee*-nee
13	kumi na tatu	*koo*-mee naa *taa*-too	80	themanini	they-maa-*nee*-nee
14	kumi na nne	*koo*-mee naa n-*ney*	90	tisini	tee-*see*-nee
15	kumi na tano	*koo*-mee naa *taa*-noh	100	mia moja	*mee*-aa *moh*-jaa
16	kumi na sita	*koo*-mee naa *see*-taa	1000	elfu	*eyl*-foo

border crossing

I'm ...	Mimi ni ...	*mee*-mee nee ...
in transit	safarini	saa-faa-*ree*-nee
on business	kwa biashara	kwaa bee-aa-*shaa*-raa
on holiday	kwa likizo	kwaa lee-*kee*-zoh

I'm here for ...	Nipo kwa ...	*nee*-poh kwaa ...
(three) days	siku (tatu)	*see*-koo (*taa*-too)
(two) weeks	wiki (mbili)	*wee*-kee (m-*bee*-lee)
(four) months	miezi (minne)	mee-*ey*-zee (mee-*n*-ney)

I'm going to (Malindi).
Naenda (Malindi).   naa-*eyn*-daa (maa-*leen*-dee)

I'm staying at (the Pendo Inn).
Nakaa (Pendo Inn).   naa-*kaa* (*peyn*-doh een)

One ... ticket	*Tiketi moja ya ...*	tee-*key*-tee *moh*-jaa yaa ...
to (Iringa), please.	*kwenda (Iringa).*	*kweyn*-daa (ee-*reen*-gaa)
one-way	*kwenda tu*	*kweyn*-daa too
return	*kwenda na kurudi*	*kweyn*-daa naa koo-*roo*-dee
I'd like to ... my	*Nataka ... tiketi*	naa-*taa*-kaa ... tee-*key*-tee
ticket, please.	*yangu, tafadhali.*	*yaan*-goo taa-faa-*dhaa*-lee
cancel	*kufuta*	koo-*foo*-taa
change	*kubadilisha*	koo-baa-dee-*lee*-shaa
confirm	*kuhakikisha*	koo-haa-kee-*kee*-shaa

I'd like a smoking/nonsmoking seat, please.
Nataka kiti kuvuta/   naa-*taa*-kaa *kee*-tee koo-*voo*-taa/
kutovuta sigara.   koo-toh-*voo*-taa see-*gaa*-raa

Is there a toilet?
Kuna choo?   *koo*-naa choh

Is there a air conditioning?
Kuna a/c?   *koo*-naa ey-*see*

How long does the trip take?
Safari huchukua muda gani?   saa-*faa*-ree hoo-choo-*koo*-aa *moo*-daa *gaa*-nee

Is it a direct route?
Njia ni moja kwa moja?   n-*jee*-aa nee *moh*-jaa kwaa *moh*-jaa

transport

Where does flight (number 432) arrive/depart?
Ndege (namba mia nne   n-*dey*-gey (*naam*-baa *mee*-aa n-ney
thelathini na mbili)   they-laa-*thee*-nee naa m-*bee*-lee)
itafika/itaondoka wapi?   ee-taa-*fee*-kaa/ee-taa-ohn-*doh*-kaa *waa*-pee

How long will it be delayed?
Itachelewa kwa muda gani?   ee-taa-chey-*ley*-waa kwaa *moo*-daa *gaa*-nee

Is this the ...	*Hii ni ... kwenda*	hee nee ... *kweyn*·daa
to (Mombasa)?	*(Mombasa)?*	(mohm·*baa*·saa)
boat	*Boti*	*boh*·tee
bus	*Basi*	*baa*·see
plane	*Ndege*	n·*dey*·gey
train	*Treni*	*trey*·nee

How much is it to ...?
Ni bei gani kwenda ...?   nee bey *gaa*·nee *kweyn*·daa ...

Please take me to (this address).
Tafadhali niendeshe   taa·faa·*dhaa*·lee nee·eyn·*dey*·shey
mpaka (anwani hii).   m·*paa*·kaa (aan·*waa*·nee hee)

I'd like to hire a car/4WD (with air conditioning).
Nataka kukodi gari/   naa·*taa*·kaa koo·*koh*·dee *gaa*·ree/
forbaifor (kwenye a/c).   fohr·baa·ee·fohr (*kwey*·nyey ey·*see*)

How much is it for (three) days/weeks?
Ni bei gani kwa siku/wiki (tatu)?   nee bey *gaa*·nee kwaa *see*·koo/*wee*·kee (*taa*·too)

directions

Where's the	*... hapo karibuni*	*... haa*·poh kaa·ree·*boo*·nee
nearest ...?	*iko wapi?*	*ee*·koh *waa*·pee
internet café	*Intaneti Kafe*	een·taa·*ney*·tee kaa·*fey*
market	*Soko*	*soh*·koh

Is this the road to (Embu)?
Hii ni barabara kwenda (Embu)?   hee nee baa·raa·*baa*·raa *kweyn*·daa (*eym*·boo)

Can you show me (on the map)?
Unaweza kunionyesha   oo·naa·*wey*·zaa koo·nee·oh·*nyey*·shaa
(katika ramani)?   (kaa·*tee*·kaa raa·*maa*·nee)

What's the address?
Anwani ni nini?   aan·*waa*·nee nee *nee*·nee

How far is it?
Ni umbali gani?   nee oom·*baa*·lee *gaa*·nee

How do I get there?
Nifikaje?   nee·fee·*kaa*·jey

Turn left/right.
Geuza kushoto/kulia.   gey·*oo*·zaa koo·*shoh*·toh/koo·*lee*·aa

It's ...	Iko ...	ee·koh ...
behind ...	nyuma ya ...	nyoo·maa yaa ...
in front of ...	mbele ya ...	m·bey·ley yaa ...
near ...	karibu na ...	kaa·ree·boo naa ...
next to ...	jirani ya ...	jee·raa·nee yaa ...
on the corner	pembeni	peym·bey·nee
opposite ...	ng'ambo ya ...	ng·aam·boh yaa ...
straight ahead	moja kwa moja	moh·jaa kwaa moh·jaa
there	hapo	haa·poh

accommodation

Where's a ...?	... iko wapi?	... ee·koh waa·pee
camping ground	Uwanja wa	oo·waan·jaa waa
	kambi	kaam·bee
guesthouse	Gesti	gey·stee
hotel	Hoteli	hoh·tey·lee
youth hostel	Hosteli ya	hoh·stey·lee yaa
	vijana	vee·jaa·naa

Can you recommend somewhere cheap/good?
Unaweza kunipendeke	oo·naa·wey·zaa koo·nee·peyn·dey·key
zea malazi rahisi/nzuri?	zey·aa maa·laa·zee raa·hee·see/n·zoo·ree

I'd like to book a room, please.
Nataka kufanya	naa·taa·kaa koo·faa·nyaa
buking, tafadhali.	boo·keeng taa·faa·dhaa·lee

I have a reservation.
Nina buking.	nee·naa boo·keeng

How much is it per night/person?
Ni bei gani kwa usiku/mtu?	nee bey gaa·ne kwaa oo·see·koo/m·too

Do you have a ... room?	Kuna chumba kwa ...?	koo·naa choom·baa kwaa ...
single	mtu mmoja	m·too m·moh·jaa
double	watu wawili,	waa·too waa·wee·lee
	kitanda kimoja	kee·taan·daa kee·moh·jaa
twin	watu wawili,	waa·too waa·wee·lee
	vitanda viwili	vee·taan·daa vee·wee·lee

I'd like to stay for (two) nights.

Nataka kukaa kwa   naa-*taa*-kaa koo-*kaa* kwaa
usiku (mbili).   oo-*see*-koo (m-*bee*-lee)

What time is check-out?

Muda wa kuachia   moo-daa waa koo-aa-*chee*-aa
chumba ni saa ngapi?   choom-baa nee saa n-*gaa*-pee

Am I allowed to camp here?

Naweza kuwa hapa kwa usiku?   naa-*wey*-zaa koo-waa haa-paa kwaa oo-*see*-koo

banking & communications

I'd like to ...	*Nataka ...*	naa-*taa*-kaa ...
cash a cheque	*kulipwa fedha*	koo-*leep*-waa *fey*-dhaa
	kutokana na hundi	koo-toh-*kaa*-naa naa *hoon*-dee
change a travellers	*kubadilisha*	koo-baa-dee-*lee*-shaa
cheque	*hundi ya msafiri*	*hoon*-dee yaa m-saa-*fee*-ree
change money	*kubadilisha hela*	koo-baa-dee-*lee*-shaa *hey*-laa
transfer money	*kufikisha hela*	koo-fee-*kee*-shaa *hey*-laa
withdraw money	*kuondoa hela*	koo-ohn-*doh*-aa *hey*-laa

I want to ...	*Nataka ...*	naa-*taa*-kaa ...
buy a phonecard	*kununua kadi*	koo-noo-*noo*-aa *kaa*-dee
	ya simu	yaa *see*-moo
call (Singapore)	*kupiga simu kwa*	koo-*pee*-gaa *see*-moo kwaa
	(Singapore)	(seen-gaa-*pohr*)
reverse the charges	*kugeuza gharama*	koo-gey-*oo*-zaa gaa-*raa*-maa
use a printer	*kutumia printa*	koo-too-*mee*-aa *preen*-taa
use the internet	*kutumia intaneti*	koo-too-*mee*-aa een-taa-*ney*-tee

How much is it per hour?

Ni bei gani kwa saa?   nee bey *gaa*-nee kwaa saa

How much does a (three)-minute call cost?

Kupiga simu kwa dakika   koo-*pee*-gaa *see*-moo kwaa daa-*kee*-kaa
(tatu) ni bei gani?   (*taa*-too) nee bey *gaa*-nee

(1000 shillings) per minute/hour.

(Shilingi elfu moja) kwa   (shee-*leen*-gee *eyl*-foo *moh*-jaa) kwaa
dakika/saa.   daa-*kee*-kaa/saa

tours

When's the next ...?	... ijayo	... ee-*jaa*-yoh
	itakuwa lini?	ee-taa-*koo*-waa *lee*-nee
day trip	*Safari ya siku*	saa-*faa*-ree yaa *see*-koo
	moja	*moh*-jaa
tour	*Safari*	saa-*faa*-ree

Is ... included?	*Inazingatia ...?*	ee-naa-zeen-gaa-*tee*-aa ...
accommodation	*malazi*	maa-*laa*-zee
food	*chakula*	chaa-*koo*-laa
the park entrance fee	*ada za hifadhi*	*aa*-daa zaa hee-*faa*-dhee
transport	*usafiri*	oo-saa-*fee*-ree

How long is the tour?
Safari itachukua   saa-*faa*-ree ee-taa-choo-*koo*-aa
muda gani?   *moo*-daa *gaa*-nee

What time should we be back?
Turudi saa ngapi?   too-*roo*-dee saa n-*gaa*-pee

shopping

I'm looking for ...
Natafuta ...   naa-taa-*foo*-taa ...

I need film for this camera.
Nahitaji filamu   naa-hee-*taa*-jee fee-*laa*-moo
kwa kemra hii.   kwaa *keym*-raa hee

Can I listen to this?
Naomba tusikilize.   naa-*ohm*-baa too-see-kee-*lee*-zey

Can I have my ... repaired?
Mnaweza kutengeneza ...   m-naa-*wey*-zaa koo-teyn-gey-*ney*-zaa ...
yangu hapa?   *yaan*-goo haa-paa

When will it be ready?
Itakuwa tayari lini?   ee-taa-*koo*-waa taa-*yaa*-ree *lee*-nee

How much is it?
Ni bei gani?   ni bey *gaa*-nee

Can you write down the price?
Andika bei.   aan·*dee*·kaa bey

What's your lowest price?
Niambie bei ya mwisho.   nee·aam·*bee*·ey bey *yaa*·koh yaa *mwee*·shoh

I'll give you (500 shillings).
Nitakupa (shilingi mia tano).   nee·taa·*koo*·paa (shee·*leen*·gee *mee*·aa *taa*·noh)

There's a mistake in the bill.
Kuna kosa kwenye bili.   *koo*·naa *koh*·saa kweyn·yey *bee*·lee

It's faulty.
Haifanyi kazi.   haa·ee·*faa*·nyee *kaa*·zee

I'd like a receipt, please.
Naomba risiti, tafadhali.   naa·*ohm*·baa ree·*see*·tee taa·faa·*dhaa*·lee

I'd like a refund, please.
Nataka unirudishie   naa·*taa*·kaa oo·nee·roo·dee·*shee*·ey
hela, tafadhali.   *hey*·laa taa·faa·*dhaa*·lee

Do you accept ...?	*Mnakubali ...*	m·naa·koo·*baa*·lee ...
credit cards	*kadi ya benki*	*kaa*·dee yaa *beyn*·kee
travellers cheques	*hundi ya msafiri*	*hoon*·dee yaa m·saa·*fee*·ree

Could you ...?	*Mnaweza ...?*	m·naa·*wey*·zaa ...
burn a CD from	*kurekodi CD*	koo·ree·*koh*·dee see·*dee*
my memory card	*kutoka kadi ya*	koo·*toh*·kaa *kaa*·dee yaa
	kunakili ya	koo·naa·*kee*·lee yaa
	kemra yangu	*keym*·raa *yaan*·goo
develop this film	*kusafisha*	koo·saa·*fee*·shaa
	picha hizi	*pee*·chaa *hee*·zee

making conversation

Hello.	*Habari.*	haa·*baa*·ree
Good night.	*Usiku mwema.*	oo·*see*·koo *mwey*·maa
Goodbye.	*Tutaonana.*	too·taa·oh·*naa*·naa
Mr	*Bwana*	*bwaa*·naa
Mrs	*Bi*	bee
Ms/Miss	*Bibi*	*bee*·bee

How are you?	*Habari?*	haa-*baa*-ree
Fine, and you?	*Nzuri, wewe je?*	n-*zoo*-ree *wey*-wey jey
What's your name?	*Jina lako nani?*	*jee*-naa *laa*-koh *naa*-nee
My name's ...	*Jina langu ni ...*	*jee*-naa *laan*-goo nee ...
I'm pleased to	*Nafurahi*	naa-foo-*raa*-hee
meet you.	*kukufahamu.*	koo-koo-faa-*haa*-moo
This is my ...	*Huyu ni ...*	*hoo*-yoo nee ...
boyfriend	*mpenzi wangu*	m-*peyn*-zee *waan*-goo
brother	*kakangu*	*kaa*-kaan-goo
daughter	*binti yangu*	*been*-tee *yaan*-goo
father	*babangu*	*baa*-baan-goo
friend	*rafiki yangu*	raa-*fee*-kee *yaan*-goo
girlfriend	*mpenzi wangu*	m-*peyn*-zee *waan*-goo
husband	*mume wangu*	*moo*-mey *waan*-goo
mother	*mamangu*	*maa*-maan-goo
sister	*dadangu*	*daa*-daan-goo
son	*mwanangu*	*mwaa*-naan-goo
wife	*mke wangu*	m-*key waan*-goo
Here's my ...	*Hii ni ... yangu.*	hee nee ... *yaan*-goo
address	*anwani*	aan-*waa*-nee
email address	*anwani ya*	aan-*waa*-nee yaa
	barua pepe	baa-*roo*-aa *pey*-pey
phone number	*simu*	*see*-moo
Where are you from?	*Unatoka wapi?*	oo-naa-*toh*-kaa *waa*-pee
I'm from ...	*Natoka ...*	naa-*toh*-kaa ...
Australia	*Australia*	aa-oo-*straa*-lee-aa
Canada	*Kanada*	*kaa*-naa-daa
New Zealand	*Nyuzilandi*	nyoo-zee-*laan*-dee
the UK	*Uingereza*	oo-een-gey-*rey*-zaa
the USA	*Marekani*	maa-rey-*kaa*-nee
I'm married.	*Nimeoa.* m	nee-mey-*oh*-aa
	Nimeolewa. f	nee-mey-oh-*ley*-waa
I'm single.	*Mimi sina mpenzi.*	*mee*-mee *see*-naa m-*peyn*-zee
Can I take a photo	*Ni sawa nikipiga*	nee *saa*-waa nee-kee-*pee*-gaa
(of you)?	*picha (ya wewe)?*	*pee*-chaa (yaa *wey*-wey)

eating out

Can you recommend a ...?	Unaweza kupendekeza ...?	oo·naa·*wey*·zaa koo·peyn·dey·*key*·zaa ...
bar	baa	baa
dish	chakula	chaa·*koo*·laa
place to eat	hoteli kwa chakula	hoh·*tey*·lee kwaa chaa·*koo*·laa

I'd like ..., please.	Naomba ..., tafadhali.	naa·*ohm*·baa ... taa·faa·*dhaa*·lee
the bill	bili	*bee*·lee
the menu	menyu	*mey*·nyoo
a table for (two)	meza kwa (wawili)	*mey*·zaa kwaa (wa·*wee*·lee)
that dish	chakula kile	cha·*koo*·la *kee*·ley

Do you have vegetarian food?	Mna chakula bila nyama?	m·naa chaa·*koo*·laa *bee*·laa *nyaa*·maa

Could you prepare a meal without ...?	Unaweza kuandaa mlo bila ...?	oo·naa·*wey*·zaa koo·aan·*daa* m·loh *bee*·laa ...
eggs	mayai	maa·*yaa*·ee
meat stock	supu ya nyama	*soo*·poo yaa *nyaa*·maa

(cup of) coffee/tea ...	(kikombe cha) kahawa/chai ...	(kee·*kohm*·bey chaa) kaa·*haa*·waa/*chaa*·ee ...
with milk	na maziwa	naa maa·*zee*·waa
without sugar	bila sukari	*bee*·laa soo·*kaa*·ree

(boiled) water	maji (ya kuchemshwa)	*maa*·jee (yaa koo·*cheym*·shwaa)

emergencies

Call an ambulance!	Ita gari la hospitali.	ee·taa *gaa*·ree laa ho·spee·*taa*·lee
Call a doctor!	Mwite daktari.	m·*wee*·tey daak·*taa*·ree
Call the police!	Waite polisi.	waa·*ee*·tey poh·*lee*·see
Help me, please.	Saidia, tafadhali.	saa·ee·*dee*·aa taa·faa·*dhaa*·lee
I'm lost.	Nimejipotea.	nee·mey·jee·poh·*tey*·aa
Where are the toilets?	Vyoo viko wapi?	vyoh *vee*·ko *waa*·pee

I have insurance.
Nina bima.   nee·naa bee·maa

I want to contact my consulate/embassy.
Nataka kuwasiliana   naa·*taa*·kaa koo·waa·see·lee·*aa*·naa
na ubalozi wangu.   naa oo·baa·*loh*·zee waan·goo

I've been assaulted.	*Nilishambuliwa.*	nee·lee·shaam·boo·*lee*·waa
I've been raped.	*Nilibakwa.*	nee·lee·*baa*·kwaa
I've been robbed.	*Niliibiwa.*	nee·lee·ee·*bee*·waa

I've lost my ...	*Nilipoteza ...*	nee·lee·poh·*tey*·zaa ...
bags	*mizigo yangu*	mee·*zee*·goh yaan·goo
credit card	*kadi ya benki*	*kaa*·dee yaa beyn·kee
handbag	*mkoba wangu*	m·*koh*·baa waan·goo
jewellery	*vipuli vyangu*	vee·*poo*·lee vyaan·goo
money	*pesa yangu*	*pey*·saa yaan·goo
passport	*pasipoti yangu*	paa·see·*poh*·tee yaan·goo
travellers	*hundi za msafiri*	*hoon*·dee zaa m·saa·*fee*·ree
cheques	*zangu*	zaan·goo
wallet	*pochi ya pesa*	*poh*·chee ya *pey*·sa

medical needs

Where's the	*... hapo karibuni*	*... haa*·poh kaa·ree·*boo*·nee
nearest ...?	*iko wapi?*	ee·koh *waa*·pee
dentist	*Daktari wa meno*	daak·*taa*·ree waa *mey*·noh
doctor	*Daktari*	daak·*taa*·ree
hospital	*Hospitali*	hoh·spee·*taa*·lee
pharmacist	*Duka la madawa*	*doo*·kaa laa maa·*daa*·waa

I need a doctor (who speaks English).
Nahitaji daktari   naa·hee·*taa*·jee daak·*taa*·ree
(anayesema Kiingereza).   (aa·naa·yey·*sey*·maa kee·een·gey·*rey*·zaa)

Could I see a female doctor?
Inawezekana nione   ee·naa·wey·zey·*kaa*·naa nee·*oh*·ney
daktari mwanamke?   daak·*taa*·ree mwaa·*naam*·key

It hurts here.
Inauma hapa.   ee·naa·*oo*·maa *haa*·paa

I'm allergic to (penicillin).
Nina mzio wa (penisilini).   nee·naa m·*zee*·oh waa (pey·nee·see·*lee*·nee)

english–swahili dictionary

Swahili verbs are shown in their root (basic) forms, with a hyphen in front. To express a series of functions in a sentence, the verb can have several elements added: prefixes, infixes and suffixes. Some adjectives also have a hyphen in front, as they take different prefixes depending on the characteristics of the thing described. Words are also marked as a (adjective), n (noun), v (verb), sg (singular) or pl (plural) as necessary.

A

accommodation *malazi* maa-*laa*-zee
adaptor *adapta* aa-*daap*-taa
after *baada* ya baa-*aa*-daa·ya
airport *uwanja wa ndege* oo-*waan*-jaa waa n-*dey*-gey
alcohol *kilevi* kee-*ley*-vee
all *zote* zoh-tey
allergy *mzio* m-*zee*-oh
and na naa
ankle *kiwiko cha mguu* kee-*wee*-koh chaa m-*goo*
antibiotic *kiuavijasumu* kee-oo-aa-vee-jaa-*soo*-moo
arm *mkono* m-*koh*-noh
aspirin *aspirini* aa-spee-*ree*-nee
asthma *pumu* poo-moo
ATM *mashine ya kutolea pesa*
    maa-*shee*-ney yaa koo-toh-*ley*-aa *pey*-saa

B

baby *mtoto mchanga* m-*toh*-toh m-*chaan*-gaa
back (body) *mgongo* m-*gohn*-goh
backpack *shanta* shaan-taa
bad *mbaya* m-*baa*-yaa
bank *benki* beyn-kee
bathroom *bafuni* baa-*foo*-nee
battery *betri* bey-tree
beautiful *ya kupendeza* yaa koo-peyn-*dey*-zaa
bed *kitanda* kee-*taan*-daa
beer *bia* bee-aa
bee *nyuki* nyoo-kee
before *kabla* kaa-blaa
bicycle *baisikeli* baa-ee-see-*key*-lee
big *kubwa* koob-waa
blanket *blanketi* blaan-key-tee
blood group *aina ya damu* aa-ee-naa yaa *daa*-moo
bottle *chupa* choo-paa
bottle opener *kifungua chupa* kee-foon-*goo*-aa *choo*-paa
boy *mvulana* m-voo-*laa*-naa
brakes (car) *breki* brey-kee
breakfast *chai ya asubuhi* chaa-ee yaa aa-*soo*-boo-hee

C

café *mgahawa* m-gaa-*haa*-waa
cancel -*futa* -*foo*-taa
can opener *opena ya kopo* oh-pey-naa yaa *koh*-poh
cash n *fedha* fey-dhaa
cell phone *simu ya mkononi* see-moo yaa m-koh-*noh*-nee
centre n *katikati* kaa-tee-*kaa*-tee
cheap *rahisi* raa-*hee*-see
check (bill) *bili* bee-lee
check-in n *mapokezi* maa-poh-*key*-zee
chest *kufua* koo-*foo*-aa
child *mtoto* m-*toh*-toh
cigarette *sigara* see-*gaa*-raa
clean a *safi* saa-fee
closed *ya kufungwa* yaa koo-*foon*-gwaa
cold a *baridi* baa-*ree*-dee
condom *kondom* kohn-dohm
constipation *uyabisi wa tumbo*
    oo-yaa-*bee*-see waa *toom*-boh
contact lenses *lenzi mboni* leyn-zee m-*boh*-nee
cough n *kikohozi* kee-koh-*hoh*-zee
currency exchange *kubadilisha hela*
    koo-baa-dee-*lee*-shaa *hey*-laa
customs (immigration) *forodha* foh-*roh*-dhaa

D

dairy products *mazao ya maziwa*
    maa-*zaa*-oh yaa maa-*zee*-waa
dangerous *hatari* haa-*taa*-ree
day *siku* see-koo
diaper *nepi* ney-pee
diarrhoea *kuhara* koo-*haa*-raa
dinner *chakula cha jioni* chaa-koo-laa chaa jee-*oh*-nee
dirty *chafu* chaa-foo
disabled *wasiojiweza* waa-see-oh-jee-*wey*-zaa
drink n *kinywaji* kee-*nywaa*-jee
drug (illicit) *madawa (ya kulevya)*
    maa-*daa*-waa (yaa koo-*ley*-vyaa)

E

ear *sikio* see-kee-oh
east *mashariki* maa-shaa-*ree*-kee
economy class *daraja la tatu* daa-*raa*-jaa laa *taa*-too
elevator *lifti* *leef*-tee
email *barua pepe* baa-*roo*-aa *pey*-pey
English (language) *Kiingereza* kee-een-*gey*-rey-zaa
exit n *kutoka* koo-*toh*-kaa
expensive *ghali* *gaa*-lee
eye *jicho* *jee*-choh

F

fast *ya kasi* yaa *kaa*-see
fever *homa* *hoh*-maa
finger *kidole* kee-*doh*-ley
first class *daraja la kwanza* daa-*raa*-jaa laa *kwaan*-zaa
fish n *samaki* saa-*maa*-kee
food *chakula* chaa-*koo*-laa
foot *mguu* m-*goo*
fork *uma* *oo*-maa
free (of charge) *bure* *boo*-rey
fruit *tunda* *toon*-daa
funny *ya kuchekesha* yaa koo-chey-*key*-shaa

G

game park *hifadhi ya wanyama*
    hee-*faa*-dhee yaa waa-*nyaa*-maa
gift *zawadi* zaa-*waa*-dee
girl *msichana* m-see-*chaa*-naa
glass (drinking) *glesi* *gley*-see
glasses *miwani* mee-*waa*-nee
good *nzuri* n-*zoo*-ree
gram *gramu* *graa*-moo
guide n *kiongozi* kee-ohn-*goh*-zee

H

hand *mkono* m-*koh*-noh
happy *mwenye furaha* mwey-nyey foo-*raa*-haa
have *-wa na* -waa naa
he *yeye* *yey*-yey
head *kichwa* *keech*-waa
headache *maumivu ya kichwa*
    maa-oo-*mee*-voo yaa *keech*-waa
heart *moyo* *moh*-yoh

heart condition *ugonjwa wa moyo*
    oo-*gohn*-jwaa waa *moh*-yoh
heat n *joto* *joh*-toh
here *hapa* *haa*-paa
high *juu* joo
highway *barabara* baa-raa-*baa*-raa
homosexual *msenge* m-*seyn*-gey
hot *joto* *joh*-toh
hungry *njaa* n-*jaa*

I

I *mimi* *mee*-mee
identification (card) *kitambulisho* e-taam-boo-*lee*-shoh
ill *mgonjwa* m-*gohn*-jwaa
important *muhimu* moo-*hee*-moo
internet *intaneti* een-ta-*ney*-tee
interpreter *mkalimani* m-kaa-lee-*maa*-nee

K

key *ufunguo* oo-foon-*goo*-oh
kilogram *kilo* *kee*-loh
kitchen *jiko* *jee*-koh
knife *kisu* *kee*-soo

L

laundry (place) *udobi* oo-*doh*-bee
lawyer *mwanasheria* mwaa-naa-shey-*ree*-aa
leg *mguu* m-*goo*
lesbian *msagaji* m-saa-*gaa*-jee
less *chache* *chaa*-chey
letter (mail) *barua* baa-*roo*-aa
like v *-penda* -*peyn*-daa
love v *-penda* -*peyn*-daa
lunch *chakula cha mchana* chaa-koo-laa chaa m-*chaa*-naa

M

man *mwanamume* mwaa-naa-*moo*-mey
matches *vibiriti* vee-bee-*ree*-tee
meat *nyama* *nyaa*-maa
medicine *dawa* *daa*-waa
message *ujumbe* oo-*joom*-bey
mobile phone *simu ya mkononi*
    see-moo yaa m-koh-*noh*-nee
month *mwezi* *mwey*-zee
morning *asubuhi* aa-soo-*boo*-hee

motorcycle *pikipiki* pee-kee-*pee*-kee
mouth *mdomo* m-*doh*-moh
movie *filamu* fee-*laa*-moo
MSG *msg* eym-eys-gee
museum *makumbusho* maa-koom-*boo*-shoh
music *muziki* moo-zee-kee

N

name n *jina* jee-naa
napkin *kitambaa cha mkono*
  kee-taam-*baa* chaa m-*koh*-noh
nappy *nepi* ney-pee
national park *hifadhi ya wanyama*
  hee-*faa*-dhee yaa waa-*nyaa*-maa
nausea *kichefuchefu* kee-chey-foo-*chey*-foo
neck *shingo* sheen-goh
new *mpya* m-pyaa
news *habari* haa-*baa*-ree
newspaper *gazeti* gaa-zey-tee
night *usiku* oo-*see*-koo
nightclub *klabu ya usiku* klaa-boo yaa oo-*see*-koo
noisy *yenye kelele* yey-nyey key-*ley*-ley
nonsmoking *hakuna sigara* haa-*koo*-naa see-*gaa*-raa
north *kaskazini* kaas-kaa-*zee*-nee
nose *pua* poo-aa
now *sasa* saa-saa
number *namba* naam-baa
nut *kokwa* kohk-waa

O

oil (engine) *mafuta* maa-*foo*-taa
OK *sawa tu* saa-waa too
old *ya zamani* yaa zaa-*maa*-nee
open a *wazi* waa-zee
outside *nje* n-jey

P

package *furushi* foo-*roo*-shee
pain *maumivu* maa-oo-mee-voo
paper *karatasi* kaa-raa-*taa*-see
park (car) v *-egesha* -ey-gey-shaa
passport *pasipoti* paa-see-*poh*-tee
pay *-lipa* -*lee*-paa
pen *kalamu* kaa-*laa*-moo
petrol *mafuta* maa-*foo*-taa
pharmacy *duka la dawa* doo-kaa laa *daa*-waa

plate *sahani* saa-*haa*-nee
postcard *postikadi* poh-stee-*kaa*-dee
post office *posta* poh-staa
pregnant *mjamzito* m-jaa-m-*zee*-toh

R

rain n *mvua* m-*voo*-aa
razor *wembe* weym-bey
registered mail *barua ya rejista*
  baa-*roo*-aa yaa *rey*-jee-staa
rent v *-kodi* -*koh*-dee
repair v *-tengeneza* -teyn-gey-*ney*-zaa
reservation *buking* boo-keeng
restaurant *mgahawa* m-gaa-*haa*-waa
return v *-rudi* -*roo*-dee
road *barabara* baa-raa-*baa*-raa
room *chumba* choom-baa

S

sad *masikitiko* maa-see-kee-*tee*-koh
safe a *salama* saa-*laa*-maa
sanitary napkin *sodo* soh-doh
seafood *vyakula kutoka baharini*
  vyaa-*koo*-laa koo-*toh*-kaa baa-haa-*ree*-nee
seat *kiti* kee-tee
send *-peleka* -*pey*-ley-kaa
sex *mapenzi* maa-*peyn*-zee
shampoo *shampuu* shaam-poo
share (a dorm, etc) *-gawana* -gaa-*waa*-naa
shaving cream *sabuni ya kunyolea*
  saa-*boo*-nee yaa koo-nyoh-*ley*-aa
she *yeye* yey-yey
sheet (bed) *shuka* shoo-kaa
shirt *shati* shaa-tee
shoes *viatu* vee-*aa*-too
shop n *duka* doo-kaa
shower n *bafuni* baa-*foo*-nee
skin *ngozi* n-*goh*-zee
skirt *skati* skaa-tee
sleep v *-sinzia* -seen-zee-aa
small *-dogo* -*doh*-goh
smoke (cigarettes) v *-vuta* -*voo*-taa
soap *sabuni* saa-*boo*-nee
some *kadhaa* kaa-*dhaa*
soon *sasa hivi* saa-saa *hee*-vee
sore throat *koo lenye maumivu*
  koh *ley*-nyey maa-oo-mee-voo

south *kusini* koo-see-nee

souvenir shop *duka la kumbukumbu*
    doo-kaa laa koom-boo-*koom*-boo

speak -*sema* -*sey*-maa

spoon *kijiko* kee-*jee*-koh

stamp v *stempu* steym-poo

station (train) *stesheni* stey-*shey*-nee

stomach *tumbo* toom-boh

stop v -*simama* -see-*maa*-maa

stop (bus) n *kituo* kee-*too*-oh

street *njia* n-jee-aa

student *mwanafunzi* mwaa-naa-*foon*-zee

sunscreen *dawa la kukinga jua*
    daa-waa laa koo-*keen*-gaa joo-aa

swim v -*ogelea* -oh-gey-*ley*-aa

T

tampon *sodo* soh-*doh*

teeth *meno* mey-noh

telephone n *simu* see-*moo*

television *televisheni* tey-ley-vee-*shey*-nee

temperature (weather) *halijoto* haa-lee-*joh*-toh

tent *hema* hey-maa

that (one) *hiyo* hee-yoh

they *wao* waa-oh

(to be) thirsty (-*sikia*) *kiu* (-see-*kee*-aa) kee-oo

this (one) *hii* hee

throat *koo* koh

ticket *tiketi/tikiti* tee-*key*-tee/tee-*kee*-tee

time *saa* saa

tired *ya kuchoka* yaa koo-*choh*-kaa

tissues *karatasi za shashi* kaa-raa-*taa*-see zaa *shaa*-shee

today *leo* ley-oh

toilet *choo* choh

tonight *usiku huu* oo-see-koo hoo

toothache *maumivu ya jino*
    maa-oo-mee-voo yaa jee-noh

toothbrush *mswaki* m-*swaa*-kee

toothpaste *dawa la meno* daa-waa laa *mey*-noh

torch (flashlight) *tochi* toh-chee

tourist office *ofisi ya watalii* o-fee-see yaa waa-taa-*lee*

towel *taulo* taa-oo-loh

translate -*tafsiri* -taaf-*see*-ree

travel agency *uwakala wa safari*
    oo-waa-*kaa*-laa waa saa-*faa*-ree

travellers cheque *hundi ya msafiri*
    hoon-dee yaa m-saa-*fee*-ree

trousers *suruali* soo-roo-*aa*-lee

twin beds *vitanda viwili* vee-*taan*-daa vee-*wee*-lee

tyre *tairi* taa-ee-ree

U

underwear *chupi* choo-pee

urgent *muhimu sana* moo-hee-moo saa-naa

V

vacant *tupu* too-poo

vegetable a *mboga* m-*boh*-gaa

vegetarian a *mlaji wa mboga za majani tu*
    m-*laa*-jee waa m-*boh*-gaa zaa maa-*jaa*-nee too

visa *viza/visa* vee-zaa/vee-saa

W

waiter *mhudumu* m-hoo-*doo*-moo

walk v -*tembea* -teym-bey-aa

warm a *ya joto* yaa joh-toh

wash (something) -*osha* -oh-shaa

watch n *saa* saa

water *maji* maa-jee

we *sisi* see-see

weekend *wikendi* wee-*keyn*-dee

west *magharibi* maa-ghaa-*ree*-bee

wheelchair *kiti cha magurudumu*
    kee-tee chaa maa-goo-roo-*doo*-moo

when *wakati* waa-*kaa*-tee

where *wapi* waa-pee

who *nani* naa-nee

why *kwa nini* kwaa *nee*-nee

window *dirisha* dee-*ree*-shaa

wine *mvinyo* m-vee-nyoh

with *na* naa

without *bila* bee-laa

woman *mwanamke* mwaan-*aam*-key

write -*andika* -aan-*dee*-kaa

Y

you sg *wewe* wey-wey

you pl *nyinyi* nyee-nyee

Wolof

Vowels		Consonants	
Symbol	**English sound**	**Symbol**	**English sound**
a	act	b	bed
aa	father	ch	cheat
ai	aisle	d	dog
aw	law	f	fun
ay	say	g	go
e	bet	h	hat
ee	see	j	jar
ey	as in 'bet', but longer	k	kit
i	hit	kh	as the 'ch' in the Scottish *loch*
o	pot	l	lot
oh	cold	m	man
oo	zoo	n	not
ow	now	ng	ring
u	put	ny	canyon
uh	ago	p	pet

In this chapter, the Wolof pronunciation is given in dark brown after each phrase.

Each syllable is separated by a dot, and the syllable stressed in each word is italicised.

For example:

Mangi.   maan-gee

r	run (trilled)
s	sun
t	top
w	win
y	yes

introduction

Dig this, man: there's an intriguing, though controversial, theory that Wolof-speaking West Africans introduced words like 'hip', 'dig' and 'jive' to American English while they were enslaved in North America in the 17th century. The origin of the name 'Wolof' (*wolof* wo-lof) itself is hotly debated, too, but perhaps the most likely suggestion is that it comes from the name of the area called 'Lof'. The Lebu people, to whom Wolof is commonly linked, were one of a number of different ethnic groups who joined together and founded the Jolof Empire in Lof at the end of the 14th century. Wolof is a member of the West Atlantic group of the Niger-Congo language family, and is the lingua franca of the northwestern African nations of Senegal and The Gambia, where it's spoken by about 80 per cent of their inhabitants (13 million people) as a first or second language. It's also spoken on a smaller scale in the neighbouring countries of Mauritania, Mali and Guinea.

wolof (native language)   **wolof** (generally understood)

language difficulties

Do you speak English?	*Ndax dégg nga angale?*	ndakh deg nguh *an*·ga·ley
Do you understand?	*Dégg nga?*	deg nguh
I understand.	*Dégg naa.*	deg naa
I don't understand.	*Dégguma.*	*deg*·goo·ma

Could you please ...?	*Ndax mën nga ...*	ndakh muhn nga ...
	su la neexee?	soo luh *ney*·khey
repeat that	*ko waxaat*	koh *wa*·khaat
speak more slowly	*wax ndànk*	wakh ndank
write it down	*ko bind*	koh bind

time, dates & numbers

What time is it?	*Ban waxtu moo jot?*	ban *wakh*·too moh jot
It's one o'clock.	*Benn waxtu moo jot.*	ben *wakh*·too moh jot
It's (two) o'clock.	*(Ñaari) waxtu moo jot.*	(nyaa·ree) *wakh*·too moh jot
Quarter past (one).	*(Benn) waxtu teggalna fukki miniit ak juróom.*	(ben) *wakh*·too *teg*·gal·na *fuk*·kee mi·*neet* ak joo·rohm
Half past (one).	*(Benn) waxtu ak xaaj.*	(ben) *wakh*·too ak khaaj
Quarter to (eight).	*(Juróom ñetti) waxtu des na fukki miniit ak juróom.*	(joo·rohm nyet·tee) *wakh*·too des nuh *fuk*·kee mi·*neet* ak joo·rohm
At what time ...?	*Ban waxtu ...?*	ban *wakh*·too ...
It's (15 December).	*Tey la (fukkeeli fan ak juróom ci weeru desaambar).*	tay luh (*fuk*·key·lee fan ak joo·rohm chee *wey*·roo dey·*saam*·bar)

yesterday	*démb*	*dem*·buh
today	*tey*	tay
tomorrow	*suba*	*soo*·ba

Monday	*altine*	*al*·ti·ney
Tuesday	*talaata*	ta·*laa*·ta
Wednesday	*àllarba*	al·*lar*·ba
Thursday	*alxames*	al·*kha*·mes
Friday	*àjjuma*	*aj*·ju·ma
Saturday	*gaawu*	*gaa*·woo
Sunday	*dibéer*	*dee*·beyr

numbers

0	tus	toos	18	fukk ak juróom ñett	fuk ak joo·rohm nyet
1	benn	ben	19	fukk ak juróom ñeent	fuk ak joo·rohm nyeynt
2	ñaar	nyaar	20	ñaar fukk	nyaar fuk
3	ñett	nyet	21	ñaar fukk ak benn	nyaar fuk ak ben
4	ñeent	nyeynt	22	ñaar fukk ak ñaar	nyaar fuk ak nyaar
5	juróom	joo·rohm	30	fan weer	fan weyr
			40	ñeent fukk	nyeynt fuk
6	juróom benn	joo·rohm ben	50	juróom fukk	joo·rohm fuk
7	juróom ñaar	joo·rohm nyaar	60	juróom benn fukk	joo·rohm ben fuk
8	juróom ñett	joo·rohm nyet	70	juróom ñaar fukk	joo·rohm nyaar fuk
9	juróom ñeent	joo·rohm nyeynt	80	juróom ñett fukk	joo·rohm nyet fuk
10	fukk	fuk	90	juróom ñent fukk	joo·rohm nyent fuk
11	fukk ak benn	fuk ak ben	90	fukk	fuk
12	fukk ak ñaar	fuk ak nyaar	100	téeméer	tey·meyr
13	fukk ak ñett	fuk ak nyet	1000	junni	jun·nee
14	fukk ak ñeent	fuk ak nyeynt			
15	fukk ak juróom	fuk ak joo·rohm			
16	fukk ak juróom benn	fuk ak joo·rohm ben			
17	fukk ak juróom ñaar	fuk ak joo·rohm nyaar			

border crossing

I'm here …	Mangi fii …	maan·gee fee …
in transit	ci transit	chee tran·seet
on business	ndax afeer	ndakh a·feyr
on holiday	ci vacances	chee wa·kaans

I'm here for …	Mangi fii ba …	maan·gee fee buh …
(10) days	(fukki) fan	(fuk·kee) fan
(three) weeks	(ñetti) ay bés	(nyet·tee) ai bes
(two) months	(ñaari) weer	(nyaa·ree) weyr

I'm going to (Dakar).
Maangi dem (Ndakaaru). maan·gee dem (nda·kaa·roo)

I'm staying at the (Ganalé Hotel).
Maangi dal ci (oteelu Ganale). maan·gee dal chee (oh·tey·lu ga·na·le)

One ... ticket (to Tambacounda), please.	*Benn ... tike (ba Tambakunda) bu la neexee.*	ben ... ti·ke (ba tam·ba·kun·da) boo la ney·khey
one-way	*benn yoon*	ben yawn
return	*dem ak dikk*	dem ak dik
I'd like to ... my ticket, please.	*Dama bëgga ... sama tike, bu la neexee.*	da·ma buhg·ga ... sa·ma ti·ke boo la ney·khey
cancel	*far*	far
change	*soppi*	sop·pee
collect	*jél*	jel
I'd like a ... seat, please.	*Dama bëgga palaas fuñu ... bu la neexee.*	da·ma buhg·ga pa·laas foo·nyoo ... boo la ney·khey
nonsmoking	*dul tóxe*	dul toh·khe
smoking	*mëna tóx*	muh·na tokh

Is there a toilet/air conditioning?
Ndax am na wanag/kilimaatisër?   ndakh am na wa·nak/ki·li·maa·ti·suhr

How long does the trip take?
Ñaata waxtu la tukki bi di jél?   nyaa·ta wakh·too la tuk·kee bee dee jel

Is it a direct route?
Ndax amul taxaaw?   ndakh a·mul ta·khow

transport

Where does flight (Air France 07) arrive/depart?
Fan la volu (Air France juróom ñaar) di eggsi/deme?   fan la vo·loo (er fa·raans joo·rohm nyaar) dee eg·see/de·mey

How long will it be delayed?
Ñaata waxtu lañu xaar balaa muy dem?   nyaa·ta wakh·tu la·nyoo khaar ba·laa mu·ee dem

Is this the ... to (Foundiougne)?	*Ndax bii ... mooy dem (Funjuñ)?*	ndakh bee ... mohy dem (*fun*-juny)
boat	*gaal*	gaal
bus	*kaar*	kaar
plane	*awiyon*	a·wee·*yong*
train	*saxaar*	sa·khaar

How much is it to ...?
Paasu fii ba ... ñaata la?   paa·soo fee ba ... *nyaa*·ta la

Please take me to (this address).
Yóbbu ma ci (adres bii).   yob·boo ma chee (*ad*·res bee)

I'd like to hire a car/4WD (with air conditioning).
Begg naa luwe oto/kat-kat   buhg naa *lu*·we *o*·to/kat·*kat*
(bu am kilimaatisër).   (boo am ki·li·*maa*·tee·suhr)

How much is it for (three) days/weeks?
Ñaata lay jar suma ko bëggee   *nyaa*·ta lai jar *su*·ma koh *buhg*·gey
luwe (ñetti) fan/ay bés?   *lu*·we (*nyet*·tee) fan/ai bes

directions

Where's the (nearest) ...?	*... (bi gëna jege fii), fan la feete?*	*... (bee guh·na je·gey fee) fan la fey·te*
internet café	*Siberkafe*	*see*·ber·ka·fey
market	*Marse*	*mar*·sey

Is this the road to (Banjul)?
Ndax yoon bii yoonu (Banjul) la?   ndakh yawn bee *yaw*·nu (*ban*·jul) la

Can you show me (on the map)?
Ndax mën nga ma   ndakh muhn nga ma
ko won(ci kart bi)?   koh won (chee kart bee)

What's the address?
Lan mooy adres bi?   lan mohy *ad*·res bee

Is it far?
Ndax sore na?   ndakh *so*·re na

How do I get there?
Naka laa fay yegge?   *na*·ka laa fai *yeg*·ge

Turn left/right.
Jaddal ci sa càmmoñ/ndeyjoor.   *jad*·dal chee sa *cham*·mony/*nday*·johr

It's ...	Mungi ...	mun·gee ...
behind ...	ci ginnaaw ...	chee gin·naaw ...
in front of ...	ci kanamu ...	chee ka·na·moo ...
near (to ...)	jégena ak ...	je·ge·na ak ...
next to ...	ci wetu ...	chee we·tu ...
on the corner	ci angal bi	chee an·gal bee
opposite ...	jàkkaarlook ...	jaak·kaar·lohk ...
straight ahead	ci sa kanam	chee sa ka·nam
there	fële	fuh·le

accommodation

Where's a ...?	Fan la ... nekk?	fan la ... nek
camping ground	kampamaan bi	kam·pa·maan bee
guesthouse	auberge bi	oh·beyrs bee
hotel	oteel	oh·teyl
youth hostel	auberge de jeunesse	oh·beyrs duh juh·nes

Can you recommend somewhere cheap/good?
Ndax mën nga ma digal   ndakh muhn nga ma dig·uhl
fu yomb/baax?   foo yomb/baakh

I'd like to book a room, please.
Bëgg naa jél ab néeg,   buhg naa jel ab neyg
su la neexee.   soo la ney·khey

I have a reservation.
Am naa reserwaasiyon ba pare.   am naa rey·ser·waa·see·yon ba pa·re

Do you have	Am ngeen	am ngeyn
a ... room?	néeg ...?	neyg ...
single	pur kenn	pur ken
double	pur ñaari nit	pur nyaa·ree nit
twin	bu am ñaari lal	bu am nyaa·ree lal

How much is it per night?
Benn bés, ñaata lay jar?   ben bes nyaa·ta lai jar

How much is it per person?
Ku nekk, ñaata lay fey?   ku nek nyaa·ta lai fay

I'd like to stay for (two) nights.
Dinaa fii nekk (ñaari) fan.   dee·naa fee nek (nyaa·ree) fan

What time is check-out?
    Ban waxtu laa wara   ban *wakh*·too laa *wa*·ra
    delloo caabi bi?   *del*·loh *chaa*·bee bee

Am I allowed to camp here?
    Ndax mën naa kampe fii?   ndakh muhn naa *kam*·pey fee

banking & communications

Note that prices in Senegal are calculated in lots of five CFA francs – so *téeméer* *tey*·meyr means '100', but in the context of money it translates as 500 CFA francs.

I'd like to ...	*Bëgg naa ...*	buhg naa ...
arrange a transfer	*jàllale xaalis*	*jaal*·la·le *khaa*·lis
cash a cheque	*aankese sek bi*	*an*·ke·sey sek bee
change a travellers cheque	*aankese* *traveler bi*	*an*·ke·sey *tra*·ve·ler bee
change money	*saanse xaalis*	*saan*·sey *khaa*·lis
withdraw money	*génne xaalis*	*gen*·ney *khaa*·lis

I want to ...	*Bëgg naa ...*	buhg naa ...
buy a phonecard	*jénd kart telefoniik*	jend kart te·le·fo·*neek*
call (the US)	*woote ci (Ameriik)*	*woh*·te chee (a·me·*reek*)
reverse the charges	*moom mu fey*	mohm moo fay
use a printer	*jëfandikoo* *amprimaan bi*	juh·*fan*·di·koh *am*·pree·maan bee
use the internet	*jëfandikoo* *anternet bi*	juh·*fan*·di·koh *an*·ter·net bee

How much is it per hour?
    Benn waxtu, ñaata lay jar?   ben *wakh*·too nyaa·ta lai jar

How much does a (three-minute) call cost?
    Wooteek (ñetti miniit), ñaata lay jar?   woh·teyk (*nyet*·tee mi·*neet*) nyaa·ta lai jar

(1000 CFA francs) per minute/hour.
    Waxtu/Miniit bu nekk,   *wakh*·too/mi·*neet* bu nek
    (ñaari téeméer) la.   (nyaa·ree *tey*·meyr) la

tours

When's the ...?	... kañ la?	kany la ...
next day trip	Beneen	ben·eyn
	exkursiyon bi	ek·skur·si·yon bee
next tour	Beneen wisiit bi	ben·eyn wi·seet bee
Is ... included?	Ndax ... dafa ci bokk?	ndakh ... da·fa chee bok
accommodation	oteel bi	oh·teyl bee
the admission charge	antere	an·te·rey
food	lekk	lek
transport	tukki	tuk·kee

How long is the tour?
Wisiiit bi ñaata waxtu lay jël?   wi·seet bee nyaa·ta wakh·too lai jel

What time should we be back?
Ban waxtu lañu wara ñibbsi?   ban wakh·too la·nyoo wa·ra nyib·see

shopping

I'm looking for ...
... laay wut.   ... lai wut

I need film for this camera.
Pelikiil laa soxla pur aparee bii.   pe·lee·keel laa sokh·la pur a·pa·rey bee

Can I listen to this?
Ndax mën naa dégglu lii?   ndakh muhn naa deg·loo lee

Can I have my ... repaired?
Ndax mën nga ma jagalal sama ...?   ndakh muhn nga ma ja·ga·lal sa·ma ...

When will it be ready?
Kañ lay pare?   kany lai pa·re

How much is it?
Ñaata lay jar?   nyaa·ta lai jar

Can you write down the price?
Ndax mën nga bind piri bi?   ndakh muhn nga bind pee·ree bee

What's your lowest price?
Lan mooy sa derñe piri?   lan mohy sa der·nye pi·ri

I'll give you (500) CFA francs.
(Téeméer) laa mën.   *(tey·meyr) laa muhn*

There's a mistake in the bill.
Dangeen juum ci adisiyon bi.   *dan·geyn joom chi a·di·si·yon bee*

It's faulty.
Baaxul.   *baa·khul*

I'd like a receipt, please.
Bindal ma resi bu la neexee.   *bin·duhl ma re·si boo la ney·khey*

I'd like a refund.
Begg naa nga delloo ma sama xaalis. *buhg naa nga del·loh ma sa·ma khaa·lis*

Do you accept ...?   *Dingeen nangu ...?*   *din·geyn nan·goo ...*
  credit cards   *kart keredi*   *kart ke·re·dee*
  debit cards   *kart bankeer*   *kart ban·keyr*
  travellers cheques   *traveleer*   *tra·ve·leer*

Could you ...?   *Ndax mën ngeen ...?*   *ndakh muhn ngeyn ...*
  burn a CD from   *sottil ma foto*   *sot·til ma fo·to*
  my memory card   *yi ci CD*   *yee chee se·de*
  develop this film   *sottil foto yi*   *sot·til fo·to yee*

making conversation

Hello.	*Salaam aleekum.*	*sa·laam a·ley·kum*
Good night.	*Fanaanleen jàmm.*	*fa·naan·leyn jam*
Goodbye.	*Mangi dem.*	*maan·gee dem*
Mr	*Góor gi*	*gohr gee*
Mrs	*Soxna si*	*sokh·na see*
Miss (young girl)	*Janq bi*	*jank bee*
How are you?	*Na nga def?*	*na nga def*
Fine, and you?	*Mangi fi rekk, na nga def?*	*maan·gee fee rek na nga def*
What's your name?	*Noo tudd?*	*noh tud*
My name's ...	*... laa tudd.*	*... laa tud*

This is my ...	Kii, sama ... la.	kee sa·ma ... la
boyfriend	far	far
brother (older)	mag	mak
brother (younger)	rakk	rak
daughter	doom bu jigéen	dohm boo ji·geyn
father	baay	ba·ai
friend	xarit	kha·rit
girlfriend	coro	cho·ro
husband	jëkkër	juhk·kuhr
mother	yaay	yaai
sister (older)	mag bu jigéen	mak boo ji·geyn
sister (younger)	rakk bu jigéen	rak boo ji·geyn
son	doom bu góor	dohm boo gohr
wife	jabar	ja·bar

Here's my ...	Sama ... angi.	sa·ma ... an·gee
What's your ...?	Lan mooy sa ...?	lan mohy sa ...
address	adres	ad·res
email address	imel	ee·mel
phone number	nimero telefon	ni·me·ro te·le·fon

Where are you from?	Fan nga joge?	fan nga jo·ge

I'm from ...	... laa joge.	... laa jo·ge
Australia	Ostrali	os·tra·lee
New Zealand	Nuwel Selaand	nu·wel se·laand
the UK	Anglateer	an·gla·teyr
the USA	Ameriik	a·me·reek

I'm married. m	Am naa Jëkër.	am naa juh·kuhr
I'm married. f	Am naa jabar.	am naa ja·bar
I'm not married.	Séyaguma.	say·a·gu·ma
Can I take a photo of you?	Ndax mën naa la foto?	ndakh muhn naa la fo·to
Can I take a photo of this?	Ndax mën naa foto lii?	ndakh muhn naa fo·to lee

eating out

Can you recommend a ...?	Mën nga ma digal ...	muhn nga ma dig·uhl ...
bar	baar	baar
dish	benn palaat	ben pa·laat
place to eat	benn restoraan	ben res·to·raan

I'd like ..., please.	Dama bëgg ...	da·ma buhg ...
the bill	adisiyon	a·di·si·yon
the menu	kart bi	kart bee
a table for (two)	taabalu (ñaari) nit	taa·ba·lu (nyaa·ree) nit
that dish	palaat bale	pa·laat ba·le

Do you have	Ndax am ngeen palaat	ndakh am ngeyn pa·laat
vegetarian food?	yu wejetariyan?	yoo we·je·ta·ri·yan

Could you prepare	Ndax men nga togg	ndakh muhn nga tog
a meal without ...?	ñam bu andul ak ...	nyam boo an·dul ak ...
eggs	nen	nen
meat stock	soos yàpp	sohs yaap

(cup of) coffee ...	(kaasu) kafe ...	(kaa·su) ka·fe ...
(cup of) Senegalese tea ...	(kaasu) àttaaya ...	(kaa·su) at·tai·ya ...
(cup of) regular tea ...	(kaasu) lipton ...	(kaa·su) lip·ton ...
with milk	ak meew	ak meyw
without sugar	bu amul suukar	boo a·mul soo·kuhr

(boiled) water	ndox mu	ndokh moo
	(ñu baxal ba pare)	(nyoo ba·khal ba pa·re)

emergencies

Help!	Wóoy!	wohy

Call ...!	Wooyal ma ...!	woh·yal ma ...
an ambulance	ambilaans bi	am·bi·laans bee
a doctor	doktoor	dok·tohr
the police	alkaati	al·kaa·tee

Could you help me, please?
Mën nga ma dimmali,   muhn nga ma dim·ma·lee
bu la neexee?   boo la ney·khey

I'm lost.
Dama réer.   da·ma reyr

Where are the toilets?
Ana wanag wi?   a·na wa·nak wee

I have insurance.
Am naa asiraans.   am naa a·si·raans

I've ...	Dañu ...	da·nyoo ...
been assaulted	dal sama kow	dal sa·ma koh
had my pockets picked	ma tafu	ma ta·foo
been raped	ma yakkataan	ma yak·ka·taan
been robbed	ma sàcc	ma sach

I've lost my ...	Sama ... daf ma réer.	sa·ma ... daf ma reyr
My ... was/were stolen.	Dañu sàcc sama ...	da·nyoo sach sa·ma ...
bags	sak yi	sak yee
credit card	kart keredi	kart ke·re·dee
handbag	sak bi	sak bee
jewellery	takkukaay	tak·koo·kaiy
money	xaalis	khaa·lis
passport	paspoor	pas·pohr
travellers cheques	traveler	tra·ve·leyr
wallet	kalpe	kal·pe

I want to contact my consulate/embassy.
Bëgg naa yéganteek sama
konsulaa/ambasaad.

buhg naa ye·gan·teyk sa·ma
kon·su·laa/am·ba·saad

medical needs

Where's the nearest ...?	... bi gëna jege fii, fan la feete?	... bee guh·na je·ge fee fan la fey·te
dentist	Daantist	daan·teest
doctor	Doktoor	dok·tohr
hospital	Opitaal	o·pi·taal
pharmacist	Farmasyeng	far·mas·yeng

I need a doctor (who speaks English).
Dama soxla doktoor
(bu dégg angale).

da·ma sokh·la dok·tohr
(boo deg an·ga·le)

Could I see a female doctor?
Ndax mën naa gis doktoor
bu jigéen?

ndakh muhn naa gis dok·tohr
boo ji·geyn

It hurts here.
Fii lay metti.

fee ley met·tee

I'm allergic to (penicillin).
Dama am alersi ci (penisilin).

da·ma am a·ler·see chee (pe·ni·si·lin)

english–wolof dictionary

In this dictionary, words are marked as n (noun), a (adjective), v (verb), sg (singular) and pl (plural) where necessary.

A

accommodation *dal* dal
adaptor *adaptër* a-dap-tuhr
airport *ayropoor* ai-roh-pawr
alcohol *sàngara* saan-ga-ra
all *lépp/yépp* sg/pl lip/yip
all (people) *ñépp* nyip
allergy *alersi* a-ler-see
and *ak* ak
ankle *waq* waak
antibiotics *antibiyotik* an-tee-bee-yoh-teek
anti-inflammatories *antianflamatwaar* an-tee-an-fla-mat-waar
arm *loxo* lo-kho
aspirin *aspiriin* as-pee-reen
asthma *asma* as-ma
ATM *masiinu xaalis* ma-see-noo khaa-lis

B

baby *bebe* be-be
back (body) *diggu-gannaaw* dig-goo-gan-now
backpack *sakado* sa-ka-doh
bad *bon* bon
baggage claim *teerukaayu bagaas* tey-roo-kai-yoo ba-gaas
bank *bank* baank
bathroom *wanag* wa-nak
battery *piil* peel
beautiful *rafet* ra-fet
bed *lal* lal
beer *beer* beyr
bees *yamb* yamb
before *balaa* ba-laa
bicycle *velo* ve-loh
big *réy* ray
blanket *mbàjj* mbaaj
blood group *xeetu deret* khey-too de-ret
bottle *butéel* boo-teyl
bottle opener *ubbikaayu butéel* ub-be-kai-yoo boo-teyl
boy *xale bu góor* kha-le boo gohr
brakes (car) *fere* fe-re
breakfast *ndekki* ndek-kee
bronchitis *bronsiit* bron-seet

C

café *kafe* ka-fay
cancel *bayyi* baiy-yee
can opener *ubbikaayu pot* ub-bee-kai-yoo pot
cash n *espes* es-pes
centre n *biir* beer
cell phone *portaabal* por-taa-bal
cheap *yomb* yomb
check (bill) *adisiyon* a-di-see-yon
check-in n *jël caabi* juhl chaa-bee
chest *dënn* duhn
child *xale* kha-le
cigarette *sigaret* see-ga-ret
city *dëkk* duhk
clean a *set* set
closed *téj* tij
codeine *kodeyin* koh-de-yeen
cold a *sedd* sed
collect call *PCV* pe-se-ve
condom *preservatif* prey-seyr-va-teef
constipation *seere* sey-re
contact lenses *lanti* lan-tee
cough n *sëgët* suh-kuht
currency exchange *dëwiis* duh-wees
customs (immigration) *duwaan* doo-waan

D

dairy products *lu jóge ci meew* loo joh-ge chee meyw
dangerous *dansërë* daa-suh-ruh
date (time) *dat* dat
day *bës* buhs
diaper *ngemb* ngemb
diarrhoea *biir buy daw* beer boo-ee dow
dinner *reer* reyr
dirty *tilim* ti-lim
disabled (person) *andikape* an-dee-ka-pey
double bed *lalu ñaari nit* la-loo nyaa-ree nit
drink n *buwaason* boo-waa-son
drivers licence *permi kondiir* per-mee kon-deer
drug (illicit) *dorog* do-rog

E

ear *nopp* nop
east *penku* pen-koo
economy class *kalaas bu yomb ka*-laas boo yomb
elevator *asansëër* a-san-suuhr
email n *imel* ee-mel
English (language) *angale* an-ga-ley
exchange rate *kuru weccee koo*-roo we-chey
exit n *bunt* bunt
expensive *jafe* ja-fe
eye *bët* buht

F

fast *gaaw* gow
fever *yaram wuy tàng ya*-ram *woo*-ee taang
finger *baaraam* baa-raam
first class *përëmiyeer kalas* puh-ruh-mee-yeyr ka-*las*
fish n *jën* juhn
food *lekk* lek
foot *tank* taank
fork *furset* fur-set
free (of charge) *amul fey a*-mul fay
fruit *furwi* fur-wee
funny *reetaanlu* rey-taan-loo

G

game park *reserv* rey-serv
gift *kado* ka-do
girl *xale bu jigéen kha*-le boo ji-geyn
glass (drinking) *kaas* kaas
glasses *linet* li-net
good *baax* baakh
gram *garam* ga-ram
guide n *njiit* njeet

H

hand *loxo* lo-kho
happy *kontaan* kon-taan
have *am* am
he *moom* mohm
head *bopp* bop
headache *bopp buy metti* bop boo-ee met-tee
heart *xol* khol
heart condition *feebaru xol fey*-ba-roo khol
heat n *tàngaay* taan-gaai
here *fii* fee
high *kawe* ka-we
highway *otoruut* o-to-root

Homosexual etc.

homosexual n&a *góor-jigéen* gohr-*ji*-geyn
hot *tàng* taang
hungry *xiif* kheef

I

I *man* maan
identification (card) *dantite* dan-tee-*te*
ill *wopp* wop
important *am solo* am so-lo
Internet *anternet* an-ter-net
interpreter *lapto* lap-to

J

job *ligéey* li-*gay*

K

key *caabi* chaa-bee
kilogram *kilo* kee-lo
kitchen *waañ* waany
knife *paaka* paa-ka

L

laundry (place) *fóotukaay* foh-too-kaai
lawyer *awokaa* a-woh-kaa
left-luggage office *konseeñ* kon-*seeny*
leg *tank* taank
lesbian n&a *lesbiyen* les-bee-*yen*
letter (mail) *bataaxal* ba-taa-khal
like v *bëgg* buhg
love v *nob* nob
lunch *añ* any

M

man *góor* gohr
matches *almet* al-*met*
meat *yàpp* yaap
medicine *garab* ga-rab
message *yóbbante* yohb-ban-te
mobile phone *portaabal* por-taa-bal
month *weer* weyr
morning *suba* soo-ba
motorcycle *moto* mo-to
mouth *gémmiñ* gem-meeny
movie *film* film
museum *mise* mee-se
music *misik* mee-seek

N

name (first) *tur* tur
name (surname) n *sant* sant
napkin *serwiyet* ser-wee-yet
nappy *ngemb* ngemb
national park *park nasyonaal*
park nas-yo-naal
nausea *xel mu teey* khel moo tey
neck *baat* baat
new *bees* beys
news *xabaar* kha-baar
newspaper *surnaal* sur-naal
night *guddi* gud-dee
nightclub *bwat* bwat
noisy *bare coow* ba-re choh
nonsmoking *fu kenn dul tóx*
foo ken dul tohkh
north *bëj-gànnaar*
buhj-*gaan*-naar
nose *bakkan* bak-kan
now *léegi* ley-gee
number *nimero* nee-me-ro
nuts (peanuts) *gerte* ger-te

O

oil (engine) *iwil* ee-weel
OK *baax na* baakh na
old *màgget* maag-get
open a *ubbi* ub-bee
outside *ci biti* chee bee-tee

P

package *paket* pa-ket
pain *mettit* met-teet
palace *pale* pa-le
paper *këyit* kuh-yit
park (car) v *gaare* gaa-re
passport *paaspoor* paas-pawr
pay v *fey* fay
pen *bindukaay* bin-doo-kai
petrol *esaas* e-saas
pharmacy *farmasi* far-ma-see
plate *palaat* pa-laat
postcard *kart postaal*
kart poh-staal
post office *post* post
pregnant *ëmb* uhmb

Q

quiet *teey* teey

R

rain n *taw* tow
razor *raasuwaar* raa-su-waar
registered mail *leetar rekomande* lee-tar re-ko-man-de
rent v *luwe* loo-we
repair v *defar* de-far
reservation *reserwaasiyon* rey-ser-*waa*-see-yon
restaurant *restoraan* res-to-*raan*
return v *dellu* del-loo
road *yoon* yawn
room *néeg* nayg

S

sad *trist* treest
safe a *wóor* woohr
sanitary napkin *fridom* free-dom
seat *toogu* taw-gu
send (someone) *yónni* yon-nee
send (something) *yónnee* yon-ney
(to have) sex *tëdd ak* tuhd ak
shampoo *sampowe* sam-po-we
share (a dorm) *bokk (néeg)* bok (neyyg)
shaving cream *krem pur watu* krem pur *wa*-too
she *moom* mohm
sheet (bed) *darab* da-rap
shirt *simis* si-mis
shoes *dàll* daal
shop n *bitik* bee-teek
shower (place) n *sanguwaay* san-goo-waai
skin *der* der
skirt *siip* seep
sleep v *nelaw* ne-low
small *tuuti* too-tee
smoke (cigarettes) v *tóx* tohkh
soap *saabu* saa-boo
some (a little) *tuuti* too-tee
soon *léegi* ley-gee
sore throat *baat bu metti* baat boo *met*-tee
south *bëj-saalum* buhj-*saa*-loom
souvenir shop *bitiku suweniir* bee-tee-koo soo-we-*neer*
speak *wax* wakh
speak (a language) *dégg* deg
spoon *kuddu* kood-doo
stamp *tambar* tam-bar
station (train) *gaar* gaar
stomach *biir* beer

stop v *taxaw* ta-khow
stop (bus) n *are kaar* a-re kaar
street *mbedd* mbed
student *jàngkat* jaang-kat
sunscreen *krem soleer* krem so-leyr
swim v *féey* faay

T

tampons *tampong* tam-pong
teeth *bëñ* buhny
telephone n *telefon* te-le-fon
television *telewisyon* te-le-wis-yon
temperature (weather) *tamperatir* tam-pe-ra-teer
tent *xayma* khai-ma
that (one) *bee* bey
that (one over there) *bële* buh-le
they *ñoom* nyohm
thirsty *mar* mar
this (one) *bii* bee
throat *put* put
ticket (admission) *tike* ti-ke
ticket (transport) *biye* bee-ye
time (for something) *jot* jot
time (o'clock) *waxtu* wakh-too
tired *sonn* son
tissues *muswaar* mus-waar
today *tey* tay
toilet *wanag* wa-nak
tonight *tey ci guddi* tay chee gud-dee
toothache *bëñ buy metti* buhny boo-ee met-tee
toothbrush *borosada* bo-ro-sa-da
toothpaste *kolgat* kol-gat
torch (flashlight) *lampu tors* lam-poo tors
tourist office *sandika dinisiativ* san-dee-ka dee-nee-see-ya-teev
towel *serwiyet* ser-wee-yet
translate *tekki* tek-kee
travel agency *asansu woyaas* a-saan-su wo-yaas
travellers cheque *traveleer* tra-ve-leyr
trousers *tubéy* too-bay
twin beds *lal* lal
tyre *pënë* puh-nuh

U

underwear (underpants) *silip* si-lip
urgent *jamp* jamp

V

vegetable n *lejum* le-jum
vegetarian a *nit ku dul lekk yàpp* nit koo dul lek yaap
visa *visa* vee-sa

W

waiter *servër* seyr-vuhr
walk v *dox* dokh
wallet *kalpe* kal-pe
warm a *tàng* taang
wash (something) *raxas* ra-khas
watch n *montar* mon-tar
water n *ndox* ndokh
we *ñun* nyun
weekend *wikend* wee-kend
west *sowu soh*-woo
wheelchair *puus-puus* poos-poos
when *kañ* kany
where *fan* fan
who *kan* kan
why *lutax* loo-takh
window *palanteer* pa-lan-teyr
wine *biñ* beeny
with *ak* ak
without *bu amul* boo a-mul
woman *jigéen ji*-geyn
write *bind* bind

Y

you sg *yow* yohw
you pl *yeen* yeyn

Xhosa

pronunciation

Vowels		Consonants	
Symbol	**English sound**	**Symbol**	**English sound**
aa	father	b	as in **rib-punch**
aw	law	b'	strong b with air sucked in
e	bet	ch'	as in '**let-show**', but spat out'
ee	see	d	as in '**hard-times**'
u	put	dl	like a voiced hl
		f	fun
		g	as in '**big-kick**'
		h	hat
		hl	as in the Welsh '**llewellyn**'
		j	jar
		k	kit
		k'	strong k
		l	lot
		m	man
		n	not
		ng	finger
		ny	canyon
		p	pet
		p'	popping p
		r	run (rolled)
		s	sun
		sh	shot
		t	top
		t'	spitting t
		ts'	as in '**lets**', but spat out
		v	very
		w	win
		y	yes
		z	zero

In this chapter,
the Xhosa pronunciation
is given in teal after each phrase.

Each syllable is separated
by a dot, and the syllable stressed
in each word is italicised.

For example:

Enkosi. e-*nk'aw*·see

Xhosa's glottalised consonants,
simplified as b', ch', k', p', t' and ts'
in our pronunciation guide,
are made by tightening and releasing
the space between the vocal cords
when you pronounce the sound,
a bit like combining it with the
sound in the middle of the word 'uh-
oh'. The sound b' has an extra twist –
instead of breathing out to make
the sound, you breathe in.

For information on Xhosa's distinctive
click sounds, see the box on page 184.

The term 'voiced' used in relation to
the dl sound means that it's produced
with the vocal cords vibrating.

introduction

Learn some Xhosa (*Funda isiXhosa* fu·*ndaa* ee·see·*kh¦aw*·saa) words and not only will you be able to communicate with the Xhosa people in their own language, but you'll have something in common with one of Africa's greatest heroes. Nelson Mandela is arguably the world's most famous Xhosa speaker – incidentally, his Xhosa name is the somewhat prophetic *Rolihlahla* raw·lee·*hlaa*·hlaa (troublemaker). Xhosa is the most widely distributed African language in South Africa (although most of its speakers live in the southeastern Cape Province) and one of the country's official languages. About 16 per cent of South Africans, or eight and a half million people, speak Xhosa as a first language. It belongs to the Nguni subfamily of the Bantu languages, along with Zulu, Swati and Ndebele. The Bantu-speaking groups migrated south over the centuries along the coast of East Africa and through Central Africa. In southern Africa, they encountered Khoisan-speaking people and borrowed elements of their language – in particular, the 'click' sounds, a distinctive feature of Xhosa and other South African languages.

■ **xhosa** (native language)   ■ **xhosa** (generally understood)

language difficulties

Do you speak English?	*Uyasithetha isingesi?*	u·yaa·see·*te*·taa ee·see·*nge*·see
Do you understand?	*Uyaqonda?*	u·yaa·*kjaw*·ndaa
I (don't) understand.	*(Andi)qondi.*	(aa·ndee·)*kjaw*·ndee
Could you please ...?	*Unakho ukunceda ...?*	u·naa·*kaw* u·k'u·*n!e*·daa ...
repeat that	*khawuphinde*	kaa·wu·*pee*·nde
speak more	*thetha ngoku*	*te*·taa *ngaw*·k'u
slowly	*cothisisa*	*k!aw*·tee·see·saa
write it down	*yibhale phantsi*	yee·*baa*·le *paa*·nts'ee

click sounds

Xhosa has a series of click sounds: some clicks are against the front teeth (like a 'tsk' sound), some are against the roof of the mouth at the front (like a 'tock' sound) and some are against the side teeth (like the chirrup you make to get a horse to start walking).

front teeth	roof of the mouth	side teeth	description
k!	kᵢ	kᶦ	voiceless
kh!	khᵢ	khᶦ	aspirated (with a puff of air)
g!	gᵢ	gᶦ	voiced
n!	nᵢ	nᶦ	nasalized voiceless
gn!	gnᵢ	gnᶦ	nasalised voiced

time, dates & numbers

What time is it?	*Ngubani ixesha?*	ngu·*b'aa*·nee ee·*kje*·shaa
It's one o'clock.	*Nguwani.*	ngu·*waa*·nee
It's (two) o'clock.	*Ngu(thu).*	ngu·(*tu*)
Quarter past (one).	*Yikota pasti (wani).*	yee·*k'aw*·t'aa p'aa·*st'ee* (*waa*·nee)
Half past (one).	*Yihaf pasti (wani).*	yee·*haaf* p'aa·*st'ee* (*waa*·nee)
Quarter to (eight).	*Yikota thu(eyithi).*	yee·*k'aw*·t'aa tu·(e·*yee*·t'ee)
At what time ...?	*Ngobani ixesha ...?*	ngaw·b'aa·nee ee·*kje*·shaa ...
At ...	*Ngo ...*	ngaw ...
It's (15 December).	*Yi(fiftini kaDisemba).*	yee·(feef·*t'ee*·nee k'aa·*dee*·se·mbaa)

yesterday	izolo	ee·*zaw*·law
today	namhlanje	naam·*hlaa*·nje
tomorrow	ngomso	ngaw·msaw
Monday	mvulo	mvu·law
Tuesday	lwesibini	lwe·see·*b'ee*·nee
Wednesday	lwesithathu	lwe·see·*taa*·tu
Thursday	lwesine	lwe·see·*ne*
Friday	lwesihlanu	lwe·see·*hlaa*·nu
Saturday	mgqibelo	m·*gjee*·b'e·law
Sunday	cawa	k!aa·waa

numbers

In Xhosa, numbers borrowed from English are commonly used and will be understood. They're also given in this chapter, rather than the more complex Xhosa forms. Numbers one to 10 are given below.

1	wani	waa·nee	6	siksi	seek'·see
2	thu	tu	7	seveni	se·*ve*·nee
3	thri	tree	8	eyithi	e·yee·tee
4	fo	faw	9	nayini	naa·yee·nee
5	fayifu	faa·yee·fu	10	teni	t'e·nee

border crossing

I'm here ...	Ndilapha ...	ndee·*laa*·paa ...
in transit	ngothutho	ngaw·*tu*·taw
on business	shishina	*shee*·shee·naa
on holiday	eholideyini	e·*haw*·lee·de·yee·nee
I'm here for ...	Ndilapha ka ...	ndee·*laa*·paa k'aa ...
(10) days	(teni) imini	(t'e·nee) ee·*mee*·nee
(three) weeks	(thri) iveki	(tree) ee·*ve*·k'ee
(two) months	(thu) inyanga	(tu) ee·*nyaa*·ngaa

I'm going to (Cintsa).
    Ndiya kwidolophu (eCintsa).   ndee·yaa k'wee·*daw*·law·pu (e·*lee*·nts'aa)

I'm staying at the (Buccaneer's).
    Ndihlala kwihotele   ndee·*hlaa*·laa k'wee·*haw*·t'e·le
    (eBuccaneer's).   (e·b'u·*k!aa*·ners)

tickets

A ... ticket (to Mdantsane), please.	Linye ... itikiti (eliya eMdantsane), nceda.	lee-*nye* ... ee-*t'ee*-k'ee-t'ee (e-lee-*yaa* e-mdaa-*nts'aa*-ne) n!e-daa
one-way	ndlelanye	ndle-laa-nye
return	buyela	b'u-ye-laa

I'd like to ... my ticket, please.	Ndingathanda uku ... itikiti lam, ndiyacela.	ndee-ngaa-*taa*-ndaa u-k'u ... ee-*t'ee*-k'ee-t'ee laam ndee-yaa-*!e*-laa
cancel	rhoxisa	khaw-k¦ee-saa
change	tshintsha	ch'ee-ntshaa
collect	qokelela	¡aw-k'e-le-laa

I'd like a ... seat, please.	Ndingathanda ... esihlalweni, ndiyacela.	ndee-ngaa-*taa*-ndaa ... e-see-*hlaa*-lwe-nee ndee-yaa-*!e*-laa
nonsmoking	ukutshaya	u-k'u-*ch'aa*-yaa
smoking	ukungatshayi	u-k'u-*ngaa*-ch'aa-yee

Is there a toilet/air conditioning?
Ikhona ithoyilethi/umoya ogudileyo?
ee-*kaw*-naa ee-*taw*-yee-le-tee/u-*maw*-yaa aw-*gu*-dee-le-yaw

How long does the trip take?
Luthatha kangakanani uhambo?
lu-*taa*-taa k'aa-ngaa-k'aa-*naa*-nee u-*haa*-mb'aw

Is it a direct route?
Yindlela ethe tse?
yee-*ndle*-laa e-*te* ts'e

transport

Where does flight (SAA59) arrive/depart?
Iflayithi (SAA fifti nayini) ifika/ihamba phi?
ee-*flaa*-yee-tee (s-aa-aa *feef*-t'ee *naa*-yee-nee) ee-*fee*-k'aa/ee-*haa*-mb'aa pee

How long will it be delayed?
Izakulibazisa kangakanani?
ee-*zaa*-k'u-lee-b'aa-zee-saa k'aa-ngaa-*k'aa*-naa-nee

Is this the ... to (Port Elizabeth)?	Yile ... eya (eBhayi)?	yee-*le* ... e-*yaa* (e-*baa*-yee)?
boat	iphenyane	ee-*pe*-nyaa-ne
bus	ibhasi	ee-*baa*-see
plane	inqwelomoya	ee-*nįwe*-law-maw-yaa
train	uloliwe	u-*law*-lee-we

How much is it to ...?
Kuxabisa njani u ...? ku-*k¡aa*-b'ee-saa *njaa*-nee u ...

Please take me to (this address).
Ndicela undise (kule dilesi). ndee-*k!e*-laa u-*ndee*-se (k'u-*le* dee-le-see)

I'd like to hire a car/4WD (with air conditioning).
Ndifuna ukuhayarisha ndee-*fu*-naa u-k'u-*haa*-yaa-ree-shaa
imoto/4WD ee-*maw*-t'aw/ee-*faw*-weel-*draa*-yee-vu
(ibe nomoya ogudileyo). (ee-*b'e* naw-*maw*-yaa aw-*gu*-dee-le-yaw)

How much is it for (three) days/weeks?
Ixabisa kangakanani ee-*k¡aa*-b'ee-saa k'aa-ngaa-*k'aa*-naa-nee
iintsuku (eziyithri)/iiveki? ee-*nts'u*-k'u (e-zee-yee-*tree*)/ee-*ve*-k'ee

directions

Where's the (nearest) ...?	Iphi e(kufutshane) ...?	ee-*pee* e-(k'u-*fu*-ch'aa-ne) ...
internet café	ikhefi	ee-*ke*-fee
	yeintanethi	ye-ee-*nt'aa*-ne-tee
market	imakhethi	ee-*maa*-ke-tee

Is this the road to (Grahamstown)?
Ingaba lendlela iya (eRhini)? ee-*ngaa*-b'aa le-*ndle*-laa ee-*yaa* (e-*khee*-nee)

Can you show me (on the map)?
Ungandibonisa (kwimaphu)? ungaa-ndee-*b'aw*-nee-saa (k'wee-*maa*-pu)

What's the address?
Ithini idilesi? ee-*tee*-nee ee-*dee*-le-see

How far is it?
Kukude kangakanani? k'u-k'u-*de* k'aa-ngaa-*k'aa*-naa-nee

How do I get there?
Ndifika njani apho? ndee-*fee*-k'aa *njaa*-nee aa-*paw*

Turn left/right.
Jika ekhohlo/ekunene. jee-k'aa e-*kaw*-hlaw/e-k'u-*ne*-ne

It's ...	/ ...	ee ...
behind ...	*emva* ...	e-*mvaa* ...
in front of ...	*ngaphambi ko* ...	ngaa-*paa*-mb'ee k'aw ...
near (to ...)	*kufutshane* ...	k'u-*fu*-ch'aa-ne ...
next to ...	*landelayo* ...	laa-*nde*-laa-yaw ...
on the corner	*ekoneni*	e-*kaw*-ne-nee
opposite ...	*chaseneyo* ...	*kh!aa*-se-ne-yaw ...
straight ahead	*nkqo-ngaphambili*	nkjaw-ngaa-*paa*-mb'ee-lee
there	*apho*	aa-*paw*

accommodation

Where's a ...?	*Iphi i ...?*	ee-*pee* ee ...
camping	*ibala*	ee-*b'aa*-laa
ground	*lokukhempisha*	law-k'u-*ke*-mp'ee-shaa
guesthouse	*indlu yamandwendwe*	ee-*ndlu* yaa-maa-*ndwe*-ndwe
hotel	*ihotele*	ee-*haw*-t'e-le
youth hostel	*ihostele yolutsha*	ee-*haw*-st'e-le yaw-lu-*ch'aa*

Can you recommend somewhere cheap/good?
Ungancoma naphina   u-ngaa-*nk!aw*-maa naa-*pee*-naa
tshipu/kakuhle?   ch'*ee*-p'u/k'aa-k'u-*hle*

I'd like to book a room, please.
Ndingathanda ukubhukisha   ndee-ngaa-*taa*-ndaa u-k'u-*bu*-k'ee-shaa
igumbi, ndiyacela.   ee-*gu*-mb'ee ndee-yaa-*k!e*-laa

I have a reservation.
Ndinamalungiselelo.   ndee-naa-maa-*lu*-ngee-se-le-law

Do you have	*Unalo*	u-*naa*-law
a ... room?	*igumbi ...?*	ee-*gu*-mb'ee ...
single	*kanye*	k'aa-*nye*
double	*kabini*	k'aa-*b'ee*-nee
twin	*wele*	*we*-le

How much is it per night/person?
Yimalini ubusuku/umntu?   yee-*maa*-lee-nee u-*b'u*-su-k'u/*um*-nt'u

I'd like to stay for (two) nights.
Ndingathanda ukuhlala   ndee-ngaa-*taa*-ndaa u-k'u-*hlaa*-laa
ubusuku ka(bini).   u-*b'u*-su-k'u k'aa-(*b'ee*-nee)

What time is check-out?

Lithini ixesha lokuphononga phandle?	lee-*tee*-nee ee-*k*ǃ*e*-shaa law-*k'u*-*paw*-naw-naw-ngaa *paa*-ndle

Am I allowed to camp here?

Ndivumelekile ukukhempisha apha?	ndee-*vu*-me-le-k'ee-le u-*k'u*-*ke*-mp'ee-shaa aa-*paa*

banking & communications

I'd like to …	Ndingathanda …	ndee-ngaa-*taa*-ndaa …
arrange a transfer	cwangcisela utshintsho	kǃwaa-*ng*ǃ*ee*-se-laa u-*ch'ee*-nch'aw
cash a cheque	itsheki yemali	ee-*ch'e*-k'ee ye-*maa*-lee
change a travellers cheque	tshintsha itsheki yabahambi	*ch'ee*-nch'aa ee-*ch'ee*-k'ee yaa-b'aa-*haa*-mb'ee
change money	tshintsha imali	*ch'ee*-nch'aa ee-*maa*-lee
withdraw money	tsala imali	ts'aa-laa ee-*maa*-lee

I want to …	Ndifuna uku …	ndee-*fu*-naa u-*k'u* …
buy a phonecard	thenga ikhadi lokufowuna	*te*-ngaa ee-*kaa*-dee law-*k'u*-*faw*-wu-naa
call (Singapore)	fowuna e (Singapore)	*faw*-wu-naa e (*see*-ngaa-p'*aw*-re)
reverse the charges	buyisela i intlawulo	b'u-*yee*-se-laa ee ee-*ntlaa*-wu-law
use a printer	sebenzisa iprinta	se-b'e-*nzee*-saa ee-*pree*-nt'aa
use the internet	sebenzisa i intanethi	se-b'e-*nzee*-saa ee ee-*nt'aa*-ne-tee

How much is it per hour?

Ingaxabisa kangakanani ngeawari?	ee-ngaa-*k*ǃ*aa*-b'ee-saa k'aa-ngaa-*k'aa*-naa-nee *nge*-aa-waa-ree

How much does a (three-minute) call cost?

Ingaba ixabisa kangakanani (imizuzu eyithri) yocingo?	ee-*ngaa*-b'aa ee-*k*ǃ*aa*-b'ee-saa k'aa-ngaa-*k'aa*-naa-nee (ee-*mee*-zu-zu e-yee-*tree*) yaw-*k*ǃ*ee*-ngaw

(One rand) per minute/hour.

(Wani randi) umzuzu/ngeawari.	(*waa*-nee *raa*-ndee) um-*zu*-zu/nge-aa-*waa*-ree

tours

When's the	Yeyiphi	ye-yee-pee
next ...?	landelayo ...?	laa-nde-laa-yaw ...
day trip	usuku lohamba	u-su-k'u law-haa-mb'aa
tour	ukhenketho	u-ke-nk'e-taw

Is ... included?	I ... idityanisiwe?	ee ... dee-ty'aa-nee-see-we
accommodation	indawo	ee-ndaa-waw
	yokuhlala	yaw-k'u-hlaa-laa
the admission	ixabiso	ee-k'¦aa-b'ee-saw
charge	elibizwayo	e-lee-b'ee-zwaa-yaw
	intlawulo	ee-ntlaa-wu-law
food	ukutya	u-k'u-ty'aa
transport	isithuthi	ee-see-tu-tee

How long is the tour?
Lude kangakanani ukhenketho? lu-de k'aa-ngaa-k'aa-naa-nee u-ke-nk'e-taw

What time should we be back?
Ngubani ixesha ngu-b'aa-nee ee-k'¦e-shaa
esinokubuya ngalo? e-see-naw-k'u-b'u-yaa ngaa-law

shopping

I'm looking for ...
Ndifuna ... ndee-fu-naa ...

I need film for this camera.
Ndifuna ifilimu yekhamera. ndee-fu-naa ee-fee-lee-mu ye-kaa-me-raa

Can I listen to this?
Ndingamamela le? ndee-ngaa-maa-me-laa le

Can I have my ... repaired?
Ndiyafuna ilungisiwe ...? ndee-yaa-fu-naa ee-lu-ngee-swe ...

When will it be ready?
Izakulunga nini? ee-zaa-k'u-lu-ngaa nee-nee

How much is it?
Yimalini? yee-maa-li-nee

Can you write down the price?
Ungabhala phantsi ixabiso? u-ngaa-baa-laa paa-nts'ee ee-k'¦aa-b'ee-saw

What's your lowest price?
Lithini ixabiso elingezantsi?   lee-*tee*-nee ee-k¦*aa*-b'ee-saw e-lee-nge-*zaa*-nts'ee

I'll give you (five) rand.
Ndizakunika (ifayifu) randi.   ndee-*zaa*-k'u-nee-k'aa (ee-*faa*-yee-fu) *raa*-ndee

There's a mistake in the bill.
Ikhona impazamo kwibhili.   ee-*kaw*-naa ee-*mp'aa*-zaa-maw k'wee-*bee*-lee

It's faulty.
Iyaphazama.   ee-ya-*paa*-zaa-maa

I'd like a receipt/refund, please.
Ndingathanda irisiti/   ndee-ngaa-*taa*-ndaa ee-*ree*-see-t'ee/
irifandi, ndiyacela.   ee-ree-*faa*-ndee ndee-yaa-*k*¦*e*-laa

Do you accept ...?	*Uyayamkela ...?*	u-yaa-*yaam*-k'e-laa ...
credit cards	*ikhredithi khadi*	ee-kre-*dee*-tee *kaa*-dee
debit cards	*idebhithi khadi*	ee-de-*bee*-tee *kaa*-dee
travellers	*itsheki*	ee-*ch'e*-k'ee
cheques	*zabahambi*	zaa-b'aa-*haa*-mb'ee

Could you ...?	*Ungakwazi uku ...?*	u-ngaa-*k'waa*-zee u-*k'u* ...
burn a CD from	*tshisa isidi*	*ch'ee*-saa ee-*see*-dee
my memory card	*kweyam imemori*	k'we-*yam* ee-*me*-maw-ree
	khadi	*ka*-dee
develop this film	*phucula le ifilimu*	pu-*k*¦*u*-laa le ee-*fee*-lee-mu

making conversation

Hello.	*Molo.*	*maw*-law
Good night.	*Ubusuku benzolo.*	u-*b'u*-su-k'u b'e-*nzaw*-law
Goodbye.	*Usale ngoxolo.*	u-*saa*-le ngaw-*k*¦*aw*-law
Mr	*Mhlekazi*	mhle-*k'aa*-zee
Mrs	*Nkosazana*	nk'*aw*-saa-zaa-naa
Ms/Miss	*Nenekazi*	ne-ne-*k'aa*-zee
How are you?	*Kunjani?*	k'u-*njaa*-nee
Fine, and you?	*Ndiyaphila,*	ndee-yaa-*pee*-laa
	unjani wena?	u-*njaa*-nee *we*-naa
What's your name?	*Ngubani*	ngu-*b'aa*-nee
	igama lakho?	ee-*gaa*-maa laa-*kaw*
My name's ...	*Igama lam ngu ...*	ee-*gaa*-maa laam ngu ...

I'm pleased to meet you.	Ndiyavuya ukukwazi.	ndee·yaa·*vu*·ya u·k'u·*k'waa*·zee
This is my ...	Yeyam le ...	ye·*yaam* le ...
boyfriend	inkwenkwe	ee·*nk'we*·nk'we
brother	mntakwethu	mnt'aa·*k'we*·tu
daughter	intombazana	ee·*nt'aw*·mb'aa·zaa·naa
father	utata	u·*t'aa*·t'aa
friend	umhlobo	um·*hlaw*·b'aw
girlfriend	intokazi	ee·*nt'aw*·k'aa·zee
husband	umyeni	u·*mye*·nee
mother	umama	u·*maa*·maa
sister	udade	u·*daa*·de
son	unyana	u·*nyaa*·naa
wife	umfazi	um·*faa*·zee
Here's my ...	Nantsi i ...	*naa*·nts'ee ee ...
What's your ...?	Ithini i ...?	ee·*tee*·nee ee ...
(email) address	idilesi (yeimeyli)	ee·*dee*·le·see (ye·*ee*·mey·lee)
phone number	inombolo	ee·naw·*mb'aw*·law
	yefowni	ye·*faw*·wu·nee
Where are you from?	Ungowaphi?	u·*ngaw*·waa·pee
I'm from ...	Ndingowase ...	ndee·*ngaw*·waa·se ...
Australia	Ostreliya	*aw*·stre·lee·yaa
Canada	Khanada	*kaa*·naa·daa
New Zealand	eNyuzilendi	e·*nyu*·zee·le·ndee
the UK	eUK	e·*uk'*
the USA	eUSA	e·u·*saa*
I'm (not) married.	(Andi)tshatanga.	(aa·ndee·)*ch'aa*·t'aa·ngaa
Can I take a photo (of you)?	Ndingayithatha ifoto (yakho)?	ndee·ngaa·yee·*taa*·taa ee·*faw*·t'aw (yaa·*kaw*)

eating out

Can you recommend a ...?	Ugakwazi ukukhuthaza ...?	u·ngaa·*k'waa*·zee u·k'u·ku·taa·zaa ...
bar	ibhari	ee·*baa*·ree
dish	isitya	ee·see·*ty'aa*
place to eat	indawo yokutya	ee·*ndaa*·waw yaw·k'u·*ty'aa*

I'd like ..., please.	Ndiyafuna ...	ndee-yaa-fu-naa ...
the bill	inkcukacha	ee-nk!u-k'aa-!haa
	ngamaxabiso	ngaa-maa-kjaa-b'ee-saw
the menu	isazisi	e-saa-zee-see
a table for (two)	itafile	ee-t'aa-fee-le
	(yababini)	(yaa-b'aa-b'ee-nee)
that dish	esasitya	e-saa-see-ty'aa

| Do you have | Unakho ukutya kwe | u-naa-kaw u-k'u-ty'aa k'we |
| vegetarian food? | vejitheriyeni? | ve-jee-te-ree-ye-nee |

Could you prepare	Ungalungiselela	u-ngaa-lu-ngee-se-le-laa
a meal without ...?	isidlo ngaphandle ...?	ee-see-dlaw ngaa-paa-ndle ...
eggs	amaqanda	aa-maa-kjaa-ndaa
meat stock	umhluzi	um-hlu-zee

(cup of) coffee ...	(ikopi) yekofu ...	(ee-k'aw-p'ee) ye-k'aw-fu ...
(cup of) tea ...	(ikopi) yeti ...	(ee-kaw-p'ee) ye-t'ee ...
with milk	nobisi	naw-b'ee-see
without sugar	ngaphandle	ngaa-paa-ndle
	kweswekile	k'we-swe-k'ee-le

| (boiled) water | amanzi (ashushu) | aa-maa-nzee (aa-shu-shu) |

emergencies

| Help! | Uncedo! | u-n!e-daw |
| I'm lost. | Ndilahlekile. | ndee-laa-hle-k'ee-le |

Call ...!	Biza ...!	b'ee-zaa ...
an ambulance	iambulensi	ee-aa-mb'u-le-nsee
a doctor	ugqirha	u-gjee-khaa
the police	amapolisa	aa-maa-paw-lee-saa

Could you help me, please?
Ungandinceda, ndiyakucela? u-ngaa-ndee-nk!e-daa ndee-yaa-k'u-k!e-laa

Where are the toilets?
Ziphi itoylethi? zee-pee ee-taw-yee-le-tee

I want to report an offence.
Ndifuna ukuchaza iofensi. ndee-fu-naa uk'u-kh!aa-zaa ee-aw-fe-nsee

I have insurance.
Ndine inshorensi. ndee-ne ee-nshaw-re-nsee

I want to contact my consulate/embassy.
Ndifuna ukhontaktha umzi/ ndee-*fu*-naa u-kaw-*nt'aa*-k'taa um-*zee*/
kamazakuzaku. kaa-maa-zaa-k'u-*zaa*-k'u

I've been assaulted. *Ndibethiwe.* ndee-be-*tee*-we
I've been raped. *Ndidlwengulwe.* ndee-*dlwe*-ngu-lwe
I've been robbed. *Ndirojiwe.* ndee-*raw*-jee-we

I've lost my ... *Ndilahlekelwe ...* ndee-*laa*-hle-k'e-lwe ...
My ... was/were stolen. *Eyam ... ibiwe.* e-*yam* ... ee-*b'ee*-we
  bags *ibhegi* ee-*be*-gee
  credit card *ikhadi lekhrediti* ee-*kaa*-dee le-kre-*dee*-tee
  handbag *ibhegi yesandla* ee-be-*gee* ye-*saa*-ndlaa
  jewellery *ijuwelari* ee-ju-we-laa-ree
  money *imali* ee-*maa*-lee
  passport *ipaspoti* ee-*paas*-paw-t'ee
  travellers cheques *iitsheki* ee-*ch'e*-k'ee
   zabahambi zaa-b'aa-*haa*-mb'ee
  wallet *iwolethi* ee-*waw*-le-tee

medical needs

Where's the *Yeyiphi* ye-*yee*-pee
nearest ...? *kufutshane ...?* k'u-*fu*-ch'aa-ne ...
  dentist *ugqirha* u-*gjee*-khaa
   wamazinyo waa-maa-*zee*-nyaw
  doctor *ugqirha* u-*gjee*-khaa
  hospital *isibhedlele* ee-see-*be*-dle-le
  pharmacist *ifamasi* ee-*faa*-maa-see

I need a doctor (who speaks English).
Ndifuna ugqirha ndee-*fu*-naa u-*gjee*-khaa
(othetha isingesi). (aw-*te*-taa ee-see-*nge*-see)

Could I see a female doctor?
Ndinakho ukubona ugqirha ndee-naa-*kaw* u-k'u-*b'aw*-naa u-*gjee*-khaa
obhinqileyo? aw-*bee*-njee-le-yaw

It hurts here.
Kubuhlungu apha. k'u-*b'u*-*hlu*-ngu aa-*paa*

I'm allergic to (penicillin).
Andidibani ne (penisilini). aa-ndee-*dee*-b'aa-nee ne (*p'e*-nee-see-lee-nee)

194

english–xhosa dictionary

In this dictionary, words are marked as n (noun), a (adjective), v (verb), sg (singular), pl (plural), inf (informal) and pol (polite) where necessary.

A

accommodation *indawo yokuhlala*
ee-*ndaa*-waw yaw-k'u-*hlaa*-laa
adaptor *iadaptha ee-aa-daa-daa-ptaa*
after *emva e-mvaa*
airport *isitishi senqwelomoya*
ee-see-t'ee-shee se-n!*lew-law-maw-*yaa
alcohol *utywala u-tywaa-*laa
all *onke aw-nk'e*
and *na* naa
ankle *iqatha ee-jaa-*taa
antibiotics *iyeza lokubulala intsholongwane*
ee-*ye-zaa law-k'u-b'u-*laa-laa
ee-*nch'aw-law-*ngwaa-ne
anti-inflammatories *amayeza okukrala*
aa-maa-*ye-zaa aw-k'u-kraa*-laa
arm *ingalo ee-ngaa-*law
aspirin *iyeza lokudambisa intlungu nefiva*
ee-*ye-zaa law-k'u-daa-mb'e-*saa ee-*ntlu-*ngu
ne-*fee*-vaa
asthma *umbefu u-mb'e-*fu
ATM *umatshini wokugcina imali*
u-maa-*ch'ee-*nee waw-k'u-*g!ee-*naa ee-*maa*-lee

B

baby *usana u-saa-*naa
back (body) *emva e-mvaa*
backpack *ingxowa oyithwala ngomqolo*
ee-*ngk!aw-*waa aw-yee-*twaa-*laa ngaw-*mjaw*law
bad *khohlakeleyo kaw-hlaa-*k'e-le-yaw
bank *ibhanki ee-baa-*nk'ee
bathroom *igumbi lokuhlamba*
ee-*gu-mb'e* law-k'u-*hlaa-*mb'aa
battery *ibhetri ee-bee-*tree
beautiful *hle* hle
bed *ibhedi ee-bee-*dee
beer *ibhiya ee-bee-*yaa
bees *iinyosi ee-nyaw-*see
before *ngaphambili ngaa-paa-mb'e-*lee
bicycle *ibhayisikili ee-baa-yee-see-k'ee-*lee
big *khulu ku-*lu
blanket *ingubo ee-ngu-b'aw*
blood group *udidi lwegazi u-dee-*dee lwe-*gaa-*zee
bottle *ibhotile ee-baw-*t'ee-le

bottle opener *isivuli bhotile ee-see-vu-*lee *baw-*t'ee-le
boy *inkwenkwe ee-nkwe-*nkwe
brakes (car) *ibreki zemoto ee-bre-k'ee* ze-*maw-*t'aw
breakfast *isidlo sakusasa ee-see-dlaw* saa-k'u-saa-*saa
bronchitis *isifo semibhobho yemiphunga*
ee-see-*faw* se-mee-*baw-*baw ye-mee-*pu*-ngaa

C

café *ikhefi ee-ke-*fee
cancel *rhoxisa khaw-k¦ee-*saa
can opener *isivuli kani ee-see-vu-*lee *k'aa-*nee
cash n *imali ee-maa-*lee
cell phone *iselifowuni ee-se-lee-faw-wu-*nee
centre n *umbindi u-mb'ee-*ndee
cheap *tshipu ch'ee-*pu
check (bill) *ibhili ee-bee-*lee
check-in n *ikhawuntara yokuzazisa*
ee-kaa-wu-nt'aa-raa yaw-k'u-zaa-zee-saa
chest *isifuba ee-see-fu-*baa
child *umntwana um-nt'waa-*naa
cigarette *isigarethi ee-see-gaa-ga-re-*tee
city *isixeko ee-see-k¦e-*kaw
clean a *coca kUaw-k*laa
closed *valiwe vaa-lee-*we
codeine *ikhowudhini ee-kaw-wu-dhee-*nee
cold a *banda b'aa-*ndaa
collect call *irivesikholi ee-ree-ve-see-kaw-*lee
condom *ikhondom ee-kaw-*ndawm
constipation *ukuqhina kwesisu*
u-k'u-jhee-naa k'we-see-su
cough n *ukhohlokhohlo u-kaw-hlaw-kaw-*hlaw
customs (immigration) *indawo yongenelelo*
ee-*ndaa-waw* yaw-nge-ne-le-*law*

D

dairy products *imveliso yasederi*
ee-mve-lee-saw yaa-se-de-ree
dangerous *ingozi ee-ngaw-*zee
date (time) *ideyithi ee-de-yee-*tee
day *usuku u-su-k'u*
diaper *isishuba ee-see-shu-*b'aa
diarrhoea *urhudo u-ru-*daw
dinner *isidlo sangokuhlwa*
ee-see-*dlaw* saa-ngaw-k'u-*hlwaa*

dirty *mdaka mdaa-k'aa*
disabled *olimazekileyo* aw-lee-maa-ze-k'ee-le-yaw
double bed *ibhedi eyenzelwe abantu ababini*
ee-be-dee e-ye-nze-lwe a-b'a-nt'u a-b'a-b'ee-nee
drink n *isiselo* ee-see-se-law
drivers licence *isazisi sokuqhuba*
ee-saa-zee-see saw-k'u-jhu-b'aa
drug (illicit) *isiyobisi* ee-see-see-yaw-b'ee-see

E

ear *indlebe* ee-ndle-b'e
east *mpumalanga* mp'u-maa-laa-ngaa
elevator *ileliveyitha* ee-le-lee-ve-yee-*taa*
email n *i-imeyili* ee-ee-me-yee-lee
English (language) *ulwimi lwesingesi*
u-*lwee*-mee lwe-se-*nge*-see
exchange rate *utshintsho mali* u-*ch'ee*-nch'aw *maa*-lee
exit n *indawo yokuphuma*
ee-*ndaa*-waw yaw-k'u-*pu*-maa
expensive *duru du*-ru
eye *imehlo* ee-me-hlaw

F

fast *khawuleza* ka-wu-*le*-zaa
fever *ifiva* ee-*fee*-vaa
finger *umnwe* um-*nwe*
first-aid kit *ikiti yoncedo lokuqala*
ee-*k'ee*-t'ee yaw-*nkfe*-daw law-k'u-*kjaa*-laa
first class *iklasi yokuqala* ee-k'*laa*-see yaw-k'u-*kjaa*-laa
fish n *intlantsi* ee-ntlaa-nts'ee
food *ukutya* u-k'u-*ty'aa*
foot *unyawo* u-*nyaa*-waw
fork *ifolokhwe* ee-*faw*-law-kwe
free (of charge) *simahla* see-maa-*hlaa*
fruit *isiqhamo* ee-see-*kjaa*-maw
funny *hlekisayo* hle-k'ee-*saa*-yaw

G

game park *indawo yokugcina izilwanyana*
ee-*ndaa*-waw yaw-k'u-*glee*-naa
ee-zee-*lwaa*-nyaa-naa
gift *isipho* ee-see-*paw*
girl *intombi* ee-nt'aw-*mb'ee*
glass (drinking) *iglasi* ee-*glaa*-see
glasses *izipeki* ee-zee-*p'e*-k'ee
gluten *ncangathi* n*laa*-ngaa-tee
good *lungileyo* lu-ngee-*le*-yaw
gram *umlinganiso wobunzima*
um-lee-ngaa-*nee*-saw waw-b'u-*nzee*-maa
guide n *inkokheli* ee-nk'aw-ke-lee

H

hand *isandla* ee-*saa*-ndlaa
happy *vuya vu*-yaa
have *ukuba na* u-k'u-*baa* naa
he *u-*(followed by name) *u-*
head *intloko* ee-*ntlaw*-k'aw
headache *intloko ebuhlungu*
ee-*ntlaw*-k'aw e-bu-*hlu*-ngu
heart *intliziyo* ee-ntlee-zee-yaw
heart condition *isifo sentliziyo*
ee-see-*faw* se-ntlee-zee-yaw
heat n *ubushushu* u-b'u-*shu*-shu
here *apha* aa-*paa*
high *phezulu* pee-zu-lu
highway *indlela enkulu* ee-*ndle*-laa e-*nk'u*-lu
hot *shushu shu*-shu
hungry *lambile* laa-*mb'ee*-le

I

I *i* ee
identification (card) *ikhadi yelD* ee-*kaa*-dee ye-*eed*
ill *gula gu*-laa
important *baluleka* b'aa-lu-*le*-k'aa
internet *intanethi* ee-*nt'aa*-ne-tee
interpreter *itoliki* ee-t'*aw*-lee-k'ee

J

job *umsebenzi* um-se-*b'e*-nzee

K

key *isitshixo* ee-see-*tsee-¦aw*
kilogram *ikhilogramu* ee-kee-law-*graa*-mu
kitchen *ikhitshi* ee-*kee*-ch'ee
knife *imela* ee-me-laa

L

laundry (place) *indawo yokuhlamba impahla*
ee-*ndaa*-waw yaw-k'u-*hlaa*-mb'aa ee-*mp'aa*-hlaa
lawyer *iqhwetha* ee-*khjwe*-taa
leg *umlenze* um-*le*-nze
less *nganeno* ngaa-ne-naw
letter (mail) *ileta* ee-*le*-t'aa
like v *thanda* taa-ndaa
love v *uthando* u-*taa*-ndaw
lunch *isidlo sasemini* ee-see-*dlaw* saa-se-*mee*-nee

M

man *indoda* ee-*ndaw*-daa
matches *imatshisi* ee-maa-ch'ee-see
meat *inyama* ee-*nyaa*-maa
medicine *iyeza* ee-ye-zaa
message *umyalezo* um-*yaa*-le-zaw
mobile phone *ifowuni onokuhambanayo*
  ee-*faw*-wu-nee aw-naw-k'u-*haa*-mb'aa-naa-yaw
month *inyanga* ee-*nyaa*-ngaa
morning *kusasa* k'u-*saa*-saa
motorcycle *isithuthuthu* ee-see-*tu*-tu-tu
mouth *umlomo* um-*law*-maw
MSG *imsg* ee-m-s-g
museum *imuziyam* ee-*mu*-zee-yam
music *umculo* um-*!u*-law

N

name n *igama* ee-*gaa*-maa
napkin *iseviyeti* ee-se-vee-ye-t'ee
nappy *isishuba* ee-see-*shu*-b'aa
nausea *ubucaphucaphu* u-bu-!aa-pu-laa-pu
neck *intamo* ee-*nt'aa*-maw
new *ntsha* nch'aa
news *indaba* ee-*ndaa*-b'aa
newspaper *iphephandaba* ee-pe-paa-ndaa-b'aa
night *ubusuku* u-b'u-su-k'u
noisy *ngxolayo* ng!aw-laa-yaw
nonsmoking *akutshaywa* aa-k'u-ch'aa-ywaa
north *entla* e-ntlaa
nose *impumlo* ee-*mp'u*-mlaw
now *ngoku* ngaw-k'u
number *inani* ee-*naa*-nee
nuts *amaqhele* aa-maa-*khje*-le

O

oil (engine) *ioyile* ee-*aw*-yee-le
old *ndala* ndaa-laa
open a *vulekileyo* vu-le-k'ee-le-yaw
outside *ngaphandle* ngaa-*paa*-ndle

P

package *impahla* ee-*mp'aa*-hlaa
pain *intlungu* ee-ntlu-ngu
palace *ibhotwe* ee-*baw*-t'we
paper *iphepha* ee-pe-paa
park (car) v *pakisha* p'aa-*k'ee*-shaa
passport *ipasipoti* ee-p'aa-see-paw-t'ee
pay *umvuzo* u-*mvu*-zaw

pen *usiba* u-*see*-b'aa
petrol *ipetroli* ee-p'e-*traw*-lee
pharmacy *ifamasi* ee-faa-*maa*-see
plate *ipleyiti* ee-*ple*-yee-t'ee
postcard *iposikhadi* ee-p'aw-see-kaa-dee
post office *iposi ofisi* ee-*p'aw*-see *aw*-fee-see
pregnant *khulelweyo* ku-le-lwe-yaw

R

rain n *imvula* ee-*mvu*-laa
razor *ireyiza* ee-re-yee-zaa
registered mail *iposi ebhaliswayo*
  ee-p'aw-see e-*baa*-lee-swaa-yaw
rent v *irente* ee-re-nt'e
repair v *lungisa* lu-*ngee*-saa
reservation *isigcinelo* ee-see-g!ee-ne-law
restaurant *irestyu* ee-re-sty'u
return v *buyela* b'u-ye-laa
road *indlela* ee-ndle-laa
room *igumbi* ee-gu-*mb'ee*

S

sad *lusizi* lu-see-zee
safe a *gcinakeleyo* g!ee-naa-k'e-le-yaw
sanitary napkin *iphedi* ee-pe-dee
seafood *ukutya kwaselwandle*
  u-k'u-ty'aa k'waa-se-*lwaa*-ndle
seat *isihlalo* ee-see-*hlaa*-law
send *thumela* tu-me-laa
sex *isini* ee-see-nee
shampoo *ishampu* ee-shaa-*mp'u*
share (a dorm, etc) *ukwabelana ngegumbi*
  uk'waa-*b'e*-laa-naa nge-*gu*-mb'ee
shaving cream *ikhrimu yokusheva*
  ee-*kree*-mu yaw-k'u-she-vaa
she *uno* (followed by name) un-aw
sheet (bed) *ishiti* ee-*shee*-t'ee
shirt *ihempe* ee-he-*mp'e*
shoes *izihlangu* ee-zee-*hlaa*-ngu
shop n *ivenkile* ee-ve-*nk'*ee-le
shower n *ishawari* ee-shaa-waa-ree
skin *ulusu* u-lu-su
skirt *isiketi* ee-see-*k'e*-t'ee
sleep v *lala* laa-laa
small *ncinci* n!ee-nlee
smoke (cigarettes) v *tshaya* tshaa-yaa
soap *isepha* ee-se-paa
some *inxenye* ee-*nje*-nye
soon *kamsinya* k'aa-*msee*-nyaa
sore throat *umqala obuhlungu*
  um-*kjaa*-laa aw-b'u-*hlu*-ngu

south *mzantsi mzaa*-nts'ee
souvenir shop *ivenkile ethengisa izikhumbuzo*
ee-*ve*-nk'ee-le e-*te*-ngee-saa e-zee-*ku*-mb'u-zaw
speak *thetha te*-taa
spoon *icephe* ee-*kʲe*-pe
stamp n *isitampu* ee-see-*t'aa*-mp'u
stand-by ticket *itikiti lokulinda*
ee-*t'e*-k'ee-t'ee law-k'u-*lee*-ndaa
station (train) *isitishi* ee-see-*t'ee*-shee
stomach *isisu* ee-*see*-su
stop v *ima* ee-*maa*
stop (bus) n *indawo yokumisa*
ee-*ndaa*-waw yaw-k'u-*mee*-saa
street *isitalato* ee-see-*t'aa*-laa-t'aw
student *umfundi u*-*mfu*-ndee
sunscreen *ikhrimu yokukhusela ilanga*
ee-*kree*-mu yaw-k'u-*ku*-se-laa ee-*laa*-ngaa
swim v *ukuqubha* u-k'u-*ku*-baa

T

tampons *iithamponi* ee-taa-*mp'aw*-nee
teeth *amazinyo* aa-maa-*zee*-nyaw
telephone n *ifowuni* ee-*faw*-wu-nee
television *umabonakude* u-maa-*b'aw*-naa-k'u-de
temperature (weather) *iqondo lobushushu*
ee-*kʲaw*-ndaw law-b'u-*shu*-shu
tent *intente* ee-*nt'e*-nt'e
that (one) *leya (inye) le*-yaa (e-*nyee*)
they *bona b'aw*-naa
thirsty *nxaniwe n*|*aa*-nee-we
this (one) *le (kanye) le* (k'aa-*nye*)
throat *umqala* um-*kʲaa*-laa
ticket *itikiti* ee-*t'ee*-k'ee-t'ee
time *ixesha* ee-*kʲe*-shaa
tired *diniwe dee*-nee-we
tissues *ithishu* ee-*tee*-shu
today *namhlanje* naam-*hlaa*-nje
toilet *ithoyilethi* ee-*taw*-yee-le-tee
tonight *ngokuhlwa* ngaw-k'u-*hlwaa*
toothache *izinyo elibuhlungu*
ee-*zee*-nyaw e-lee-b'u-*hlu*-ngu
toothbrush *ibrashi yokuxukuxa amazinyo*
ee-*b'raa*-shee yaw-k'u-*kʲu*-k'u-*kʲaa* aa-maa-*zee*-nyaw
toothpaste *intlama yamazinyo*
ee-*ntlaa*-maa yaa-maa-*zee*-nyaw
torch (flashlight) *itotshi* ee-*t'aw*-ch'ee
tourist office *iofisi yabacandi-zwe*
ee-*aw*-fee-see yaa-b'aa-*klaa*-ndee-zwe
towel *itawuli* ee-*t'aa*-wu-lee
translate *guqula* gu-*kʲu*-laa

travel agency *umlungiseleli hambo*
um-lu-ngee-se-le-lee *haa*-mb'aw
travellers cheque *itsheki yabahambi*
ee-*ch'e*-k'ee yaa-b'aa-haa-mb'ee
trousers *iibhulukhwe* ee-bu-lu-kwe
twin beds *iibhedi ezimbini ezifanayo*
ee-*be*-dee e-zee-*mb'ee*-nee e-zee-*faa*-naa-yaw
tyre *ithayara* ee-*taa*-yaa-raa

U

underwear *isinxibo sangaphantsi*
ee-see-*nʲee*-b'aw saa-ngaa-*paa*-nts'ee
urgent *ngxamiseka ng*|*aa*-mee-se-k'aa

V

vacant *ngenanto* nge-naa-*nt'aw*
vegetable n *umfuno* um-*fu*-naw
vegetarian a *utya izihluma* u-*ty'aa* ee-zee-*hlu*-maa
visa *iviza* ee-*vee*-zaa

W

waiter *iweyita* ee-we-yee-*t'aa*
walk v *hamba haa*-mb'aa
wallet *isipaji* ee-see-*p'aa*-jee
warm a *fudumeleyo* fu-du-me-*le*-yaw
wash (something) *vasa vaa*-saa
watch n *iwotshi* ee-*waw*-ch'ee
water *amanzi* aa-*maa*-nzee
we *thina tee*-naa
weekend *impelaveki* ee-*mp'e*-laa-*ve*-k'ee
west *ntshona* nch'*aw*-naa
wheelchair *isitulo esinamavili*
ee-see-*t'u*-law e-see-naa-maa-*vee*-lee
when *nini nee*-nee
where *phi* pee
who *bani b'aa*-nee
why *kutheni* k'u-*te*-nee
window *ifestile* ee-fe-*st'ee*-le
wine *iwayini* ee-*waa*-yee-nee
with *na* naa
without *ngaphandle* ngaa-*paa*-ndle
woman *umfazi* um-*faa*-zee
write *bhala baa*-laa

Y

you sg inf/pol *wena/nawe* we-naa/naa-*we*
you pl inf/pol *nina/thina* nee-*naa*/tee-*naa*

Yoruba

pronunciation

Vowels		Consonants	
Symbol	**English sound**	**Symbol**	**English sound**
a	**a**ct	b	**b**ed
ang	as in '**a**ct', but nasal	d	**d**og
ay	s**ay**	f	**f**un
e	b**e**t	g	**g**o
eng	as in 'b**e**t', but nasal	gb	rug**b**y
i	h**i**t	h	**h**at
ing	as in 'h**i**t', but nasal	j	**j**ar
o	p**o**t	k	**k**it
oh	c**o**ld	kp	ba**ckp**ack
ong	as in 'p**o**t', but nasal	l	**l**ot
u	p**u**t	m	**m**an
ung	as in 'p**u**t', but nasal	n	**n**ot

	r	**r**un

The Yoruba pronunciation is given in light green after each phrase.

Each syllable is separated by a dot.

For example:

	s	**s**un
	sh	**sh**ot
	t	**t**op
Ọṣẹ́.	oh·shay	w	**w**in

Yoruba's nasal vowels, indicated with ng after the vowel symbol, are pronounced as if you're trying to force the sound out of your nose.

y	**y**es

There are a range of accent marks above and below vowels. You won't need to worry about using these, if you follow the pronunciation guides you'll be understood.

YORÙBÁ – pronunciation

introduction

There's a Yoruba proverb, *Ohun tí o bá gbìn ni wàá ká* o-hung ti o ba gbing ni wa-a ka, which means 'Whatever you sow, you will reap' – and any efforts to speak to locals in Yoruba will be greatly appreciated. Yoruba (*Yorùbá* yoh-ru-ba), a language from the Niger-Congo family, is spoken by almost 30 million people in West Africa. The Yoruba nation consists of a number of tribes which trace their origins to a leader called Oduduwa, the founder of the city Ile-Ife in what is now southwestern Nigeria, where Yoruba is primarily spoken. There are also Yoruba speakers in the Benin Republic and eastern Togo, and a variety of the language is spoken in Sierra Leone. Yoruba was one of the first West African languages to have a written grammar and a dictionary in the 1840s. It's also one of the first African languages with a novel published in it, and is the mother tongue of Nobel-prize-winning writer Wole Soyinka.

■ **yoruba** (native language)   ■ **yoruba** (generally understood)

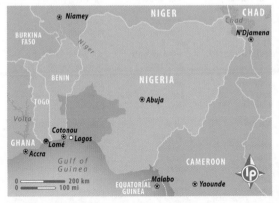

language difficulties

Do you speak English?
Ṣé o ń sọ gèésì? shay o n so ge·e·si

Do you understand?
Ṣé ó yé ọ? shay oh yay o

I (don't) understand.
Èmi (kò) gbọ́. ay·mi (koh) gbo

Could you please ...? *Jòwó ṣé o lè ...?* jo·wo shay on lay ...
  repeat that *tun sọ* tung so
  speak more slowly *rọra sọ̀rọ̀* ro·ra so·ro
  write it down *kọ ọ sílẹ̀* ko o si·le

time, dates & numbers

What time is it?	*Kí ni aago sọ?*	ki ni a·a·goh so
It's one o'clock.	*Aago kan ni.*	a·a·goh kang ni
It's (two) o'clock.	*Aago (méjì) ni.*	a·a·goh (may·ji) ni
Quarter past (one).	*Aago (kan) kojá iṣéjú méèdógún.*	a·a·goh (kang) ko·ja i·she·ju me·e·doh·gung
Half past (one).	*Aago (kan) àbọ̀.*	a·a·goh (kang) a·bo
Quarter to (eight).	*Aago (méjọ) ku ìṣéjú méèdógún.*	a·a·goh (me·jo) ku i·she·ju me·e·doh·gung
At what time ...?	*Nígbà wo ...?*	ni·gba woh ...
At ...	*Ní ...?*	ni ...
It's (15 December).	*Ní (ojó keèdógún oṣù dìsẹ́mbà).*	ni (o·jo ke·e·doh·gung oh·shu di·se·m·ba)

yesterday	*àná*	a·na
today	*òní*	oh·ni
tomorrow	*ọla*	o·la

Monday	*ojó ajé*	o·jo a·jay
Tuesday	*ojó iségun*	o·jo i·she·gung
Wednesday	*ojórú*	o·jo·ru
Thursday	*ojóbò*	o·jo·bo
Friday	*ojó ẹtì*	o·jo e·ti
Saturday	*ojó abámẹ́ta*	o·jo a·ba·me·ta
Sunday	*ojó àìkú*	o·jo a·i·ku

0	*òdo*	o·do	16	*èrìndínlógún*	e·ring·ding·loh·gung
1	*òkan*	o·kang	17	*ètàdínlógún*	e·ta·ding·loh·gung
2	*èjì*	ay·ji	18	*èjìdínlógún*	ay·ji·ding·loh·gung
3	*èta*	e·ta	19	*òkàndínlógún*	o·kang·ding·loh·gung
4	*èrin*	e·ring	20	*ogún*	oh·gung
5	*àrun*	a·rung	21	*òkànlélógún*	o·kang·lay·loh·gung
6	*èfà*	e·fa	22	*èjìlélógún*	ay·ji·lay·loh·gung
7	*èje*	ay·jay	30	*ogbòn*	o·gbong
8	*èjo*	e·jo	40	*ogójì*	oh·goh·ji
9	*èsan*	e·sang	50	*àádóta*	a·a·do·ta
10	*èwá*	e·wa	60	*ogóta*	o·go·ta
11	*òkànla*	o·kang·la	70	*àádórin*	a·a·do·ring
12	*èjìlá*	ay·ji·la	80	*ogórin*	o·go·ring
13	*ètàlá*	e·ta·la	90	*àádòrún*	a·a·do·rung
14	*èrínlá*	e·ring·la	100	*ogòrùn-ún*	o·go·rung·ung
15	*èdógún*	e·do·gung	1000	*egbèrúng*	e·gbe·rung

border crossing

I'm here ...	*Mo wà níbí ...*	moh wa ni·bi ...
in transit	*lénu ìrìn-àjò*	le·nu i·ring·a·joh
on business	*fún isé*	fung i·she
on holiday	*fún ìsimi*	fung i·si·mi
I'm here for ...	*Mo wà níbí fún ...*	moh wa ni·bi fung ...
(10) days	*ojó (méwàá)*	o·jo (me·wa·a)
(three) weeks	*òsè (méta)*	o·se (me·ta)
(two) months	*osù (méjì)*	oh·shu (may·ji)

I'm going to (Òyó).
Mò ń lo sí (Òyó).   moh n lo si (o·yo)

I'm staying at the (Premier Hotel).
Mò ń gbé ní (Ilé Ìtura Pírémìà).   moh n gbay ní (i·lay i·tu·ra kpi·re·mi·a)

tickets

A ... ticket	Ìwé ìwọlé ...	i·way i·wo·lay ...
(to Ìbàdàn), please.	lọ (sí Ìbàdàn).	lo (si i·ba·dang)
one-way	àlọ nìkan	a·lo ni·kang
return	àtàlọ-àtàbọ	a·ta·lo·a·ta·bo

I'd like to ... my	Jọwọ mà á fé láti ...	jo·wo ma a fe la·ti ...
ticket, please.	ìwé ìwọlé mi.	i·way i·wo·le mi
cancel	fagilé	fa·gi·lay
change	pààrọ̀	kpa·a·ro
collect	gba	gba

Is there a ...?	Sé ... wa?	shay ... wa
air conditioning	èrọ amúlétutù	e·ro a·mu·lay·tu·tu
toilet	ilé ìgbònsè	i·le i·gbong·se

I'd like a smoking/nonsmoking seat, please.
Jòwó, mà á fé ìjókòó   jo·wo ma a fe i·joh·koh·oh
amusìgá/mámusìgá.   a·mu·si·ga/ma·mu·si·ga

How long does the trip take?
Báwo ni ìrìnàjò yìí sẹ jìnnà sí?   ba·woh ni i·ring·a·joh yi·i shay jing·na si

Is it a direct route?
Sé tààràtà ni?   shay ta·a·ra·ta ni

transport

Where does the (Virgin Nigeria) flight arrive/depart?
Ibo ni bàálù (fájìnì ti Nàijíríà)   i·boh ni ba·a·lu (fa·ji·ni ti na·i·ji·ri·a)
yóò ti gbéra/kúrò?   yoh·oh ti gbay·ra/ku·roh

How long will it be delayed?
Fún àkókò wo ni ìdádúró bàálù?   fung a·koh·koh woh ni i·da·du·roh ba·a·lu

Is this the ...	Sé èyí ni ...	shay ay·yi ni ...
to (Èkó)?	sí (Èkó)?	si (ay·ko)
boat	ọkọ̀ ojú-omi	o·ko oh·ju·oh·mi
bus	bọọ̀sì	bo·o·si
plane	bàálù	ba·a·lu
train	ọkọ̀ ojú-irin	o·ko oh·ju·i·ring

How much is it to ...?
Èló ni dé ...?   ay·loh ni day ...

Please take me to (this address).
Jòwó gbé mi lo sí (àdírésí yìí).   jo·wo gbay mi lo si (a·di·re·si yi·i)

I'd like to hire a car (with air conditioning).
Mà á fé gba okò tí ó   ma a fe gba o·ko ti oh
(ni èrọ amúlétutù).   (ni e·ro a·mu·lay·tu·tu)

How much is it for (three) days/weeks?
Èló ni fún òjó/òsè (méta)?   ay·loh ni fung o·jo/o·se (me·ta)

directions

Where's the	*Ibo ni ...*	i·boh ni ...
(nearest) ...?	*(tí ó súnmó wà)?*	(ti oh sung·mo wa)
internet café	*búkà ìtàkùn àgbáyé*	bu·ka i·ta·kung a·gba·yay
market	*ojà*	o·ja

Is this the road to (Òyó)?
Se ònà (Òyó) nìyí?   shay o·na (o·yo) ni·yi

Can you show me (on the map)?
Sé o lè fi hàn mí (lórí àwòrán)?   shay oh lay fi hang mi (loh·ri a·woh·rang)

What's the address?
Kí ni àdírésí?   ki ni a·di·re·si

How far is it?
Báwo ni ó se jìnnà sí?   ba·woh ni oh shay jing·na si

How do I get there?
Báwo ni mà á se dé ibè?   ba·woh ni ma a shay day i·be

Turn left/right.
Yà sósì/sótùn-ún.   ya soh·si/so·tung·ung

It's ...	*Ó wà ...*	oh wa ...
behind ...	*lé·yìn ...*	le·ying ...
in front of ...	*níwájú ...*	ni·wa·ju ...
near (to ...)	*légbèé ...*	le·gbe·e ...
next to ...	*légbèé ...*	le·gbe·e ...
on the corner	*légbèé ...*	le·gbe·e ...
opposite ...	*níwájú ...*	ni·wa·ju ...
straight ahead	*lòkánkán*	lo·kang·kang
there	*níbè*	ni·be

accommodation

Where's a ...?	*Níbo ni ... wà?*	ni·boh ni ... wa
camping ground	*ilè ìpàgó*	i·le i·kpa·go
guesthouse	*ilé ìtura*	i·lay i·tu·ra
hotel	*ìlé ìtura*	i·lay i·tu·ra
youth hostel	*ilé itura òdó*	i·lay i·tu·ra o·do

Can you recommend somewhere cheap/good?
Ṣe o lè júwe ibi tí ó ti   shay oh lay ju·way i·bi ti oh ti
dínwo/dára?   ding·woh/da·ra

I'd like to book a room, please.
Jòwó mà á fẹ́ gba yàrá kan.   jo·wo ma a fe gba ya·ra kang

I have a reservation.
Mo ti gba yàrá sílẹ̀ télẹ̀.   moh ti gba ya·ra si·le te·le

Do you have a ... room?	*Ṣe ẹ ní yàrá ...?*	shay e ni ya·ra ...
single	*elénìkan*	e·le·ni·kang
double	*elénìméjì*	e·le·ni·may·ji
twin	*oníbejì*	oh·ni·bay·ji

How much is it per ...?	*Èló ni fún ...?*	ay·loh ni fung ...
night	*alé ojó kan*	a·le o·jo kang
person	*ẹnì kan*	e·ni kang

I'd like to stay for (two) nights.
Mà á fẹ́ sun ibí fún ojó (méjì).   ma a fe sung i·bi fung o·jo (may·ji)

What time is check-out?
Ìgbà wo ni kíkẹ́ rú jáde nínú ilé ìtura?   i·gba woh ni ki·ke ru ja·de ni·nu i·lay i·tu·ra

Am I allowed to camp here?
Ṣe àyè wà láti pàgó síbí?   shay a·yay wa la·ti kpa·go si·bi

banking & communications

I'd like to ... | Mà á fẹ́ ... | ma a fe ...
arrange a transfer | fi owó ránṣẹ́ | fi oh·woh rang·she
cash a cheque | fi sòwédowó | fi so·way·doh·woh
 | gba owó | gba oh·woh
change a travellers cheque | pààrò sòwédowó | kpa·a·ro so·way·doh·woh
 | arìnrìnàjò | a·ring·ring·a·jo
change money | pààrò owó | kpa·a·ro oh·woh
withdraw money | gba owó ní bánkì | gba oh·woh ni bang·ki

I want to ... | Mo fẹ́ ... | mo fe ...
buy a phonecard | ra káàdì ìfóònù | ra ka·a·di i·foh·oh·nu
call (Singapore) | pe (Singapore) | kpay (sing·a·po)
reverse the charges | yi owó padà | yi oh·woh kpa·da
use a printer | lo ìtèwé | loh i·te·way
use the internet | lo ìtàkùn àgbáyé | loh i·ta·kung a·gba·yay

How much is it per hour?
Èló ni fún wákàtí kan? — ay·loh ni fung wa·ka·ti kang

How much does a (three-minute) call cost?
Èló ni pípè fún (ìṣẹ́jú méta) jé? — ay·loh ni kpi·kpay fung (i·she·ju me·ta) je

(100 naira) per minute/hour.
(Ogórùn-ún náírà) fún ìṣẹ́jú/wákàtí kan. — (o·go·rung·ung na·i·ra) fung i·she·ju/wa·ka·ti kan

tours

When's the next ...? | Ìgbà wo ni ...? | i·gba woh ni ...
day trip | ìrìn-ojó kan | i·ring·o·jo kang
tour | ìrìn-àjò afẹ́ | i·ring·a·joh a·fe

Is ... included? | Ṣé ẹ fi ... si? | shay e fi ... si
accommodation | ibùgbé | i·bu·gbay
the admission charge | owó ìgbàwọlé | oh·woh i·gba·wo·lay
food | oúnje | oh·ung·je
transport | ìrìn-àjò | i·ring·a·joh

How long is the tour?
Báwo ni ìrìn-àjò náà ṣe jìnnà sí?   ba·woh ni i·ring·a·joh naa shay jing·na si

What time should we be back?
Ìgbà wo ni ó yẹ kí á padà?   i·gba woh ni oh yę ki a kpa·da

shopping

I'm looking for ...
Mò ń wá ...   moh n wa ...

I need film for this camera.
Mo fẹ́ fíìmù fún ẹ̀rọ ayàwòrán yìí.   moh fe fi·i·mu fung e·ro a·ya·woh·rang yi·i

Can I listen to this?
Ṣe mo lè gbọ́ èyí?   shay moh lay gbo ay·yi

Can I have my ... repaired?
Ṣé mo lè tún ... mi ṣe?   shay moh lay tung ... mi shay

When will it be ready?
Ìgbà wo ni yóò ṣe tán?   i·gba woh ni yoh·oh shay tang

How much is it?
Èló ni?   ay·loh ni

Can you write down the price?
Ṣé o lè kọ iye owó rẹ̀ sílẹ̀?   shay oh lay ko i·yay oh·woh re si·le

What's your lowest price?
Èló ni jálẹ̀?   ay·loh ni ja·le

I'll give you (800) naira.
Màá fún ọ ní (ẹgbẹ̀rin) náírà.   ma a fung o ni (e·gbe·ring) na·i·ra

There's a mistake in the bill.
Àṣìṣe wà nínú iwé owó yìí.   a·shi·she wa ni·nu i·way oh·woh yi·i

It's faulty.
Ó ti bàjé.   o ti ba·je

I'd like a ..., please.   *Jọ̀wọ́ mà á fẹ́ gba ...*   jo·wo ma a fe gba ...
   receipt   *rìsíìtì*   ri·si·i·ti
   refund   *owó padà*   oh·woh kpa·da

Do you accept ...?	Sé ẹ gba ...?	shay e gba ...
credit cards	káàdì moyáwó	ka-a-di moh-ya-woh
debit cards	káàdì mojẹgbèsè	ka-a-di moh-je-gbay-say
travellers	iwé sòwédowó	i-way so-way-doh-woh
cheques	arin-rìn-àjò	a-ring-ring-a-joh

Could you ...?	Sé o lè ...?	shay oh lay ...
burn a CD from my	da rékòdù yìí ko	da re-ko-du yi-i ko
memory card	láti inú fón rán	la-ti i-nu fong rang
develop this film	fò fíìmù	fo fi-i-mu

making conversation

Hello.	Pèlé o.	kpe-le o
Good night.	Ó dààrò.	oh da-a-ro
Goodbye.	Ó dàbò.	oh da-bo

Mr	Ògbéni	o-gbe-ni
Mrs	Aya	a-ya
Ms/Miss	Omidan	oh-mi-dang

How are you?	Sẹ dáádá ni?	shay da-a-da-a ni
Fine, and you?	Bééni, ìwo ń kó?	be-e-ni i-wo n ko
What's your name?	Kí ni orúkọ rẹ?	ki ni oh-ru-ko re
My name's ...	Orúkọ mi ni ...	oh-ru-ko mi ni ...
I'm pleased to meet you.	Inú mi dùn láti pàde rẹ.	i-nu mi dung la-ti kpa-day re

This is my ...	Èyí ni ... mi.	ay-yi ni ... mi
boyfriend	òrékùnrin	o-re-kung-ring
brother	arakunrin	a-ra-kung-ring
daughter	ọmọ mi obìnrin	o-mo mi oh-bing-ring
father	bàbá	ba-ba
friend	òrẹ́	o-re
girlfriend	òrébìnrin	o-re-bing-ring
husband	ọkọ	o-ko
mother	ìyá/màmá	i-ya/ma-ma
sister	arábìnrin	a-ra-bing-ring
son	ọmọ mi ọkùnrin	o-mo mi o-kung-ring
wife	ìyàwó	i-ya-woh

Here's my ...	Eyi ni ...	a·yi ni ...
What's your ...?	Kí ni ... re?	ki ni ... re
address	àdírésì	a·di·re·si
email address	àdírésì ìtàkùn	a·di·re·si i·ta·kung
	àgbayé	a·gba·yay
phone number	nómbà fóònù	no·m·ba foh·oh·nu
Where are you from?	Ibo ni ìlú re?	i·boh ni i·lu re
I'm from ...	Ìlú mi ni ...	i·lu mi ni ...
Australia	Osirélíà	o·si·ray·li·a
Canada	Kánádà	ka·na·da
New Zealand	Nìù sìlandì	ni·u si·la·n·di
the UK	Ìlú òyìnbó	i·lu oh·ying·boh
the USA	Améríkà	a·me·ri·ka
I'm (not) married. m	Mi (ò) tí ì láya.	mi (oh) ti i la·ya
I'm (not) married. f	Mi (ò) tí ì ní oko.	mi (oh) ti i ni o·ko
Can I take a photo (of you)?	Sé mo lè yà (ó) ní fótò?	shay moh lay ya (o) ni fo·toh

eating out

Can you recommend a ...?	Ǹ jé o le júwe ...?	n je oh lay u·way ...
bar	iléotí	i·lay·o·ti
dish	oúnje	oh·un·je
place to eat	iléoúnje	i·lay·oh·ung·je
I'd like ..., please.	Jòwó, mà á fé ...	jo·wo ma a fe ...
the bill	íwe owó	i·we oh·woh
the menu	àwon oúnje tí ó wà	a·wong oh·ung·je ti oh wa
a table for (two)	ìjokòò fún (eni méjì)	i·joh·koh·oh fung (e·ni me·ji)
that dish	oúnje yen	o·ung·je yeng
Do you have vegetarian food?	Ǹ jé e ní oúnje aláìjeran?	n je e ni oh·ung·je a·la·i·je·rang
Could you prepare a meal without ...?	Jòwó ba mi se oúnje lai fi ... si?	jo·wo ba mi shay oh·ung·je lai fi ... si
eggs	eyin	e·ying
meat stock	eran	e·rang

(cup of) coffee ...	(ife) kọfí ...	(i·fay) ko·fi ...
(cup of) tea ...	(ife) tíì ...	(i·fay) ti·i ...
with milk	pèlú mílííki	kpe·lu mi·li·i·ki
without sugar	láì sí súgà	la·i si su·ga
(boiled) water	omi (gbígbóná)	oh·mi (gbi·gboh·na)

emergencies

Help!	Ẹ ràn mí lọ́wọ́ o!	e rang mi lo·wo o
Call ...!	Ẹ pe ...!	e kpay ...
an ambulance	ọkọ̀ gbókùùgbokùú	o·ko gboh·ku·u·gboh·ku·u
a doctor	dókítà	doh·ki·ta
the police	ọlọ́pàá	o·lo·kpa·a

Could you help me, please?
Jòwọ́ṣe o lè ràn mí lọ́wọ́?   jo·wo·shay oh lay rang mi lo·wo

I'm lost.
Mo ti sọnù.   moh ti so·nu

Where are the toilets?
Ibo ni ilé ìgbònsẹ̀ wà?   i·boh ni i·lay i·gbong·se wa

I want to report an offence.
Mo fẹ́ fi ẹjọ́ kan sùn.   moh fe fi e·jo kang sung

I have insurance.
Mo ní ìwé adójútòfò.   moh ni i·way a·do·ju·to·fo

I want to contact my consulate/embassy.
Mo fẹ́ bá aṣojú ilẹ̀   mo fe ba a·shoh·ju i·le
òkèèrè ìlú mi sọ̀rọ̀.   o·kay·ay·ray i·lu mi so·ro

I've been ...	Wọn ti ...	wong ti ...
assaulted	fìyà je mí	fi·ya je mi
raped	fipá bá mi lò pọ̀	fi·kpa ba mi loh kpo
robbed	jà mí lólè	ja mi loh·lay

I've lost my ...	Mo ju ... nù.	moh ju ... nu
bags	àpò	a·kpoh
credit card	káàdì moyáwó	ka·a·di moh·ya·woh
handbag	àpamówó	a·kpa·mo·wo
jewellery	ohun-oṣo	oh·hung·o·sho
money	owó	oh·woh
passport	ìwé ìrìnnà	i·way i·ring·na
travellers	ìwé sòwédowó	i·way so·way·doh·woh
cheques	arin-rìn-àjò	a·ring·ring·a·joh
wallet	póòsì	kpo·o·si

My (money) was stolen.   *Owó mi ti sọnu.*   (oh·woh) mi ti so·nu

medical needs

Where's the nearest ...?	Ibo ni ... tí ó súnmọ ibi?	i·boh ni ... ti oh sung·mo i·bi
dentist	dókítà eléyín	doh·ki·ta ay·lay·ying
doctor	dókítà	doh·ki·ta
hospital	ilé-ìwòsàn	i·lay·i·woh·sang
pharmacist	apògùn	a·kpoh·gung

I need a doctor (who speaks English).
*Mo fé dókítà (tí ó
lè sọ èdè òyìnbó).*
moh fe doh·ki·ta (ti oh
lay so ay·day oh·ying·boh)

Could I see a female doctor?
Ṣe mo lè rí dókítà obìnrin?
shay moh lay ri doh·ki·ta oh·bing·ring

It hurts here.
O ń dùn mí níbí.
oh n dung mi ni·bi

I'm allergic to (penicillin).
(Ògùn) yìí ṣe ọwó òdì sí mi.
(oh·gung) yi·i shay o·wo oh·di si mi

english–yoruba dictionary

In this dictionary, words are marked as n (noun), a (adjective), v (verb), sg (singular) and pl (plural) where necessary.

A

accommodation *ibùgbé* i-bu-gbay
adaptor *ìbádógba* i-ba-do-gba
after *léyìn* le-ying
airport *ibùdókò òfurufu* i-bu-doh-ko oh-fu-ru-fu
alcohol *otí* o-ti
all *gbogbo* gboh-gboh
allergy *èhun* e-hung
and *àti* a-ti
ankle *orùn-esè* o-rung-e-se
antibiotics *ògùn-èyà wuuru* oh-gung-e-ya wu-u-ru
anti-inflammatories *ògùn-ara wíwú* oh-gung-a-ra wi-wu
arm *apá* a-kpa
aspirin *asipirínìnì* a-si-kpi-ring-ing-ni
asthma *ikó-fée* i-ko-fay-ay
ATM *èro kàádì agbówójáde* e-ro ka-a-di a-gboh-woh-ja-de

B

baby *omo-owó* o-mo-o-wo
back (body) *eyìn* e-ying
backpack *apo ìgbèrùsìléyìn* a-kpoh i-gbe-ru-si-le-ying
bad *burú* bu-ru
baggage claim *ìbìlgberù* i-bi-i-gbe-ru
bank *ilé-ìfowópamósí* i-lay-i-foh-woh-kpa-mo-si
bathroom *ilé-ìwè* i-lay-i-we
battery *bátìrì* ba-ti-ri
beautiful *dára* da-ra
bed *ibùsùn* i-bu-sung
beer *bìà* bi-a
bees *oyin* oh-ying
before *télètélè* te-le-te-le
bicycle *kèké* ke-ke
big *tóbi* toh-bi
blanket *aso-ìbora òtútù* asho-i-boh-ra oh-tu-tu
blood group *orísí-èjè* oh-ri-shi-e-je
bottle *ìgò* i-goh
bottle opener *Ìsìtí* i-shi-ti
boy *omokùnrin* o-mo-kung-ring
brakes (car) *bìréèkì-okò* bi-ray-ay-ki-o-ko
breakfast *oúnje-àárò* oh-ung-je-a-a-ro
bronchitis *àìsàn ìnú èdòfóró* a-i-sang i-n-e-do-foh-roh

C

café *búkà* bu-ka
cancel *fagìlé* fa-gi-le
can opener *isí-agolo* i-shi-a-goh-loh
cash n *owó* oh-woh
cell phone *telifóònù aláàgbékà* te-li-foh-oh-nu a-la-a-gbay-ka
centre n *àárin* a-a-ring
cheap *pò* kpo
check (bill) *ìwé sòwédowó* i-way so-way-doh-wo
check-in n *kérùsókò* ke-ru-so-ko
chest *àyà* a-ya
child *odómodé* o-do-mo-day
cigarette *sigá* si-ga
city *ìlú* i-lu
clean a *mó* mo
closed *padé* kpa-day
codeine *kodìnì* koh-di-i-ni
cold a *tútù* tu-tu
condom *kóndóòmù* ko-n-do-o-mo-mu
constipation *inúkíkún* i-nu-ki-kung
contact lenses *igò-ojú* i-goh-oh-ju
cough n *ikó* i-ko
currency exchange *ìséwó ilè òkèèrè* i-she-woh i-le oh-kay-ay-ray
customs (immigration) *asóbodè* a-sho-boh-day

D

dairy products *èròjà wàrà* ay-roh-ja wa-ra
dangerous *léwu* lay-wu
date (time) *àkókò* a-koh-koh
day *ojó* o-jo
diaper *aso-ìléèdí* a-sho-i-lay-ay-di
diarrhoea *ìgbé-gbuuru* i-gbe-gbu-u-ru
dinner *oúnje-alé* oh-ung-je-a-le
dirty *dòtí* do-ti
disabled *abirùn* a-bi-rung
double bed *ibùsùn aláàgbékà* i-bu-sung a-la-a-gbay-ka
drink n *ohun mímu* oh-hung-mi-mu
drivers licence *ìwé erí awakò* i-way e-ri a-wa-ko
drug (illicit) *ògùn olóró* o-gung oh-loh-roh

E

ear *etí* ay-ti
east *ìlà oòrùn* i-la oh-oh-rung
economy class *ìjókòó alábóodé*
i-joh-koh-oh a-la-bo-o-day
elevator *èro-òkàbà* e-ro-a-ka-ba
email n *létà orí ìtàkùn àgbayé*
le-ta oh-ri i-ta-kung a-gba-yay
English (language) *èdè gèésì* ay-day ge-e-si
exchange rate *pàsìpààrò owó ilè òkèèrè*
kpa-shi-kpa-a-ro oh-woh i-le oh-kay-ay-ray
exit n *ònà àbájáde* o-na a-ba-ja-deh
expensive *òwón* o-wong
eye *ojú* oh-ju

F

fast *yá* ya
fever *ibà* i-ba
finger *ika owó* i-ka o-wo
first-aid kit *àpò ìsègùn wàràwéré*
a-kpoh i-she-gung wa-ra-way-ray
first class *ipò kíínì* i-kpoh ki-i-ni
fish n *eja* e-ja
food *oúnje* oh-ung-je
foot *esè* e-se
fork *èmúga* e-mu-ga
free (of charge) *òfé* o-fe
fruit *èso* ay-soh
funny *panilérìnín* kpa-ni-le-ring-ing

G

game park *ogba-erankò* o-gba-e-rang-koh
gift *èbùn* e-bung
girl *omobìnrin* o-mo-bing-ring
glass (drinking) *ife-ìmumi* i-fay-i-mu-mi
glasses *dígí-ojú* di-gi-oh-ju
gluten *gulutìnì* gu-lu-ti-i-ni
good *dára* da-ra
gram *gírààmù* gi-ra-a-mu
guide n *amònà* a-mo-na

H

hand *owó* o-wo
happy *ìdùnnú* i-dung-nu
have *ní* ni

he *òun* oh-ung
head *orí* oh-ri
headache *èfórí* e-fo-ri
heart *okàn* o-kang
heart condition *ipò okàn* i-kpoh o-kang
heat n *ooru* oh-oh-ru
here *ibí* i-bi
high *gíga* gi-ga
highway *òpópónà* oh-kpoh-kpoh-na
homosexual n&a *okùnrin asebíabo*
o-kung-ring a-shay-bi-a-boh
hot *gbóná* gboh-na
hungry *ebi* ay-bi

I

I *èmi* ay-mi
identification (card) *káàdì ìdánimò* ka-a-di i-da-ni-mo
ill *àìsàn* a-i-sang
important *pàtàkì* kpa-ta-ki
internet *ìtàkùn àgbáyé* i-ta-kung a-gba-yay
interpreter *ògbufò* oh-gbu-fo

J

job *isé* i-she

K

key *kókóró* ko-ko-ro
kilogram *kílò* ki-loh
kitchen *ilé ìdáná* i-lay i-da-na
knife *òbe* o-be

L

laundry (place) *ibi ìfoso* i-bi i-fo-sho
lawyer *agbejórò* a-gbe-jo-roh
left-luggage office *ófíìsì ìkérùsì* o-fi-i-si i-ke-ru-si
leg *esè* e-se
lesbian n&a *obìnrin asebíako*
oh-bing-ring a-shay-bi-a-ko
less *dín* ding
letter (mail) *létà* le-ta
like v *féràn* fe-rang
lost-property office *ófíìsì ìkérùtónù-sí*
o-fi-i-si i-ke-ru-toh-nu-si
love v *fé* fe
lunch *oúnje òsán* oh-ung-je o-sang

M

man *okùnrin* o-kung-ring
matches *ìsáná* i-sha-na
meat *ẹran* e-rang
medicine *òògùn* oh-gung
message *iṣé* i-she
mobile phone *telifóònù-aláàgbékà* te-li-foh-oh-nu-a-la-a-gbay-ka
month *oṣù* oh-shu
morning *àárò* a-a-ro
motorcycle *alùkpùkpù* a-lu-kpu-kpu
mouth *ẹnu* e-nu
movie *sinimá* si-ni-ma
MSG *amóbèdùn* a-mo-be-dung
museum *ilé-ìṣẹ̀mbáyé* i-lay-i-she-m-ba-yay
music *orin* oh-ring

N

name ⊓ *orúkọ* oh-ru-ko
napkin *aṣọ inuwó* a-sho-i-nu-wo
nappy *aṣọ ìléèdí ọmọdé* a-sho-i-lay-ay-di o-mo-day
national park *gbàgede ìgbàfé* gba-gay-day i-gba-fe
nausea *èèbì* ay-ay-bi
neck *ọrùn* o-rung
new *tuntun* tung-tung
news *ìròyìn* i-roh-ying
newspaper *ìwé-ìròyìn* i-way-i-roh-ying
night *alé* a-le
nightclub *ilé ìgbafé alé* i-lay i-gba-fe a-le
noisy *pariwo* kpa-ri-woh
nonsmoking *mámusìgá* ma-mu-si-ga
north *àaréwà* a-a-ray-wa
nose *imú* i-mu
now *nísinsìnyí* ni-sing-sing-yi
number *nónbà* no-n-ba
nuts *nóòtì* no-o-ti

O

oil (engine) *epo* ay-kpoh
OK *ódára* oh-da-ra
old *gbó* gboh
open a *ṣí* shi
outside *ìta* i-ta

P

package *ẹrù* e-ru
pain *irora* i-roh-ra

palace *ààfin òba* a-a-fing o-ba
paper *ìwé* i-way
park (car) v *yàrá ìgbókòsí* ya-ra i-gbo-ko-si
passport *ìwé ìrìnnà* i-we i-ring-na
pay *san* sang
pen *kálàmù* ka-la-mu
petrol *epo betiróòlù* ay-kpoh be-ti-roh-oh-lu
pharmacy *ilé ìpòògùn* i-lay kpoh-oh-gung
plate *àwo/abó* a-woh/a-bo
postcard *pádí ìkíní* kpa-a-li i-ki-ni
post office *ilé ìfowópamoósí* i-lay i-foh-woh-kpa-mo-si
pregnant *oyún* oh-yung

Q

quiet *dáké* da-ke

R

rain ⊓ *òjò* oh-joh
razor *abẹfélé* a-be-fe-le
registered mail *ìwé ìfíránṣẹ́* i-way i-fi-rang-she
rent v *yá lò* ya loh
repair v *tún ṣe* tung shay
reservation *gbà sìlè* gba si-le
restaurant *ilé ìtura* i-lay i-tu-ra
return v *padà* kpa-da
road *ònà* o-na
room *yàrá* ya-ra

S

sad *banújé* ba-nu-je
safe a *fi pamó* fi-kpa-mo
sanitary napkin *aṣọ nìkan-oṣù* a-sho n-n-kang-oh-shu
seafood *àwọn-ohun-jìje-inú-òkun* a-wong-oh-hung-ji-je-i-nu-oh-kun
seat *ijókòó* i-joh-koh-oh
send fi *ìránṣẹ́* fi rang-she
sex *bá sùn* ba sung
shampoo *oṣeìfọrun* o-she-i-fo-rung
share (a dorm, etc) *bá pín* ba-kping
shaving cream *oṣeìfárun* o-she-i-fa-rung
she *òun* oh-ung
sheet (bed) *aṣọ ibora* a-sho i-boh-ra
shirt *ṣẹ̀tí* she-e-ti
shoes *bàtà* ba-ta
shop ⊓ *ṣọ́bù* sho-o-bu
shower ⊓ *ṣáwà* sha-wa
skin *awọ* a-wo
skirt *aṣọ àwọsódò obìnrin* a-sho-a-wo-soh-doh oh-bing-ring
sleep v *sùn* sung

small *kéré* kay-ray
smoke (cigarettes) v *mu* mu
soap *ose* o-she
some *diè* di-e
soon *láìpé* la-i-kpe
sore throat *egbò òfun* ay-gboh-o-fung
south *gúsù* gu-su
souvenir shop *sóòbù ìtajà* sho-o-bu i-ta-ja
speak *sòrò* so-ro
spoon *síbí* shi-bí
stamp *òòtè* oh-oh-te
stand-by ticket *tíkèètì sì-dúródìè* ti-ke-e-ti sì-du-roh-di-e
station (train) *ibudoko rélùwéè* i-bu-doh-ko ray-lu-way-ay
stomach *ìkùn* i-kung
stop v *dúró* du-roh
stop (bus) n *ibúdókò* i-bu-doh-ko
street *òpópó* oh-kpoh-kpoh
student *akékòo* a-ke-ko-o
sunscreen *ìpara-agbòòrùn* i-kpa-ra-a-gboh-oh-rung
swim v *lúwèé* lu-we-e

T

tampons *aso nnkan-osù* a-sho n-n-kang-oh-shu
teeth *eyín* ay-ying
telephone n *telifóònù* te-li-foh-oh-nu
television *amóhùnmáwòràn* a-moh-hung-ma-woh-rang
temperature (weather) *ojú ojó* oh-ju o-jo
tent *àgó* a-go
that (one) *iyen* i-yeng
they *àwon* a-wong
thirsty *òungbè* oh-ung-gbe
this (one) *èyí* ay-yi
throat *òfun* o-fung
ticket *iwé iwolé* i-way i-wo-le
time *ìgbà* i-gba
tired *rè* re
tissues *ìsù ara* i-shu a-ra
today *òní* oh-ni
toilet *ilé ìgbònsè* i-lay i-gbong-se
tonight *alé òní* a-le oh-ni
toothache *akokoro* a-koh-koh-roh
toothbrush *bùróòsì ifoyín* bu-ro-o-shi i-fo-ying
toothpaste *ose ifoyín* o-she i-fo-ying
torch (flashlight) *tóòsì* to-o-shi
tourist office *ofíísì arin-rìn-àjò* o-fi-i-si a-ring-ring-a-joh
towel *táwèlì* ta-we-li

translate *túmò* tu-mo
travel agency *asètò arin-rìn-àjò* a-she-toh a-ring-rìn-a-joh
travellers cheque *iwé sòwédowo arin-rìn-àjò* i-we so-way-doh-woh a-ring-ring-a-joh
trousers *sòkòtò* shoh-koh-toh
twin beds *béédì oníbejì* be-e-di oh-ni-bay-ji
tyre *táyà* ta-ya

U

underwear *àwòtélè* a-wo-te-le
urgent *kíákiá* ki-a-ki-a

V

vacant *sí sìlè* shi si-le
vegetable n *èfó* e-fo
vegetarian a *aládíjeran* a-la-i-je-rang
visa *iwé àse ìrìnnà* i-we a-she i-ring-na

W

waiter *agbótí* a-gbo-ti
walk v *rìn* ring
wallet *àpò owó* a-kpoh oh-woh
warm a *ooru* oh-oh-ru
wash (something) *fò* fo
watch n *isó* i-sho
water *omi* oh-mi
we *àwa* a-wa
weekend *òpin-òsè* oh-ping-o-se
west *ìwò oòrùn* i-wo oh-oh-rung
wheelchair *kèké abirùn* ke-ke a-bi-rung
when *nígbàwo* ni-gba-woh
where *níbo* ni-boh
who *ta ni* ta ni
why *nítorí kí ni* ni-toh-ri ki ni
window *fèrésé* fay-ray-say
wine *otí lile* o-ti li-lay
with *pèlú* kpe-lu
without *láìsí* la-i-si
woman *obìnrin* oh-bing-ring
write *ko* ko

Y

you sg *ìwo* i-wo
you pl *èyin* e-ying

Zulu

pronunciation

Vowels		Consonants	
Symbol	English sound	Symbol	English sound
aa	father	b	rib-punch
aw	law	b'	strong b with air sucked in
e	bet	ch'	as in 'let-show' but spat out
ee	see	d	as in 'hard-times'
u	put	dl	like a voiced hl
		f	fun
		g	as in 'big-kick'
		h	hat
		hl	as in the Welsh 'llewellyn'
		j	jar
		k	kit
		k'	k, but spat out
		l	lot
		m	man
		n	not
		ng	finger
		ny	canyon
		p	pet
		p'	popping p
		r	run (rolled)
		s	sun
		sh	shot
		t	top
		t'	spitting t
		ts'	as in 'lets', but spat out
		v	very
		w	win
		y	yes
		z	zero

In this chapter,
the Zulu pronunciation
is given in pink after each phrase.

Each syllable is separated
by a dot, and the syllable stressed in
each word is italicised.

For example:

Uxolo.　　u-k'*aw*-law

Note also that Zulu has no word stress
in questions.

The term 'voiced' applied to consonant
and clicks in this chapter means 'said
with the vocal cords vibrating'.

Zulu's glottalised consonants,
simplified as b', ch', k', p', t' and ts'
in our pronunciation guide,
are made by tightening and releasing
the space between the vocal cords
when you pronounce the sound,
a bit like combining it with the
sound in the middle of the word
'uh-oh'. The sound b' has an extra twist
– instead of breathing out to make
the sound, you breathe in.

For information on Zulu's distinctive
click sounds, see the box on page 220.

introduction

The name of the Zulu language (*isiZulu* ee·see·*zu*·lu) comes from the word *izulu* ee·*zu*·lu – literally 'heaven', or, more poetically, 'the people of heaven'. About 10 million Africans speak Zulu as a first language, with the vast majority (more than 95 per cent) in South Africa. Other speakers are in Botswana, Lesotho, Malawi, Mozambique and Swaziland. Zulu, an Nguni language belonging to the Southern Bantu group, is closely related to other Bantu languages in southern Africa, particularly Xhosa. Zulu-speaking people are descendents of the Nguni people who inhabited coastal regions of southeastern Africa from the 16th century. Some linguists believe that during the 16th and 17th centuries, the Nguni dialects acquired their distinctive 'click' sounds, which still feature in Zulu. Another theory claims that Zulu and Xhosa women borrowed the clicks from neighbouring Khoisan languages to disguise taboo words in their own languages. The Zulu Empire was established in the second quarter of the 19th century, a time in which foreign missionaries were recording and documenting the language and culture of the Zulu people. Several spelling systems were in use by 1860, and a standardised writing system was implemented in 1921.

■ **zulu** (native language)　　■ **zulu** (generally understood)

language difficulties

Do you speak English?	*Uyasikhuluma isiNgisi?*	u·yaa·see·ku·lu·maa ee·see·ngee·see
Do you understand?	*Uyezwa?*	u·ye·zwaa
I understand.	*Ngiyezwa.*	ngee·ye·zwaa
I don't understand.	*Angizwa.*	aa·ngee·zwaa
Could you please ...?	*Ake ...?*	aa·ge ...
repeat that	*uphinde*	u·pee·nde
speak more slowly	*ukhulume kancane kakhulu*	u·ku·lu·me gaa·nk!aa·ne gaa·ku·lu
write it down	*uyibhale phansi*	u·yee·baa·le paa·nts'ee

click sounds

Zulu has a series of click sounds: some clicks are against the front teeth (like a 'tsk' sound), some are against the roof of the mouth at the front (like a 'tock' sound) and some are against the side teeth (like the chirrup you make to get a horse to start walking).

front teeth	roof of the mouth	side teeth	description
k!	k¡	k¦	voiceless
kh!	kh¡	kh¦	aspirated (with a puff of air)
g!	g¡	g¦	voiced
n!	n¡	n¦	nasalized voiceless
gn!	gn¡	gn¦	nasalised voiced

time, dates & numbers

What time is it?	*Ngubani isikhathi?*	ngu·b'aa·nee ee·see·kaa·tee
It's one o'clock.	*Nguwani.*	ngu·*waa*·nee
It's (two) o'clock.	*Ngu(thu).*	ngu·(*thu*)
It's quarter past (one).	*Yingokhotha-phasi (wani).*	yee·ngaw·kaw·taa·paa·see (*waa*·nee)
Half past (one).	*Ngophasi-(wani).*	ngaw·paa·see·(*waa*·nee)
Quarter to (eight).	*Ngokhotha-thu (eyithi).*	ngaw·kaw·taa·tu (e·*yee*·tee)
At what time ...?	*Ngasikhathi bani ...?*	ngaa·see·kaa·tee b'aa·nee ...
At ...	*Ngo-...*	ngaw·...
It's (17 December).	*Ngumhla ka-(seventini Disemba).*	ngu·*m*·hlaa gaa·(se·ve·*nt*'ee·nee dee·*se*·mbaa)

yesterday	*izolo*	ee-*zaw*-law
today	*namhlanje*	naa-m-hlaa-*nje*
tomorrow	*kusasa*	gu-*saa*-saa
Monday	*uMsombuluko*	u-m-saw-mbu-*lu*-gaw
Tuesday	*uLwesibili*	u-lwe-see-*b'ee*-lee
Wednesday	*uLwesithathu*	u-lwe-see-*taa*-tu
Thursday	*uLwesine*	u-lwe-*see*-ne
Friday	*uLwesihlanu*	u-lwe-see-*hlaa*-nu
Saturday	*uMgqibelo*	u-m-gjee-*b'e*-law
Sunday	*iSonto*	ee-*saw*-nt'aw

numbers

In Zulu, numbers borrowed from English are commonly used and will be understood. They're also given in this chapter, rather than the more complex Zulu forms. See below for numbers one to 10.

1	*uwani*	u-*waa*-nee	**6**	*usiksi*	u-*seek*-see
2	*uthu*	u-*tu*	**7**	*usevene*	u-se-*ve*-nee
3	*uthri*	u-*three*	**8**	*u-eyithi*	u-e-*yeet*
4	*ufo*	u-*faw*	**9**	*unayini*	u-*naa*-yee-nee
5	*ufayifi*	u-*faa*-yee-fee	**10**	*utheni*	u-*the*-nee

border crossing

I'm here ...	*Ngilapha ...*	ngee-*laa*-paa ...
in transit	*ngidlula nje*	ngee-*dlu*-laa nje
on business	*ngebhizinisi*	nge-bee-zee-*nee*-see
on holiday	*ngeholide*	nge-haw-*lee*-de
I'm here for ...	*Ngizoba lapha ...*	ngee-*zaw*-b'aa *laa*-paa ...
(10) days	*amalanga*	aa-maa-*laa*-ngaa
	(ayishumi)	(a-yee-*shu*-mee)
(three) weeks	*amasonto*	aa-maa-*saw*-nt'aw
	(amathathu)	(aa-maa-*taa*-tu)
(two) months	*izinyanga*	ee-zee-*nyaa*-nga
	(ezimbili)	(e-zee-*mbee*-lee)

I'm going to (the Drakensberg).
  Ngiya (oKhahlamba).　　ngee-yaa (aw-kaa-*hlaa*-mbaa)

I'm staying at the (Durban Sun).
  Ngihlala (e-Durban Sun).　　ngee-*hlaa*-laa (e-de-ben *saa*-nee)

tickets

A one-way ticket to (Eshowe), please.
*Ngicela ithikithi elilodwa
ukuya (eShowe).*
ngee-*k!e*-laa ee-tee-*gee*-tee e-lee-*law*-dwaa
u-gu-yaa (e-*shaw*-we)

A return ticket to (Ulundi), please.
*Ngicela ithikithi elilodwa
ukuya nokubuya (oLundi).*
ngee-*k!e*-laa ee-tee-*gee*-tee e-lee-*law*-dwaa
u-gu-yaa naw-gu-*b'u*-yaa (aw-*lu*-ndee)

I'd like to ... my ticket, please.	*Ngicela uku-...
ithikithi lami.*	ngee-*k!e*-laa u-gu-...
ee-tee-*gee*-tee *laa*-mee
cancel	*khansela*	kaa-*nts'e*-laa
change	*shintsha*	*shee*-nch'aa
collect	*landa*	*laa*-ndaa

Is there a toilet?
Kukhona ithoyilethi?
gu-kaw-naa ee-taw-yee-le-tee

Is there air conditioning?
Kukhona umoya opholisiwe?
gu-kaw-naa u-maw-yaa aw-paw-lee-see-we

How long does the trip take?
*Uhambo luthatha isikhathi
esingakanani?*
u-haa-mbaw lu-taa-taa ee-see-kaa-tee
e-see-ngaa-gaa-naa-nee

Is it a direct route?
Yindlela eqondile?
yee-ndle-laa e-k¡aw-ndee-le

transport

Where does flight (BA325) arrive/depart?
*Lifikela/Lisukekela kuphi
ibhanoyi u-(BA325)?*
lee-fee-ge-laa /lee-su-ge-ge-laa gu-pee
ee-ba-naw-yee u-(bee ey three tu faiv)

How long will it be delayed?
*Lizomiswa isikhathi
esingakanani?*
lee-zaw-mee-swaa ee-see-kaa-tee
e-see-ngaa-gaa-naa-nee

Is this the boat/train to (Cape Town)?
*Yiso isikebhe/isitimela
esiya (eKipi)?*
yee-saw ee-see-k'e-be/ee-see-t'ee-me-laa
e-see-yaa (e-k'ee-p'ee)

Is this the bus/plane to (Johannesburg)?
*Yilo ibhasi/ibhanoyi
eliya (eGoli)?*
yee-law ee-baa-see/ee-baa-naw-yee
e-lee-yaa (e-gaw-lee)

I'd like to hire a ... (with air conditioning).	*Ngicela ukuqasha ... (enomoya opholisiwe).*	ngee-*kle*-laa u-gu-*kjaa*-shaa ... (e-naw-*maw*-yaa aw-paw-lee-*see*-we)
4WD	*i-fo-bhayi-fo*	ee-*faw*-baa-yee-*faw*
car	*imoto*	ee-*maw*-t'aw

How much is it for (three) days/weeks?
Malini amalanga/amasonto (amathathu)?
maa·lee·nee aa·maa·laa·ngaa/aa·maa·saw·nt'aw (aa·maa·taa·tu)

How much is it to (Umvoti)?
Malini ukuya (eMvoti)?
maa·lee·nee u·gu·yaa (em·vaw·tee)

Please take me to (this address).
Ake ungise ku-(lelikheli).
aa·ge u·*ngee*·se gu·(le·lee·*ke*·lee)

directions

Where's the (nearest) ...?	*Ingakuphi ... (eseduzana)?*	ee·ngaa·gu·pee ... (e·se·du·zaa·naa)
internet café	*i-Internet café*	ee·een·ter·net kaa·fe
market	*imakethe*	ee·maa·ge·te

Is this the road to (Hluhluwe)?
Yiyo indlela eya (eHluhluwe)?
yee·yaw ee·ndle·laa e·yaa (e·hlu·hlu·we)

Can you show me (on the map)?
Ungangibonisa (kumephu)?
u·ngaa·ngee·b'aw·nee·saa (gu·me·pu)

What's the address?
Lithini ikheli?
lee·tee·nee ee·ke·lee

How far is it?
Kukude kangakanani?
gu·gu·de gaa·ngaa·gaa·naa·nee

How do I get there?
Ngifika kanjani lapho?
ngee·fee·gaa gaa·njaa·nee laa·paw

Turn left/right.
Jikela kwesokunxele/ kwesokunene.
jee·*ge*·laa gwe·saw·gu·n¦e·le/ gwe·saw·gu·*ne*·ne

It's ...	Ku-...	gu-...
behind ...	semva kwa-...	se·mbvaa gwaa·...
in front of ...	phambi kwa-...	paa·mbee gwaa·...
near (to ...)	seduze (na-)...	se·du·ze (naa·)...
next to ...	secaleni kwa-...	se·k!aa·le·nee gwaa·...
on the corner	sekhoneni	se·kaw·ne·nee
opposite ...	bhekene na-...	be·ge·nee naa·...
straight ahead	ngaphambili	ngaa·paa·mbee·lee
there	laphaya	laa·paa·yaa

accommodation

Where's a ...?	Ingakuphi ...?	ee·ngaa·gu·pee ...
camping ground	indawo yokukhempa	ee·ndaa·waw yaw·gu·ke·mpaa
guesthouse	indlu yezivakashi	ee·ndlu ye·zee·vaa·gaa·shee
hotel	ihhotela	ee·haw·t'e·laa
youth hostel	ihostela labasha	ee·haw·st'e·laa laa·b'aa·shaa

Can you recommend somewhere cheap/good?
Ikhona indawo eshibhile/   ee·kaw·naa ee·ndaa·waw e·shee·bee·le/
enhle oyaziyo?   e·ntl'e aw·yaa·zee·yaw

I'd like to book a room, please.
Ngingathanda ukubekisa   ngee·ngaa·taa·ndaa u·gu·b'e·gee·saa
ikamelo.   ee·k'aa·me·law

I have a reservation.
Ngibekelwe indawo.   ngee·b'e·ge·lwe ee·ndaa·waw

Do you have a ... room?	Ninekamelo ...?	nee·ne·k'aa·me·law ...
single	lomuntu oyedwa	law·mu·nt'u aw·ye·dwaa
double	labantu ababili	laa·b'aa·nt'u aa·b'aa·b'ee·lee
twin	elinemibhede emibili	e·le·ne·mee·be·de e·mee·b'ee·lee

How much is it per ...?	Malini ...?	maa·lee·nee ...
night	ubusuku obubodwa	u·b'u·su·gu aw·b'u·b'aw·dwaa
person	umuntu oyedwa	u·mu·nt'u aw·ye·dwaa

I'd like to stay for (two) nights.
Ngingathanda ukulala   ngee·ngaa·taa·ndaa u·gu·laa·laa
izinsuku (ezimbili).   ee·zee·nts'u·gu (e·zee·mbee·lee)

What time is check-out?
Kufanele kuphunywe   gu·faa·ne·le gu·pu·nywe
ngasikhathi bani?   ngaa·see·kaa·tee b'aa·nee

Am I allowed to camp here?
Kuvunyelwa ukumisa   gu·vu·nye·lwa u·gu·mee·saa
ikamu lapha?   ee·k'aa·mu laa·paa

banking & communications

I'd like to ...	*Ngicela uku-...*	ngee·*k!e*·laa u·gu·...
arrange a transfer	*shintshwa*	*shee*·nch'waa
cash a cheque	*phendula isheke*	pe·*ndu*·laa i·*she*·ge
change a travellers cheque	*phendula isheke lesihambi*	*phe*·ndu·laa ee·*she*·ge le·see·*haa*·mbee
change money	*shintsha imali*	*shee*·nch'aa ee·*maa*·lee
withdraw money	*khipha imali*	*kee*·paa ee·*maa*·lee

I want to ...	*Ngifuna uku-...*	ngee·*fu*·naa u·gu·...
buy a phonecard	*thenga ikhadi*	*te*·ngaa ee·*kaa*·dee
call (London)	*locingo fowunela ku(Landani)*	law·*k!e*·ngaw faw·wu·ne·laa gu·(laa·*ndaa*·nee)
reverse the charges	*buyisela izindleko emuva*	b'u·yee·*se*·laa ee·zee·*ndle*·gaw e·*mu*·vaa
use a printer	*sebenzisa iphrinta*	se·b'e·*ndzee*·saa ee·*phree*·nt'aa
use the internet	*sebenzisa i-intanethi*	se·b'e·*ndzee*·saa ee·ee·*nt'aa·ne*·tee

How much is it per hour?
Malini nge-awa?   maa·lee·nee nge·aa·waa

How much does a (three-minute) call cost?
Malini ucingo (lwemizuzu   maa·lee·nee u·k!ee·ngaw (lwe·mee·zu·zu
emithathu)?   e·mee·taa·tu)

(One rand) per minute/hour.
(Irandi) ngomzuzu/nge-awa.   (ee·*raa*·ndee) ngaw·m·*zu*·zu/nge·*aa*·waa

tours

When's the next ...?	*Luzokuba nini ...?*	lu·zaw·gu·baa nee·nee ...
day trip	*uhambo lwemini*	u·haa·mbaw lwe·mee·nee
	yonke	yaw·nk'e
tour	*uhambo*	u·haa·mbaw

Is ... included?	*Sekuhlangene imali ...?*	se·gu·hlaa·nge·ne ee·maa·lee ...
accommodation	*yokuhlala*	yaw·gu·hlaa·laa
the admission charge	*yokungena*	yaw·gu·nge·naa
food	*yokudla*	yaw·gu·dlaa
transport	*yokuthuthwa*	yaw·gu·tu·twaa

How long is the tour?
*Uhambo luthatha isikhathi
esingakanani?*
u·haa·mbaw lu·taa·taa ee·see·kaa·tee
e·see·ngaa·gaa·naa·nee

What time should we be back?
*Kufanele sibuye
ngasikhathi bani?*
gu·faa·ne·le see·b'u·ye
ngaa·see·kaa·tee b'aa·nee

shopping

I'm looking for ...
Ngifuna ...
ngee·*fu*·naa ...

I need film for this camera.
*Ngidinga ifilimu
lale khamera.*
ngee·*dee*·ngaa ee·fee·*lee*·mu
laa·*le* kaa·*me*·raa

Can I listen to this?
Ngingalalela le na?
ngee·ngaa·laa·le·laa le naa

Can I have my ... repaired?
Ngingalungiselwa ... na?
ngee·ngaa·lu·ngee·se·lwaa ... naa

When will it be ready?
Izobe ilungile nini?
ee·zaw·b'e ee·lu·ngee·le nee·nee

How much is it?
Yimalini?
yee·maa·lee·nee

Can you write down the price?
Ungangibhalela inani?
u·ngaa·ngee·baa·le·la ee·naa·nee

What's your lowest price?		
Yini intengo ephansi?		yee·nee een·t'e·ngaw e·paa·nts'ee

I'll give you (five) rands.		
Ngizokunika amarandi (amahlanu).		nge·zaw·gu·nee·gaa aa·maa·*raa*·ndee (aa·ma·*hlaa*·nu)

There's a mistake in the bill.		
Kunesiphosiso esikwenetwini.		gu·ne·see·paw·*see*·saw e·see·kwe·ne·*twee*·nee

It's faulty.		
Ayisebenzi kahle.		a·yee·se·*b'e*·ndzee *gaa*·hle

I'd like a receipt, please.		
Ngicela irisidi.		ngee·*k!e*·laa ee·ree·*see*·dee

I'd like a refund, please.		
Ngicela ukubuyiselwa imali.		ngee·*k!e*·laa u·gu·b'u·yee·*se*·lwaa ee·*maa*·lee

Do you accept ...?	*Nithatha ... na?*	nee·taa·taa ... naa
credit cards	*amakhadi ekhrediti*	aa·maa·kaa·dee e·khre·dee·tee
debit cards	*amakhadi edebithi*	aa·maa·kaa·dee e·de·b'ee·tee
travellers cheques	*amasheke esihambi*	aa·maa·she·ge e·see·haa·mbee

Could you ...?	*Unga-... na?*	u·ngaa·... naa
burn a CD from	*wathatha amafayili*	waa·taa·taa aa·maa·faa·yee·lee
my memory	*ekhadini lami*	e·kaa·dee·nee laa·mee
card	*le-memory*	le·me·maw·ree
	uwabhale ku-CD	u·waa·baa·le gu·see·dee
develop this film	*khulisa leli filimu*	ku·lee·saa le·lee fee·lee·mu

making conversation

Hello.	*Sawubona.* sg	saa·wu·*b'aw*·naa
Hello.	*Sanibonani.* pl	saa·nee·b'aw·*naa*·nee
Good night.	*Lala/Lalani kahle.* sg/pl	laa·laa/laa·laa·nee *gaa*·hle
Goodbye (stay well).	*Sala/Salani kahle.* sg/pl	saa·laa/saa·laa·nee *gaa*·hle
Goodbye (go well).	*Hamba/Hambani kahle.* sg/pl	haa·mbaa/haa·mbaa·nee *gaa*·hle

Mr	*(u)Mnumzane*	(u)·m·nu·m·*zaa*·ne
Mrs	*(u)Nkosikazi*	(u)·nk'aw·see·*gaa*·zee
Ms/Miss	*(u)Nkosazana*	(u)·nk'aw·saa·*zaa*·naa

(the *u* in the Zulu title is omitted when you actually address someone)

How are you?	*Unjani?/Ninjani?* sg/pl	u·njaa·nee/nee·njaa·nee
Fine. And you?	*Sikhona. Nawe/Nani?* sg/pl	see·*kaw*·naa naa·we/naa·nee
What's your name?	*Ngubani igama lakho?*	ngu·*b'aa*·nee ee·*gaa*·maa *laa*·kaw
My name's ...	*Igama lami ngu-...*	ee·*gaa*·maa *laa*·mee ngu·...
I'm pleased to meet you.	*Ngiyajabula ukukwazi/ukunazi.* sg/pl	ngee·yaa·jaa·*b'u*·laa u·gu·*gwaa*·zee/u·gu·*naa*·zee

This is my ...	*Lo ... wami.*	law ... *waa*·mee
brother	*ngumfowethu*	ngu·m·faw·*we*·tu
father	*ngubaba*	ngu·*b'aa*·b'aa
friend	*ngumngane*	ngu·m·*ngaa*·ne
husband	*ngumyeni*	ngu·m·*ye*·nee
mother	*ngumama*	ngu·*maa*·maa
sister	*udadewethu*	u·daa·de·*we*·tu
wife	*ngunkosikazi*	ngu·nk'aw·see·*gaa*·zee

Here's my ...	*Nayi ...*	*naa*·yee ...
What's your ...?	*Lithini ... lakho?*	lee·tee·nee ... laa·kaw
address	*ikheli*	ee·ke·lee
email address	*ikheli le-email*	ee·ke·lee le·e·me·yee·lee

Where are you from?	*Uvelaphi?*	u·ve·laa·pee
I'm from (Australia).	*Ngivela (e-Ostrelia).*	ngee·*ve*·laa (e·aw·stre·*lee*·yaa)

I'm married.	*Ngishadile.*	ngee·shaa·*dee*·le
I'm not married.	*Angishadanga.*	aa·ngee·shaa·*daa*·ngaa
Can I take a photo (of you)?	*Ngicela uku(ku)- thatha isithombe.*	ngee·*kle*·laa u·gu·(gu)· *taa*·taa ee·see·*taw*·mbe

eating out

Can you recommend a ...?	*Ungasitshela ... na?*	u·ngaa·see·ch'e·laa ... naa
bar	*ngendawo yokuphuza oyithandayo*	nge·ndaa·waw yaw·gu·pu·zaa aw·yee·taa·ndaa·yaw
dish	*ngesidlo osithandayo*	nge·see·dlaw aw·see·taa·ndaa·yaw
place to eat	*ngendawo yokudla oyithandayo*	nge·ndaa·waw yaw·gu·dlaa aw·yee·taa·ndaa·yaw

I'd like ..., please.	Ngicela ...	ngee-k!e-laa ...
the bill	irisidi lokukhokha	ee-ree-see-dee law-gu-kaw-kaa
the menu	imenyu	ee-me-nyu
a table (for two)	itafula (yabantu ababili)	ee-t'aa-fu-laa (yaa-b'aa-nt'u aa-b'aa-b'ee-lee)
that dish	leso sidlo	le-saw see-dlaw

Do you have vegetarian food?	Ninokudla kwabangadli nyama?	nee-naw-gu-dlaa gwaa-b'aa-ngaa-dlee nyaa-maa

Could you prepare a meal without ...?	Ungakupheka ukudla ngaphandle kokusebenzisa ... na?	u-ngaa-gu-pe-gaa u-gu-dlaa ngaa-paa-ndle gaw-gu-se-b'e-ndzee-saa ... naa
eggs	amaqanda	aa-maa-kǃaa-ndaa
meat stock	isobho lenyama	ee-saw-baw le-nyaa-maa

(cup of) coffee/tea ...	ikhofi/itiye ...	ee-kaw-fee/ee-t'ee-ye ...
with milk	elinobisi	e-lee-naw-b'ee-see
without sugar	elingenashukela	e-lee-nge-naa-shu-ge-laa

(boiled) water	amanzi (abilisiweyo)	aa-maa-ndzee (aa-b'ee-lee-see-we-yaw)

emergencies

Call ...!	Biza ...!	b'ee-zaa ...
an ambulance	i-ambulense	ee-aa-mbu-le-nts'e
a doctor	udokotela	u-daw-gaw-t'e-laa
the police	amaphoyisa	aa-maa-paw-yee-saa

Could you help me, please?
Ake ungisize/ningisize. sg/pl   aa-ge u-ngee-see-ze/nee-ngee-see-ze

I'm lost.
Ngilahlekile.   ngee-laa-hle-gee-le

Where are the toilets?
Ziphi izindlu zangasese?   zee-pee ee-zee-ndlu zaa-ngaa-se-se

I want to report an offence.
Ngifuna ukubika icala.   ngee-fu-naa u-gu-b'ee-gaa ee-k!aa-laa

I have insurance.
Nginomshwayilense.   ngee-naw-m-shwaa-yee-le-nts'e

I've been assaulted.	Ngilinyaziwe.	ngee·lee·nyaa·zee·we
I've been raped.	Ngidlwenguliwe.	ngee·dlwe·ngu·lee·we
I've been robbed.	Ngigetshengiwe.	ngee·ge·ch'e·ngee·we

| I've lost my ... | | |
| Ngilahlekelwe yi-... | | ngee·laa·hle·ge·lwe yee·... |

| My bags were stolen. | | |
| Amapotimende ami ebiwe. | | aa·maa·p'aw·tee·me·nde aa·mee e·b'ee·we |

| My passport was stolen. | | |
| Iphasiphothi lami lebiwe. | | ee·paa·see·paw·tee laa·mee le·b'ee·we |

| My wallet was stolen. | | |
| Isikhwama sami semali sebiwe. | | ee·see·kwaa·maa saa·mee se·maa·lee se·b'ee·we |

I want to contact my consulate/embassy.		
Ngifuna ukuthintana		ngee·fu·naa u·gu·tee·nt'aa·naa
ne-consulate/ne-embassy.		ne·kaw·nsu·laa·tee/ne·e·mbaa·see

medical needs

Where's the	Ikuphi indawo	ee·gu·pee ee·ndaa·waw
nearest ...?	... eseduzane?	... e·se·du·zaa·ne
dentist	kadokotela	gaa·daw·gaw·te·laa
	wamazinyo	waa·maa·zee·nyaw
doctor	kadokotela	gaa·daw·gaw·te·laa

Where's the nearest hospital?
Sikuphi isibhedlela esiseduzane? see·gu·pee ee·see·be·dle·laa e·see·se·du·zaa·ne

Where's the nearest pharmacist?
Likuphi ikhemisi eliseduzane? lee·gu·pee ee·ke·mee·see e·lee·se·du·zaa·ne

I need a doctor (who speaks English).
Ngidinga udokotela (okwazi ngee·dee·ngaa u·daw·gaw·te·laa (aw·gwaa·zee
ukukhuluma isiNgisi). u·gu·ku·lu·maa ee·see·ngee·see)

Could I see a female doctor?
Ngingabona udokotela ngee·ngaa·b'aw·naa u·daw·gaw·te·laa
wesifazane na? we·se·faa·zaa·ne naa

It hurts here.
Kubuhlungu lapha. gu·b'u·hlu·ngu laa·paa

I'm allergic to (penicillin).
Angizwani na-(nephenisilini). aa·ngee·zwaa·nee naa·(ne·pe·nee·see·lee·nee)

english–zulu dictionary

In this dictionary, words are marked as n (noun), a (adjective), v (verb), sg (singular) and pl (plural) where necessary. Note that in Zulu the pronouns are prefixes attached to the beginning of a verb, as indicated with hyphens in this dictionary. Zulu adjectives usually come after the noun and the form of the adjective changes according to the class of the noun. Just use the form of the adjective given in this dictionary and remember to have it after the noun – it won't be completely correct grammatically, but you should be understood.

A

accommodation *indawo yokulala*
ee-ndaa-waw yaw-gu-*laa*-laa
after *emva kwa-* e-mbvaa gwaa-
airport *isikhumulo samabhanoyi*
ee-see-ku-*mu*-law saa-maa-baa-*naw*-yee
alcohol *utshwala* u-*ch'waa*-laa
all -*onke* -*aw*-nk'e
and (joins nouns) *na-* naa-
and (joins sentences) *futhi* fu-tee
ankle *iqakala* ee-kjaa-*gaa*-laa
arm *ingalo* ee-*ngaa*-law
aspirin *i-aspirin* ee-es-pee-*ree*-nee
asthma *umbefu* u-m-*b'e*-fu
ATM *i-ATM* ee-e-yee-tee-*em*

B

baby *usana* u-*saa*-naa
back (body) *umhlane* u-m-*hlaa*-ne
backpack *unxazisuka* u-n'jaa-zee-*su*-gaa
bad -*bi* -*b'ee*
baggage claim *ithikithi yempahla*
ee-tee-gee-tee ye-*mp'aa*-hlaa
bank *ibhange* ee-*baa*-nge
bathroom *ibhavulumu* ee-baa-vu-*lu*-mu
battery *ibhetri* ee-be-tree
beautiful -*hle* -hle
bed *umbhede* u-m-*be*-te
beer *ubhiya* u-*bee*-ya
bees *izinyosi* ee-zee-*nyaw*-see
before *phambi kwa-* paa-mbee gwaa-
bicycle *ibhayisikili* ee-baa-yee-see-*gee*-lee
big -*khulu* -*ku*-lu
blanket *ingubo* ee-*ngu*-b'aw
blood group *uhlobo lwegazi* u-hlaw-b'aw lwe-*gaa*-zee
bottle *ibhodlela* ee-baw-*dle*-laa
bottle opener *isivulo sebhodlela*
ee-see-*vu*-law se-baw-*dle*-laa
boy *umfana* u-m-*faa*-naa
brakes (car) *amabhuleki* aa-maa-bu-*le*-gee

breakfast *ibhulakufesi* ee-bu-laa-gu-*fe*-see
bronchitis *ukucinana kwesifuba*
u-gu-k!ee-*naa*-naa gwe-see-fu-b'aa

C

café *ikhefi* ee-*ke*-fee
cancel -*khansela* -kaa-*nts'e*-laa
can opener *isivulo sethini* ee-see-*vu*-law se-*tee*-nee
cash n *ukheshe* u-*ke*-she
cell phone *isele* ee-*se*-le
centre n *iphakathi* ee-paa-*gaa*-tee
cheap -*shibhile* -shee-*bee*-le
check (bill) *irisidi lokukhokha*
ee-ree-*see*-dee law-gu-*kaw*-kaa
check-in n *ukubhalisa* u-gu-baa-*lee*-saa
chest *isifuba* ee-see-fu-b'aa
child *umntwana* u-m-*nt'waa*-naa
cigarette *usikilidi* u-see-gee-*lee*-dee
city *idolobha* ee-daw-*law*-baa
clean a -*hlanzekile* -hlaa-ndze-*gee*-le
closed -*valiwe* -vaa-*lee*-we
codeine *i-codeine* ee-kaw-*dee*-nee
cold a -*bandayo* -b'aa-*ndaa*-yaw
collect call *ucingo olukhokhelwa ngolutholayo*
u-k!ee-ngaw aw-lu-kaw-*ke*-lwaa ngaw-lu-taw-*laa*-yaw
condom *ikhondomu* ee-kaw-*ndaw*-mu
constipation *ukuqunjelwa* u-gu-qu-*nje*-lwaa
contact lenses *ama-contact lens* aa-maa-kawn-tekt *lens*
cough n *umkhuhlane* u-m-ku-*hlaa*-ne
currency exchange *ukushintshwa kwezimali*
u-gu-*shee*-nch'waa gwe-zee-*maa*-lee

D

dairy products *imikhiqizo yobisi*
ee-mee-kee-*k!ee*-zaw yaw-*b'ee*-see
dangerous -*nengozi* -ne-*ngaw*-zee
date (time) *usuku* u-*su*-gu
day *ilanga* ee-*laa*-ngaa
diaper *inabukeni* ee-naa-b'u-*k'e*-nee
diarrhoea *uhudo* u-*hu*-daw
dinner *idina* ee-dee-naa

dirty *-ngcolile* -ng!aw-*lee*-le
disabled *-nobulima* -naw-b'u-*lee*-maa
double bed *umbhede wedabuli* u-m-*be*-de we-daa-*b'u*-lee
drink n *isiphuzo* ee-see-*pu*-zaw
drivers licence *ilayisense lokuqhuba*
ee-laa-yee-se-nts'e yaw-gu-*kıhu*-b'aa
drugs (illicit) *izidakamizwa* ee-zee-daa-gaa-*mee*-zwaa

E

ear *indlebe* ee-*ndle*-b'e
east *impumalanga* ee-mp'u-maa-*laa*-ngaa
economy class *iklasi elishibhile*
ee-*klaa*-see e-lee-shee-*bee*-le
elevator (lift) *ikhesi* ee-*ke*-shee
email n *i-e-mail* ee-ee-me-yee-lee
English (language) *isiNgisi* ee-see-*ngee*-see
exchange rate *izinga loshintsho lwezimali*
ee-zee-ngaa law-*shee*-nch'aw lwe-zee-*maa*-lee
exit n *umnyango wokuphuma*
u-m-*nyaa*-ngaw yaw-gu-*pu*-maa
expensive *-dulile* -du-*lee*-le
eye *iso* ee-*saw*

F

fast *ngokusheshisa* ngaw-gu-she-*shee*-saa
fever *imfiva* ee-mpf'ee-vaa
finger *umunwe* u-*mu*-nwe
first-aid kit *ibhokisi losizo lokuqala*
ee-baw-*gee*-see law-see-zaw law-gu-*kıaa*-laa
first class *ufesi* u-*fe*-see
fish n *inhlanzi* ee-*ntl'aa*-ndzee
food *ukudla* u-gu-*dlaa*
foot *unyawo* u-*nyaa*-waw
fork *imfologo* ee-mpf'aw-*law*-gaw
free (of charge) *mahhala* maa-*haa*-laa
fruit *isithelo* ee-see-*te*-law
funny *-hlekisayo* -hle-gee-*saa*-yaw

G

game park *indawo yezilwane zasendle*
ee-*ndaa*-waw ye-zee-*lwaa*-ne zaa-se-ndle
gift *isipho* ee-*see*-paw
girl (older) *intombi* ee-*nt'aw*-mbee
girl (young) *intombazana* ee-nt'aw-mbaa-*zaa*-naa
glass (drinking) *ingilazi* ee-ngee-*laa*-zee
glasses *izibuko* ee-zee-*b'u*-gaw
good *-hle* -hle
gram *igramu* ee-*graa*-mu
guide n *umphelezeli* u-m-pe-le-ze-*lee*

H

hand *isandla* ee-*saa*-ndlaa
happy *-jabule* -jaa-*b'u*-le
have *-na-* -naa-
he *u-* u-
head *ikhanda* ee-*kaa*-ndaa
headache *ikhanda* ee-*kaa*-ndaa
heart *inhliziyo* ee-ntlee-*zee*-yaw
heart condition *isifo senhliziyo*
ee-see-faw se-ntl'ee-*zee*-yaw
heat n *ukushisa* u-gu-*shee*-saa
here *lapha* *laa*-paa
high *-phakamileyo* -paa-gaa-mee-*le*-yaw
highway *umgwaqomkhulu* u-m-gwaa-kıaw-m-*ku*-lu
homosexual n *inkonkoni* ee-nk'aw-*nk'aw*-nee
hot *-shisa* -shee-saa
hungry *-lambile* -laa-*mbee*-le

I

I *ngi-* ngee-
identification (card) *i-ID* ee-aa-yee-*dee*
(be) ill *-gula* -gu-laa
important *-balulekile* -b'aa-lu-le-*gee*-le
internet *i-intanethi* ee-ee-nt'aa-*ne*-tee
interpreter *ihumusha* ee-hu-*mu*-shaa

J

job *umsebenzi* u-m-se-*b'e*-ndzee

K

key *isikhiye* ee-see-*kee*-ye
kilogram *ikhilogramu* ee-kee-law-*graa*-mu
kitchen *ikhishi* ee-*kee*-shee
knife *umese* u-*me*-se

L

laundry (place) *ilondolo* ee-law-*ndaw*-law
lawyer *ummeli* u-m-*me*-lee
leg *umlenze* u-m-*le*-ndze
lesbian n *inkonkoni yesifazane*
ee-nk'aw-*nk'aw*-nee ye-see-faa-*zaa*-ne
less a *-ncane* -*nkıaa*-ne
letter (mail) *incwadi* ee-*nkıwaa*-dee
like v *-thanda* -*taa*-ndaa
love v *-thanda* -*taa*-ndaa
lunch *ilantshi* ee-laa-*nch'ee*

M

man *indoda* ee-*ndaw*-daa
matches *umentshisi* u-me-*nch'ee*-see
meat *inyama* ee-*nyaa*-maa
medicine *umuthi* u-*mu*-tee
message *umlayezo* u-m-laa-*ye*-zaw
mobile phone *isele* ee-*se*-le
month *inyanga* ee-*nyaa*-ngaa
morning *intsasa* ee-*nts'aa*-saa
(in the) morning *ekuseni* e-gu-*se*-nee
motorcycle *isithuthuthu* ee-see-tu-*tu*-tu
mouth *umlomo* u-m-*law*-maw
movie *ibhayisikobho* ee-baa-yee-see-*k'aw*-baw
MSG *i-MSG* ee-em-es-*jee*
museum *imnyuziyamu* ee-m-nyu-zee-*yaa*-mu
music *umculo* u-m-*k͡gu*-law

N

name *igama* ee-*gaa*-maa
napkin (serviette) *iseviyethe* ee-se-vee-*ye*-te
nappy *inabukeni* ee-naa-b'u-*ge*-nee
national park *iphaki elivikelwe lezwe lonke*
  ee-*paa*-gee e-lee-vee-*ge*-lwe *le*-zwe *law*-nk'e
nausea *isicasucasu* ee-see-k!aa-su-*k!aa*-su
neck *intamo* ee-*nt'aa*-maw
new *-sha* -shaa
news *izindaba* ee-zee-*ndaa*-b'aa
newspaper *iphephandaba* ee-pe-paa-*ndaa*-b'aa
night *ubusuku* u-b'u-*su*-gu
nightclub *iklabhu yasebusuku*
  ee-*klaa*-bu yaa-se-b'u-*su*-gu
noisy *-nomsindo* -naw-m-see-ndaw
nonsmoking *lapho kungebhenywe khona*
  laa-paw gu-nge-*be*-nywe *kaw*-naa
north *inyakatho* ee-nyaa-*gaa*-taw
nose *impumulo* ee-mp'u-*mu*-law
now *manje* maa-*nje*
number (numeral) *inombolo* ee-naw-*mbaw*-law
number (quantity) *inani* ee-*naa*-nee
nuts *amantongomane* aa-maa-nt'aw-ngaw-*maa*-ne

O

oil (engine) *uwoyela* u-waw-*ye*-laa
OK *kulungile* gu-lu-*ngee*-le
old (objects) *-dala* -*daa*-laa
old (people) *-khulile* -ku-*lee*-le
open a *-vuliwe* -vu-*lee*-we
outside *ngaphandle* ngaa-*paa*-ndle

P

package *iphasela* ee-paa-*se*-laa
pain *ubuhlungu* u-b'u-*hlu*-ngu
paper *iphepha* ee-*pe*-paa
park (car) v *-paka* -*paa*-gaa
passport *iphasiphothi* ee-paa-see-*paw*-tee
pay *-khokha* -*kaw*-kaa
pen *ipeni* ee-*pe*-nee
petrol *uphethilolo* u-pe-tee-*law*-law
pharmacy *ikhemisi* ee-ke-*mee*-see
plate *isitsha* ee-see-*ch'aa*
postcard *iposikhadi* ee-p'aw-see-*kaa*-dee
post office *iposi* ee-*paw*-see
pregnant *-khulelwe* -ku-*le*-lwe

R

rain n *imvula* ee-*mbvu*-laa
razor *ireza* ee-*re*-zaa
registered mail *iposi elirejistiwe*
  ee-*p'aw*-see e-lee-re-jee-*st'ee*-we
rent v *-qashisa* -k꞉aa-*shee*-saa
repair v *-lungisa* -lu-*ngee*-saa
reservation (place) *indawo ebhukiwe*
  ee-*ndaa*-waw e-bu-*gee*-we
reservation (table) *itafula elibhukiwe*
  ee-t'aa-*fu*-laa e-lee-bu-*gee*-we
restaurant *ikhefi* ee-*ke*-fee
return (come back) *-buya* -*b'u*-yaa
return (give back) *-buyisa* -b'u-*yee*-saa
road *indlela* ee-*ndle*-laa
room *ikamelo* ee-k'aa-*me*-law

S

sad *-dabukile* -daa-b'u-*gee*-le
safe a *-ngenangozi* -nge-naa-*ngaw*-zee
sanitary napkins *amaphede* aa-maa-*pe*-te
seafood *ukudla okuvela olwandle*
  u-gu-dlaa aw-gu-ve-laa aw-*lwaa*-ndle
seat *isihlalo* ee-see-*hlaa*-law
send (someone) *-thuma* -tu-maa
send (something) *-thumela* -tu-*me*-laa
sex *ukalalana* u-gu-laa-*laa*-naa
shampoo *ishampu* ee-*shaa*-mp'u
share (a dorm, etc) *ukulala sibaningi ekamelweni*
  u-gu-*laa*-laa see-b'aa-*nee*-ngee e-k'a-me-*lwe*-nee
shaving cream *umuthi wokushefa*
  u-*mu*-tee waw-gu-*she*-faa
she *u-* u-
sheet (bed) *ishidi* ee-*shee*-dee

shirt *iyembe* ee-ye-mbe
shoes *izicathulo* ee-zee-k!aa-*tu*-law
shop n *ivenkile* ee-ve-*nk'ee*-le
shower n *ishawa* ee-*shaa*-waa
skin *isikhumba* ee-see-*ku*-mbaa
skirt *isiketi* ee-see-*k'e*-tee
sleep v -*lala* -*laa*-laa
small -*ncane* -*nk!aa*-ne
smoke (cigarettes) v -*bhema* -*be*-maa
smoking a *lapho kungabhenywa khona*
  laa-paw gu-ngaa-*be*-nywaa *kaw*-naa
soap *insipho* ee-*nts'ee*-paw
some -*nye* -nye
soon *masinyane* maa-see-*nyaa*-ne
sore throat *umphimbo obuhlungu*
  u-*m-pee*-mbaw aw-*b'u-hlu*-ngu
south *iningizimu* ee-nee-ngee-*zee*-mu
speak -*khuluma* -ku-lu-maa
spoon *ukhezo* u-*ke*-zaw
stamp *isitembu* ee-see-*t'e*-mbu
station (train) *isiteshi* ee-see-*t'e*-shee
stomach *isisu* ee-*see*-su
stop v -*ma* -maa
stop (bus) n *isitobhi (sebhasi)*
  ee-see-*t'aw*-bee (se-*baa*-see)
street *umgwaqo* u-*m-gwaa*-kjaw
student *umfundi* u-*m-fu*-ndee
sunscreen *i-sunscreen* ee-saan-*skree*-nee
swim v -*bhukuda* -bu-*gu*-daa

T

tampons *amathemponi* aa-maa-te-*mp'aw*-nee
teeth *amazinyo* aa-maa-*zee*-nyaw
telephone n *ucingo* u-*klee*-ngaw
television *umabonakude* u-maa-*b'aw*-naa-*gu*-de
temperature (weather) *izinga lokushisa*
  ee-zee-ngaa law-gu-*shee*-saa
tent *itende* ee-*t'e*-nde
that (one near you) *leyo* le-yaw
that (one in the distance) *leya* le-*yaa*
they (animals & objects) *zi-* zee-
they (people) *ba-* b'aa-
thirsty -*omile* -aw-*mee*-le
this (one) *le* le
throat *umphimbo* u-*m-pee*-mbaw
ticket *ithikithi* ee-tee-*gee*-tee
time *isikhathi* ee-see-*kaa*-tee
tired -*khathele* -kaa-*te*-le
today *namhlanje* naa-m-hlaa-*nje*

toilet *indlu yangasese* ee-ndlu yaa-ngaa-*se*-se
tonight *namhlanje ebusuku* naa-m-hlaa-*nje* e-b'u-*su*-gu
toothbrush *isixubho* ee-see-*kju*-baw
toothpaste *umuthi wokugeza amazinyo*
  u-*mu*-tee waw-gu-*ge*-zaa aa-maa-*zee*-nyaw
torch (flashlight) *ithoshi* ee-*taw*-shee
towel *ithawula* ee-taa-wu-laa
translate -*humusha* -hu-*mu*-sha
travellers cheque *isheke lezihambi*
  ee-*she*-ge le-*zee-haa*-mbee
trousers *ibhulukwe* ee-bu-*lu*-gwe
tyre *ithaya* ee-*taa*-yaa

V

vacant -*ngenamuntu* -nge-naa-*mu*-nt'u
vegetable n *umfino* u-m-*fee*-naw
vegetarian a *okungenanyama* aw-gu-nge-na-*nyaa*-maa
visa *iviza* ee-*vee*-zaa

W

waiter *uweta* u-*we*-t'aa
walk v -*hamba ngezinyawo*
  -*haa*-mbaa nge-zee-*nyaa*-waw
wallet *isikhwama* ee-see-*kwaa*-maa
warm a -*fudumele* -fu-du-*me*-le
wash (something) -*geza* -*ge*-zaa
watch n *iwashi* ee-*waa*-shee
water *amanzi* aa-*maa*-ndzee
weekend *impelasonto* ee-mp'e-laa-*saw*-nt'aw
west *intshonalanga* ee-nch'aw-naa-*laa*-ngaa
wheelchair *isitulo esinamasondo*
  ee-see-*t'u*-law e-see-naa-maa-*saw*-ndaw
when *nini* nee-nee
where *kuphi* gu-*pee*
who sg *ubani* u-*b'aa*-nee
who pl *obani* aw-*b'aa*-nee
why *yini* yee-nee
window *ifasitela* ee-faa-see-*t'e*-laa
wine *iwayini* ee-waa-*yee*-nee
with *na-* naa-
without (someone) *engekho* e-*nge*-kaw
without (something – eg milk, sugar)
  -*ngena* -nge-naa-
woman *inkosikazi* ee-*nk'aw*-see-*gaa*-zee
write -*bhala* -*baa*-laa

Y

you sg *u-* u-
you pl *ni-* nee-

Culture

The glory of Africa is the sheer diversity of its myriad cultures – from rich **histories** and varied **cuisines** to colourful **festivals**, Africa has it all. Here we present you with a cultural snapshot of the region and give you the tools to communicate and travel in an exciting, respectful and **sustainable** way.

history timeline

Take a wander through the rich history of Africa …

1 million – 10,000 BC	The evolution and rise of *Homo sapiens* (modern man), who, most scientists agree, originated in Africa and then spread around the world.
9000 – 3000 BC	Agricultural development begins in the Sahel, the Sahara desert and North Africa, which were home to lakes, rainforests and a pleasant Mediterranean climate.
5000 BC	Global climate change initiates the long process of turning the Sahara into a desert, and people begin migrating south towards the Gulf of Guinea.
4000 – 3000 BC	West Africa's peoples forsake nomadic life and settle in communities, domesticating cattle and cultivating native plants.
2000 BC	The Bantu people begin migrating from West Africa, eventually reaching East Africa by 100 BC and Southern Africa by AD 300.
1000 BC	The Aksum Empire is established in Ethiopia by the son of the Queen of Sheba. It lasts until 1974, when the 237th emperor, Haile Selassie, is deposed.
800 BC	Phoenicians from Tyre in modern-day Lebanon establish the colony of Carthage in Tunisia.
6th century BC	At this point, the Phoenicians control much of the trade taking place in the Mediterranean.
500 – 400 BC	Iron smelting has been established in Nigeria, central Niger and southern Mali.
AD 300	The Ghana Empire is founded. By the 8th century it has profited from its control of trans-Saharan trade and from its legendary gold deposits.
333	The Aksum Empire's King Ezana adopts Christianity as the official religion of his kingdom.
639	Islam sweeps through North Africa, largely displacing Christianity. By AD 1000, traders from the north have introduced it to West Africa via the Saharan trade routes.
750	The Swahili civilisation – a rich mixture of Bantu, Arabic, Persian and Asian influences – begins to flourish in East Africa.

11th century	Great Zimbabwe attains power and wealth by trading gold and ivory with Swahili traders. It triumphs for 400 years, but collapses by the 16th century.
late 11th century	The Ghana Empire is defeated by the Muslim Berbers of the Almoravid Empire from Mauritania and Morocco.
13th century	Eleven rock-hewn churches are built in Lalibela, Ethiopia. Stunning examples of monolithic architecture, they are cut straight from the bedrock, with their roofs at ground level.
c. 1235	Sundiata Keita, the leader of the Malinké people, establishes the Mali Empire. He adopts the 'Charter of Kurukanfuga', which includes a clause prohibiting slavery.
from 1235	The Mali Empire has expanded to control almost all trans-Saharan trade. This brings great wealth to its rulers, who enthusiastically embrace Islam.
14th century	The Dogon people first move into central Mali, where they build unique rock and mud villages consisting of buildings for each sex and a central square where most ceremonies are held.
1325	The Arab architect Abu Ishap Es-Saheli Altouwaidjin constructs Timbuktu's oldest mosque, Dyingerey Ber Mosque.
early 15th century	The Sankoré Mosque is built in Timbuktu. Also functioning as a university, it becomes one of the largest schools of Arabic learning in the Muslim world by the 16th century.
1443	The Portuguese, while seeking to exploit the Arab and Muslim-dominated gold trade, reach the mouth of the Senegal River.
1444	The first slaves are brought to Portugal from Mauritania.
mid-15th century	The power of the Mali Empire has declined. The Songhaï Empire, also established in Mali, is at the height of its powers and rules over much of West Africa.
1482	The Portuguese build St George's Castle – the earliest European structure in Sub-Saharan Africa – at Elmina, Ghana.
1487	The Portuguese explorer Bartholomeu Dias successfully navigates the Cape of Good Hope in Southern Africa.
1490	The first Christian missionaries come to Sub-Saharan Africa at the request of King Nzinga of Kongo (also known as the Manikongo) and rebuild the capital in stone at Mbanza Kongo.
1510	The Spanish start shipping the first African slaves to their colonies in South America.

17th century	Islam becomes the Sahel's dominant religion. The Tofinu in Benin flee from slave hunters to the swampy Ganvié region, and establish Africa's only village of bamboo huts on stilts.
1699	Tulbagh in South Africa is first settled. It is famous for Church Street, one of the most complete examples of an 18th- and 19th-century Cape Dutch village in South Africa.
1728	East Africa's first known Swahili manuscript, an epic poem written in Arabic script, is penned.
early 19th century	Bioko Island in Equatorial Guinea becomes an important slave-trading base for many European nations.
1813	One of the earliest written accounts of the highly-symbolic mural art (*litema*) of the Basotho people of southern Africa appears. The art's bright colours and geometric shapes were originally painted on houses as a plea for rain and good fortune.
1816	Shaka Zulu becomes chief of the Zulu kingdom in southern Africa, sparking the *difaqane* (or forced migration) that accelerates the formation of Sotho (Lesotho) and Swazi (Swaziland).
1850–80s	The 'Marabout Wars' are fought between Islam's holy warriors and Europeans in Senegal.
1860	Livingstone House – which was later used a base by many European missionaries, including David Livingstone – is built in Zanzibar for Sultan Majid.
1870	The slave trade is officially abolished.
1871	Anthropologist EB Tylor coins the term 'animism'. It can be used to describe almost all traditional African religions, which attribute life or consciousness to natural objects or phenomena.
1881	Adventurer and explorer Henry Morgan Stanley allegedly utters the famous words 'Dr Livingstone, I presume' after he journeys into Congo (Zaïre) in search of the good doctor Livingstone.
1884–85	Africa is split into French, British, German, Portuguese, Italian, Spanish and Belgian colonies at the Berlin Conference.
1893	The Grande Mosquée is built in Burkina Faso. Designed in the Sahel mud-brick style, it consists of conical towers and wooden struts that support the structure.
1907	The Djenné Mosque, another classic of Sahel mud-brick architecture, is built in Mali. It is based on the design of an older mosque (built in 1280) that once stood on the site.
1910	Union of South Africa created, with no voting rights for blacks.

1913	Theologian, philosopher and musician Albert Schweitzer moves to Lambaréné, Gabon, and builds a hospital to serve humanity in what is regarded as the heart of 'darkest, savage' Africa.
1948	Apartheid is institutionalised in South Africa.
1951	Libya becomes the first African country to win independence.
1960	Independence is granted to a host of African nations, including Mali, Senegal, Madagascar, Niger, Nigeria and Mauritania.
1970s	Oil is discovered in Gabon. The discovery helps make the central African nation one of the richest in Sub-Saharan Africa.
1974	The Aksum empire ends when Emperor Haile Selassie is deposed.
1975	The Portuguese exit their colony at São Tomé & Príncipe, leaving it with virtually no skilled labour, a 90 per cent illiteracy rate, only one doctor and many derelict cocoa plantations.
1976	The Soweto uprising, which protests against the use of the Afrikaans language in black schools, begins in South Africa.
1977	Central African Republic dictator Jean-Bédel Bokassa has himself crowned 'emperor' of a renamed Central African Empire. France pays most of the US$20 million coronation bill.
1990–91	The legal apparatus of apartheid is abolished in South Africa.
1994	Nelson Mandela, president of the African National Congress, is elected president in South Africa's first democratic elections.
1996	Voodoo (or *vodou*) is formally recognised as a religion in Benin. Its followers believe in a supreme god, and a host of lesser spirits that are ethnically specific to them and their ancestors.
1999	South African novelist JM Coetzee is awarded the Booker Prize for a second time for *Disgrace*.
2001	Kenya's Lamu Old Town, the oldest and best-preserved Swahili settlement in East Africa, becomes a Unesco World Heritage Site.
2011	The 'Arab Spring' series of popular uprisings sees long-time African leaders Zine El Abidine Ben Ali in Tunisia, Hosni Mubarak in Egypt and Colonel Qaddafi in Libya ousted from power.

food

Africa, the second-largest landmass on Earth, is home to hundreds of tribes, ethnic and social groups with traditions that have been influenced by Arab, European and Asian colonisers. From desert areas to verdant coasts, it's also a land of extremes that affect the range of ingredients available to its inhabitants. Still, as you travel through this great continent, you are sure to encounter staples peculiar to the region you are in.

Starch forms the basis of all African meals and has many regional variations. *Ugali* is generally made from maize (corn) flour and has a consistency varying from porridge to a stiff dough. Also referred to as *posho* (Uganda), *nshima* (Zambia), *nsima* (Mali), *sadza* (Zimbabwe), *mealie pap* (South Africa) and *chakula* (Tanzania), *ugali* is an important part of the diet of east and southern Africans, as the crops that produce corn flour grow well in poor conditions. Millet and rice are both popular in West Africa, as is *foufou*, a thick paste (a bit like mashed potatoes mixed with gelatine) made with root vegetables like yam or cassava. To eat *ugali* or *foufou* local-style, grab a portion and roll it into a ball before dipping it with your right hand into the accompanying sauce or vegetable or meat stew. If you can, try *sauce arachide*, a thick brown paste made from groundnuts (peanuts) – it may stain your fingers, but the taste is well worth it!

Couscous is ubiquitous in North Africa, particularly in Morocco, where it's the national dish. It's both an ingredient (a semolina native in varying forms in North Africa) and the name of a dish (the semolina topped with a rich stew). The holy grail is Moroccan couscous, a perfumed, spicy and fragrant concoction that includes any number of elements such as meat, seasonal vegetables, dried fruit and nuts. Another delectable Moroccan speciality is *pastilla*, a rich savoury-sweet dish with a filling made from pigeon meat and lemon-flavoured eggs plus almonds, cinnamon, saffron and sugar, encased in layers of paper-fine pastry.

Once famously mistaken by an American tourist for the tablecloth, *injera* is a large, thin, slightly bitter pancake that forms the base of almost every Ethiopian meal. Quite a clever invention, *injera* does away with the need for plates, bowls and even utensils: it's either wrapped around small pieces of food or simply heaped with the food. Good-quality *injera* is pale (the paler the better), regular in thickness, smooth and always made with the cereal *tef*, native to the Ethiopian highlands. The favourite companion of *injera* is *wat*, Ethiopia's version of stew. Most commonly made with *bege* (lamb), *wat* can also consist of *bure* (beef), *figel* (goat) or *doro* (chicken). It can also be boiled in a spicy sauce made with oodles of *berbere*, a red powder containing up to 16 spices.

Chillies or *jaxatu* (similar to a green or yellow tomato but extremely bitter) are used to flavour dishes in Nigeria and other coastal regions of West Africa, where seafood is abundant. Okra, which is native to Africa, is also popular – the cooked result is a slimy green concoction that tastes a whole lot better than it looks – as are black-eyed peas. These ingredients feature in dishes widely available in West Africa, including the ubiquitous *jollof* (rice and vegetables with meat or fish), *kedjenou* (Côte d'Ivoire's national dish of slowly simmered chicken or fish with peppers and tomatoes) and *poulet yassa* (a Senegalese dish of rice baked in a thick sauce of fish and vegetables).

In South Africa, you will not only encounter the unusual *biltong* (dried meat), but a fusion of culinary influences: the hearty meat-and-vegetable stews dating from the early days of Dutch settlement, spicy curries from India, and the melange of local produce and Asian spices that is Cape (Malay) cuisine. Cape dishes to watch out for include *bobotie* (a curried mince pie topped with egg custard, usually served with rice and chutney), *waterblommetjie bredie* (lamb stew mixed with water-hyacinth flowers and white wine) and *malva* (a delicious sponge dessert with apricot jam and vinegar).

Tea and coffee are standard drinks throughout the continent, but there are some interesting variations. These include Swahili tea or coffee spiced with lemongrass or cardamom in East Africa, coffee flavoured with a woody leaf called *kinkiliba* in West Africa, and a marriage of black tea with mint in Morocco. In Ethiopia, where coffee was discovered between the 5th and 10th centuries, the coffee ceremony elevates coffee drinking to an art form. After a meal, the host invokes nature by sprinkling freshly cut grass on the ground, then roasts coffee beans in a pan over a tiny charcoal stove. The roasted beans are ground up with a mortar and pestle before being brewed, and the coffee is served in tiny china cups. The guest is obliged to accept at least three cups – the third in particular is considered to bestow a blessing upon the drinker.

While imported alcoholic drinks are available in most African countries, it's worth trying the local brew. *Tej*, the Ethiopian honey mead, used to be the drink of Ethiopian kings. It's a delicious and pretty powerful drink, fermented using a local shrub known as *gesho*. In the Sahel region of West Africa, locals make a rough, brown, gritty beer (called *chakalow* or *kojo*) using millet. However, the most popular drink in West Africa is palm wine, a milky-white low-strength brew made from the sap from palm trees.

Argungu Fishing Festival (Argungu, Nigeria)

First held in 1934 to mark peace between the former Sokoto Caliphate and the Kebbi kingdom, the Argungu Fishing Festival is the climax of an annual four-day cultural event held in Nigeria's Kebbi state. Thanks to a fishing ban along a one-mile stretch of the Sokoto River, a plentiful bounty of fish is ensured for the thousands of local fisherman who, armed with nets and gourds, compete to find the biggest fish. The event begins with the competitors leaping into the Sokoto River at the sound of a starting gun. As the men madly scramble to find the 'catch of the day', drummers move through the surging water on canoes, providing a soundtrack to the proceedings. After an hour, the men stagger up stone steps with their fish for the verdict. One year the winning fish weighed 75 kilos, for which the fisherman was awarded a brand new bus and one million *naira* (about $US7000).

Cape Town New Year Karnaval (South Africa)

On 2 January each year from the early 19th century, Cape Town slaves celebrated a day of freedom they christened *Tweede Nuwe Jaar* (Second New Year), a kind of independence day for the coloured community. Today, each 31 December and 2 January, Capetonians honour this tradition with noisy, joyous and disorganised parades of marching troupes made up of members from a particular neighbourhood of the city and decked out in make-up and colourful costumes in every colour of satin, sequin and glitter. Throughout January and early February these troupes also participate in a minstrel competition, where they perform ribald song-and-dance routines inspired by American minstrels who visited the Cape in the early 20th century. Even if they don't emerge victorious, they are still winners in the eyes of their local communities, who provide them with booze and an array of delicious Cape cuisine.

Djenné Festival (Djenné, Mali)

Each spring, members of Djenné's community work together to maintain the city's Great Mosque. It's a festive occasion accompanied by music, food and fun for all involved. The focus of the renovations is the replastering of the mosque – but first the plaster, which cures for days in large vats, has to be prepared. During this time, boys caked with mud from head to toe stir the mixture by playing barefoot in the vats. The actual plastering work begins before dawn, and is heralded with chanting, drumming and flute playing. Young women carry buckets of water to the mosque on their head, while one group of men carries plaster from the pits to other men who climb onto the mosque's built-in scaffolding to smear the plaster on its walls. This all happens under the gaze of elderly community members, who sit in a place of honor in the town's market square.

Festival au Désert (Essakane, Mali)

Held in the desert oasis of Essakane, 65 kilometres from Timbuktu, the Festival au Désert focuses on the culture of the Tuareg nomads of the Sahara, who traditionally held festivals to race camels, stage sword fights, settle scores, make policy and play music. The Festival au Désert allows outsiders, including Westerners and other tribes, to experience these customs for the first time. The festival straddles the traditional and modern, with daytime cultural events (including dancing, swordplay, camel races and artisans' exhibits) and electrifying music after the sun goes down. Western artists like Robert Plant and Damon Albarn (of the band Blur) have played at the festival, but with their gourd guitars plugged into amps and screaming against a hypnotising backdrop of indigenous rhythms supplied by tom-toms, bongos, tindé drums and water drums, the traditional Saharan and African musicians are the real stars of the show.

Fez Sacred Music Festival (Fez, Morocco)

Sufi whirling dervishes, Berber trance music, Arab-Andalusian music, Hindustani chants, Celtic sacred music, Christian gospel, flamenco, and the Philharmonic Orchestra of Morocco: all have featured at the Fez Sacred Music Festival. Renowned as one of the world's greatest music festivals, the Fez Festival brings together the musical traditions of religions from across the globe in a fitting setting – the ancient holy city of Fez, where Christian, Jewish and Islamic communities have coexisted peacefully for centuries. The festival is held each June/July and features both paid and free performances . The paid performances are held under a majestic Barbary oak in the gardens of the 100-year-old Hispano-Moorish Batha Museum, and in the courtyard of the splendid Bab Makina palace, while the free performances are staged in the grand Bab Bou Jeloud Square and Dar Tazi Gardens.

Imilchil Marriage Feast (Marrakech, Morocco)

According to legend, a man and a woman from two local Moroccan tribes once fell in love, but were forbidden to marry by their families. The man and woman cried themselves to death, creating the neighbouring lakes of Issly and Tisslit near Imilchil in the Middle-High Atlas Mountains. The devastated families honoured the anniversary of the lovers' deaths by establishing a day on which members of the two tribes could marry each other. On this day – the Imilchil Marriage Feast – potential husbands survey the single women done up in traditional dress by their families (their pointed head apparel gives them away). Once a man has found a suitor, he makes his proposal. The woman can either refuse the offer, or accept it by uttering the words, 'You have captured my liver.' And so with these immortal words, the pair joins the 40 other couples tying the knot on this festive day.

La Cure Salée (In-Gall, Niger)

La Cure Salée (The Salt Cure) is a sort of homecoming for the nomadic Fula and Tuareg peoples, who bring their animals to the area around In-Gall during the rainy season. Supervised by their owners – who sit on camels, catching up with old friends and frequently camel racing – the animals partake in the 'salt cure', slurping up a healthy dose of minerals to sustain them during the dry months ahead. For the Wodaabé sect of the Fulani, it is also the time of the Gerewol festival, an event in which Wodaabé men aim to impress eligible women by participating in a 'beauty contest' featuring a dance intended to display their beauty, charisma and charm. The women are looking for tall lean bodies, long slender noses, white even teeth and bright eyes – the men oblige by preening themselves for hours in an effort to highlight their assets. The prize? A highly-sought-after marriage proposal.

The Maitisong Festival (Gaborone, Botswana)

Back in the 1980s, when officials of the Maru-a-Pula School were planning to build a hall, they decided it should be available to the whole community of Gaborone, which at the time had nowhere to stage professional performances. The hall was completed at the beginning of 1987, and was introduced to the public with the Maitisong Festival shortly after. Testament to the saying, 'From little things big things grow', the festival is now the largest arts festival in Botswana, and attracts big names from all over the nation and region. Featuring a range of films, dance troupes, drama and music, the festival is renowned for the huge gospel and pop performances to which thousands of locals flock. Locals also get in on the act themselves – to keep everyone happy during the intervals of free outdoor concerts, they get up on stage and perform impromptu music, dance and comedy acts!

The Serengeti-Masai Mara Wildebeest Migration (Tanzania-Kenya)

According to African legend, the curious-looking wildebeest was created using left-over parts. Still he is the undeniable star of one of nature's most stunning spectacles. It is difficult to pinpoint when the wildebeest – who are accompanied by small numbers of zebras, elands and Thompson's gazelles – will begin their exodus from the dry plains of Serengeti National Park to the nutrient-rich grassy landscape of Kenya's Masai-Mara region, but the best time to see the migration is usually between June and August, when the animals congregate and prepare to cross the Grumeti River enroute to the Masai-Mara. Here gigantic crocodiles await their prey and the animals try not to stumble as they cross the teeming waters. Witnessing animals fall victim to the hungry crocodiles can be upsetting, but being in the Masai-Mara area as up to one and a half million animals pour in is truly mind-blowing.

Timkat (Feast of Epiphany) Festival (Ethiopia)

Held on 19 January each year, Timkat commemorates John the Baptist's blessing of Jesus Christ. On the eve of Timkat, *ketera* (priests) remove the *tabot* (symbolizing the Ark of the Covenant containing the Ten Commandments) from each church and cover it in layers of rich cloth to protect it from impious eyes. Accompanied by men, women and children dressed in dazzling white traditional dress – a dramatic contrast to the jewelled colours of the priests' ceremonial robes and sequinned velvet umbrellas – the *tabot* is carried to a pool of water or river to be blessed for the next day's celebration. People camp here throughout the night, eating and drinking by fire- and torch-light. Towards dawn, members of the congregation gather around the blessed water, and are symbolically baptised by the priest. The *tabots* are then taken back to their respective churches and the festivities ramp up.

Umhlanga (Reed) Dance (Lombaba, Swaziland)

In August or September each year, young maidens from all parts of Swaziland gather in the nation's royal heartland. They come voluntarily in their thousands to learn skills that will help them to handle married life in a dignified manner, and to perform a traditional 'reed dance' for the Swazi King. From this performance, the King, who typically takes over 400 wives during his lifetime, chooses a bride. For their big moment, the women wear a traditional costume of *ligcebesha* (a beaded necklace with colours of the Swazi flag), *umgaco* (colourful beads with wooly tassels that hang from the left shoulder to the right hip) and *indlamu* (short beaded skirts) and perform with reeds they have hand-picked. The dance attracts many tourists and, when it is over, the reeds are taken to the royal village where they are used to make wind breakers for the queen mother's house.

sustainable travel

What is sustainable travel and responsible tourism?

Being a responsible tourist in Africa means acknowledging that travel inevitably impacts on the host communities and environment you visit – when you travel, you're not only embracing the diversity of this big, wide wonderful world, but you're adding your footprints to those left by some of the 1-billion-plus people who travel internationally each year. This runaway juggernaut affects wilderness, native species and traditional cultures. The goal is to make the impact as positive as possible by giving back to local communities and acting to minimise negative outcomes. In doing so, you are helping to make your steps lighter, greener and friendlier.

How can travel to Africa have a positive effect on local African industries and wildlife?

A land of stunning geography, all-night partying and wondrous architecture, Africa is also the ultimate destination to observe the 'Big Five' (elephant, rhinoceros, leopard, lion and Cape buffalo) in their natural habitat. However, with the global inequities of wealth distribution so pronounced in Africa, it's particularly important to ensure that your travel enjoyment is not at the expense of locals and their environment.

At one level, the impact of tourism can be positive – it can provide an incentive for locals to preserve environments and wildlife by generating employment, while enabling them to maintain their traditional lifestyles. However, the negative impacts of tourism can be substantial and contribute to the gradual erosion of traditional life. You can try to keep your impact as low as possible by considering the following tips:

- Support local enterprise. Use locally owned hotels and restaurants and buy souvenirs directly from the tradespeople and craftspeople who make them.
- Don't buy items made from natural materials such as ivory, skins and shells.
- Choose safari and trekking operators that treat local communities as equal partners, and that are committed to protecting local ecosystems.
- Question any so-called eco-tourism operators for specifics about what they're really doing to protect the environment and the people who live there.
- Instead of giving cash, food or medicines to locals, make a donation to a recognised project such as a health centre or school.
- Try to get a balanced view of life in developed countries, and focus on the strong points of local culture.
- Resist the local tendency to be indifferent to littering. On treks, in parks or when camping, carry out your litter and leave areas cleaner than you found them.
- In order to help minimise land degradation, keep to the tracks when walking or when on safari, or encourage your driver to do so.

safari

What are the main safari regions in Africa?

East and Southern Africa have a clutch of popular parks showcasing some of the greatest wildlife spectacles on earth. Highlights in East Africa, where Swahili is commonly spoken, are the magnificent Serengeti–Masai Mara ecosystem; the wildlife-packed Ngorongoro Crater and Tarangire National Park in Tanzania; Parc National de Volcans, Rwanda's original *Gorillas in the Mist* backdrop; and the hippo-, crocodile- and elephant-filled Murchison Falls and Budongo Central Forest Reserve with its chimpanzees and dense forest, in Uganda. In Southern Africa, where Afrikaans, Xhosa and Zulu are the most common languages, you'll find world-class wildlife watching at South Africa's Madikwe Game Reserve, Pilanesberg National Park, and its safari showpiece Kruger National Park; in Swaziland, there's the wildlife-rich Mkhaya Game Reserve, noted for its black rhinos, and the evocative Phinda Resource Reserve.

In the following, we give you the vocabulary you need to communicate effectively and respectfully in the two main languages spoken in these popular safari areas. The symbol ⓐ indicates Afrikaans and ⓢ indicates Swahili.

safari animals		
buffalo	*buffel* ⓐ	*bi*·fil
	mbogo ⓢ	m·*boh*·goh
camel	*kameel* ⓐ	ka·*meyl*
	ngamia ⓢ	ngaa·*mee*·aa
crocodile	*krokodil* ⓐ	kraw·ku·*dil*
	mamba ⓢ	*maam*·baa
elephant	*olifant* ⓐ	*oo*·lee·fant
	ndovu/tembo ⓢ	n·*doh*·voo/*teym*·boh
giraffe	*kameelperd* ⓐ	ka·*meyl*·pert
	twiga ⓢ	*twee*·gaa
leopard	*luiperd* ⓐ	*lay*·pirt
	chui ⓢ	*choo*·ee
lion	*leeu* ⓐ	*ley*·u
	simba ⓢ	*seem*·baa
monkey	*tumbili* ⓢ	toom·*bee*·lee
	apie ⓐ	*aa*·pi
rhinoceros	*renoster* ⓐ	ri·*naws*·tir
	kifaru ⓢ	kee·*faa*·roo
zebra	*sebra* ⓐ	*sey*·bra
	punda milia ⓢ	*poon*·daa mee·*lee*·aa

I'd like to stay at a locally run safari park.

Ek wil in 'n safaripark bly wat deur   ek vil in i sa·*faa*·ree·park blay vat deyr
plaaslike mense bestuur word. ⓐ   *plaas*·li·ki *men*·si bi·*stewr* vort

I'd like to visit a native-style tourist station.

Ningependa kufikia kwenye   neen·*gey*·*peyn*·daa koo·*fee*·kaa *kweyn*·yey
kituo cha kitalii cha   kee·*too*·oh chaa kee·taa·*lee* chaa
kienyeji. ⓢ   kee·*eyn*·*yey*·jee

Are there any eco-lodges at the park?

Is daar enige eko-hutte in die park? ⓐ   is daar *ee*·ni·khi *ee*·ku·hi·ti in dee park

Are there any local-style guesthouses in the park?

Kuna nyumba za wageni za   koo·naa *nyoom*·baa zaa waa·*gey*·nee zaa
kienyeji ndani ya hifadhi? ⓢ   kee·*eyn*·*yey*·jee n·*daa*·nee yaa hee·*faa*·dhee

Are there fair working standards at this park?

Is die werksomstandighede   is dee *verks*·om·*stan*·dikh·hee·di
in hierdie park billik? ⓐ   in *heer*·dee park *bi*·lik
Kuna viwango vya kazi za   koo·naa vee·*waan*·goh vyaa *kaa*·zee zaa
kistaarabu ndani ya   kee·staa·*raa*·boo n·*daa*·nee yaa
hifadhi? ⓢ   hee·*faa*·dhee

Does your business have responsible tourism policies?

Het julle besigheid 'n   het *ji*·li *bey*·sikh·hayt i
verantwoordelike toerismebeleid? ⓐ   fir·ant·*voor*·di·li·ki tu·*ris*·mi·bi·*layt*

Is your business involved in tourism activities that protect the environment?

Biashara yako   bee·aa·*shaa*·raa *yaa*·koh
inajihusisha na shughuli   ee·naa·jee·hoo·*see*·shaa naa shoo·*goo*·lee
za kitalii kuhifadhi   zaa kee·taa·*lee* koo·hee·*faa*·dhee
mazingira? ⓢ   maa·zeen·*gee*·raa

I'd like to hire a local guide.

Ek wil 'n plaaslike gids huur. ⓐ   ek vil i *plaas*·li·ki khits hewr
Nataka kuajiri kiongozi   naa·*taa*·kaa koo·aa·*jee*·ree kee·ohn·*goh*·zee
kutoka hapo jirani. ⓢ   koo·*toh*·kaa *haa*·poh jee·*raa*·nee

I'd like to go somewhere off the beaten track.

Ek wil êrens anders as na   ek vil *e*·rins an·dirs as naa
die gewone plekke toe gaan. ⓐ   dee khi·*voo*·ni *ple*·ki tu khaan
Nataka kuenda mahali   naa·*taa*·kaa koo·*eyn*·daa maa·*haa*·lee
ambapo siyo kawaida   aam·*baa*·poh *see*·yoh kaa·waa·*ee*·daa
kwa watalii. ⓢ   kwaa waa·taa·*lee*

Is it safe to walk around this section of the park?

Is dit veilig om in hierdie deel   is dit *fay*·likh om in *heer*·dee deyl
van die park rond te loop? ⓐ   fan dee park ront ti loop
Ni salama nikitembea kwa   nee saa·*laa*·maa nee·kee·teym·*bey*·aa kwaa
miguu katika sehemu hii ya   mee·*goo* kaa·*tee*·kaa sey·*hey*·moo hee yaa
hifadhi? ⓢ   hee·*faa*·dhee

Do you have information about the preservation of wildlife at this park?

Het julle inligting oor die   het *ji*·li *in*·likh·ting oor dee
bewaring van wild in hierdie park? ⓐ   bi·*vaa*·ring fan vilt in *heer*·dee park
Je, unazo taarifa   jey oo·*naa*·zoh taa·*ree*·faa
zinazohusiana na   zee·naa·zoh·hoo·see·*aa*·naa naa
utunzaji wa wanyama   oo·toon·*zaa*·jee waa waan·*yaa*·maa
pori ndani ya hifadhi hii? ⓢ   *poh*·ree n·*daa*·nee yaa hee·*faa*·dhee hee

Do you have any endangered species at this park?

Het julle enige bedreigde   het *ji*·li *ey*·ni·khi bi·*draykh*·di
spesies in hierdie park? ⓐ   *spey*·sees in *heer*·dee park
Je, unao viumbe   jey oo·*naa*·oh vee·*oom*·bey
walioko hatarini katika   waa·lee·*oh*·koh haa·taa·*ree*·nee kaa·*tee*·kaa
hifadhi hii? ⓢ   hee·*faa*·dhee hee

Do you have the Big Five animals at this park?

Het julle die Groot Vyf in   het *ji*·li dee khroot fayf in
hierdie park? ⓐ   *heer*·dee park
Je, unao wanyama wakuu   jey oo·*naa*·oh waan·*yaa*·maa waa·*koo*
watano katika hifadhi hii? ⓢ   waa·*taa*·noh kaa·*tee*·kaa hee·*faa*·dhee hii

Can you recommend a company that organises safaris?

Kan julle 'n maatskappy aanbeveel   kan *ji*·li i maat·ska·*pay* aan·bi·feyl
wat safari's organiseer? ⓐ   vat sa·*faa*·rees awr·kha·nee·*seer*
Unaweza kupendekeza   oo·naa·*wey*·zaa koo·peyn·dey·*key*·zaa
kampuni ya safari kwa miguu? ⓢ   kaam·*poo*·nee yaa saa·*faa*·ree kwaa mee·*goo*

Can you recommend a 4WD/walking safari?

Kan julle 'n vier-by-vier/   kan *ji*·li i feer bay feer/
stapsafari aanbeveel? ⓐ   stap·sa·*faa*·ree aan·bi·feyl

Can you recommend a camel/walking safari?

Unajua safari ya ngamia/ oo·naa·*joo*·aa saa·*faa*·ree yaa n·gaa·*mee*·aa/
kutembea nzuri? ⑤ koo·teym·*bey*·aa n·*zoo*·ree

When's the next safari?

Wanneer is die volgende safari? ⓐ va·nir is dee *fol*·khin·di sa·*faa*·ree
Safari ijayo itakuwa lini? ⑤ saa·*faa*·ree ee·*jaa*·yoh ee·taa·*koo*·waa *lee*·nee

Are park fees included?

Is parkfooie ingesluit? ⓐ is *park*·foy·i *in*·khi·slayt
Inazingatia ada za hifadhi? ⑤ ee·naa·zeen·gaa·*tee*·aa *aa*·daa zaa hee·*faa*·dhee

How many people will be in the group?

Hoeveel mense sal in die groep *hu*·fil *men*·si sal in dee khrup
wees? ⓐ veys
Kundi itakuwa na watu *koon*·dee ee·taa·*koo*·waa naa *waa*·too
wangapi? ⑤ waan·*gaa*·pee

We'd like to go wildlife spotting.

Ons wil gaan diere kyk. ⓐ awns vil khaan *dee*·ri kayk
Tunataka kwenda kutafuta too·naa·*taa*·kaa *kweyn*·daa koo·taa·*foo*·taa
wanyama pori. ⑤ waa·*nyaa*·maa *poh*·ree

What animals are we likely to see?

Watter diere gaan ons sien? ⓐ va·tir *dee*·ri khaan ons seen
Tutegemee kuona wanyama too·tey·gey·*mey* koo·*oh*·naa waa·*nyaa*·maa
gani? ⑤ *gaa*·nee

We're very keen to see (elephants).

Ons wil graag (olifante) sien. ⓐ awns vil khraakh (*oo*·lee·fan·ti) seen
Tunataka sana kuona (tembo). ⑤ too·naa·*taa*·kaa *saa*·naa koo·*oh*·naa (*teym*·bo)

What animal is that?

Watter dier is dit? ⓐ va·tir deer is dit
Ni mnyama gani? ⑤ nee m·*nyaa*·maa *gaa*·nee

Is it a protected park/species?

Is dit 'n beskermde park/spesie? ⓐ is dit i bi·*ske*·rim·di park/*spey*·see
Mbuga/Spishi m·*boo*·gaa/*spee*·shee
inahifadhiwa? ⑤ ee·naa·hee·faa·*dhee*·waa

INDEX